T0361554

PRAISE FOR *HABS 365*

Most Montreal Canadiens fans probably think they know everything there is to know about the franchise's storied history, but Mike Commito has produced a daily reminder that there is always more to know. Even if you know the "what" of many of the moments he has captured, Commito provides some of the "how" and the "why" behind those moments in short, digestible bites. A fun read for any Canadiens fan.

— ARPON BASU, senior columnist on the
Montreal Canadiens for The Athletic

Habs 365 is a great resource for new fans wanting to immerse themselves in the rich history that defines the franchise, while offering an opportunity for long-time hockey fans to learn something new about the most successful hockey team in NHL history. From championships to trades and everything in between, *Habs 365* has you covered.

— MARC DUMONT, manager, Montreal Hockey Now

365 days doesn't seem like enough to tell the stories of this fabled franchise, but Mike has filled his Canadiens calendar with the best of them. A must-have for all who bleed bleu, blanc, et rouge.

— JAMES DUTHIE, commentator, TSN, and author of
Beauties: Hockey's Greatest Untold Stories

365 well-told stories — a most unique way of zooming into over 100 years of rich Montreal Canadiens history. This is a book Habs fans will thoroughly enjoy.

— ERIC ENGELS, senior columnist, Sportsnet

As a hockey historian, I've come to learn that I should never stop learning. That explains why the books in Mike Commito's 365 series have become NHL "bibles" for me. They, including this latest, have been great reading but also an inspiration for me to write more stories about our favourite sport. Keep 'em coming, Mike.

— STAN FISCHLER, author and historian

If you're a Montreal Canadiens fan, you'll want to read *Habs 365*. You'll get to relive your favourite moments in the team's history and learn a thing or two along the way. Mike does a great job at picking the right stories and bringing them to life.

— MITCH GALLO, radio host, TSN 690

Habs 365 highlights some quirky moments that may not all have a meaningful impact in hockey history but that truly resonate with Canadiens fans, such as Alex Kovalev's retaliation hit on Darcy Tucker, or Erik Cole high-fiving a referee after a goal. Oh, the legendary moments are there, and they are numerous. But the format also allows us to stop and pay attention to former players and coaches who wouldn't usually be discussed in a Canadiens history book. I mean, John Scott? Paul Masnick? Karri Rämö?

Some of the unlikeliest of heroes are remembered — and a few painful trades and signings are, too — as we time travel through 115 years of Montreal Canadiens hockey with light and well-chosen stories. Habs fans are obsessed with hockey all year round — it only makes sense that a book would give them something for every single day!

— MARC ANTOINE GODIN, Radio-Canada

Just when you think you know everything about your favourite hockey team along comes Mike Commito to open your eyes. Turn every page in *Habs 365* and see for yourself.

— JEFF MAREK, host of *The Jeff Marek Show* and co-host of *32 Thoughts*

This book is an absolute must for any Montreal Canadiens fan, full of little-known facts and anecdotes.

— GORD MILLER, NHL, TSN, and international commentator

It's fitting that Mike has so nicely assembled 365 days of Montreal Canadiens history here, because many fans of this team live — and perish — with the Canadiens 25 hours a day, eight days a week. A perfect, breezy addition to the library of any Habs fan or anyone with a love of hockey history.

— DAVE STUBBS, columnist and historian, NHL.com

It is a momentous job to whittle Montreal's glorious history down to 365 easy-to-consume bite-size morsels of Canadiens glory, but Mike Commito did the deed in the latest installment of his Hockey 365 series. So whether you want a jumping-on point for the bandwagon or are simply looking for a conversation starter around the water cooler at work, this book is a great reference to keep on your shelf.

— ANDREW ZADARNOWSKI, historian and writer for
Habs Eyes on the Prize

HABS 365

The Hockey 365 Series

Habs 365
Leafs 365
Hockey 365, The Second Period
Hockey 365

MIKE COMMITO

HABS 365

DAILY STORIES FROM THE ICE

DUNDURN
PRESS

Publisher: Meghan Macdonald | Acquiring editor: Kathryn Lane | Editor: Patricia MacDonald

Library and Archives Canada Cataloguing in Publication

Title: Habs 365 : daily stories from the ice / Mike Commito.
Names: Commito, Mike, author.
Identifiers: Canadiana (print) 20240380509 | Canadiana (ebook) 20240380533 | ISBN 9781459753570 (hardcover) | ISBN 9781459753587 (PDF) | ISBN 9781459753594 (EPUB)
Subjects: LCSH: Montreal Canadiens (Hockey team)—Miscellanea. | LCSH: Hockey teams—Québec (Province)—Montréal—Miscellanea.
Classification: LCC GV848.M6 C68 2024 | DDC 796.962/640971428—dc23

We acknowledge the support of the Canada Council for the Arts and the Ontario Arts Council for our publishing program. We also acknowledge the financial support of the Government of Ontario, through the Ontario Book Publishing Tax Credit and Ontario Creates, and the Government of Canada.

Care has been taken to trace the ownership of copyright material used in this book. The author and the publisher welcome any information enabling them to rectify any references or credits in subsequent editions.

The publisher is not responsible for websites or their content unless they are owned by the publisher.

Printed and bound in Canada.

Dundurn Press
1382 Queen Street East
Toronto, Ontario, Canada M4L 1C9
dundurn.com, @dundurnpress

For Moe, who has forgotten more
Habs stories than I'll ever know

PRE-GAME SKATE

et's get this out of the way. I am not a Montreal Canadiens fan. Now before you close the book, let me explain. I consider myself a hockey historian, and the Canadiens are one of the most storied franchises in hockey history, so when there was a chance to expand the Hockey 365 series to the bleu, blanc, et rouge, I jumped at the opportunity.

If you're still holding this book, chances are you probably didn't pick up a copy of my last offering, *Leafs 365*, which featured 365 short stories about the Toronto Maple Leafs. That one was my first foray into a team-specific book, and it was a natural fit for me.

For as long as I can remember, I have been a Leafs fan because of my mother. Growing up, I even had the same bed set that John Tavares made infamous when he declared he was going to Toronto as a free agent. And while my mom set me on a path to join Leafs Nation, there was a moment when I could have been a Habs fan. My godfather, Barry, was an avid Canadiens fan, and one Christmas he and my godmother gifted me a pair of Habs pajamas. I am not sure how my mom let me try them on, but she did, and there's photographic proof that I still have somewhere.

There was even one time when I went to Montreal for a friend's bachelor party, and while I was there, the Canadiens were hosting the Sabres. I borrowed a leather Habs jacket for the trip from my father-in-law, Maurice, who is a dyed-in-the-wool Canadiens fan, and I gotta say, I rocked that thing. I got compliments from people on the street, and I definitely cheered for the Canadiens while wearing it that night at the game. When I got home, I almost didn't want to give it back.

But I want to make something absolutely clear: I did not write this book from the perspective of a Leafs fan because, honestly, who would want to read that? Certainly not Habs fans. So I went into it with an open mind. While the Leafs and Canadiens have certainly had a long-standing rivalry, I put that baggage aside to focus on how I could come up with 366 stories (don't forget those pesky leap years) about the Habs that you would actually want to read.

When I first started the process, I was a little reticent. Since I am not a Habs fan myself, I knew there would be blind spots for me. Would I know enough about the team's history and its players to do them justice? But as a professionally trained historian, this is exactly what I was taught to do. I have researched moments in history that I didn't experience or wasn't familiar with, but you do your due diligence, interpret the facts as best as you can, and always try to tell a compelling story.

But I certainly wasn't a blank slate. I had been telling hockey history stories for nearly a decade, and growing up as a hockey fan in Canada, even if you didn't root for the bleu, blanc, et rouge, the Habs still loomed large on the hockey landscape, especially when they battled my beloved Leafs on *Hockey Night in Canada*. And, of course, as a student of Canadian history long before I poured myself into hockey history, I knew that figures like Maurice Richard transcended the game. He was much more than simply a hockey player for a generation of French Canadians, and some scholars believe the Richard Riot — in response to his suspension in 1955 by NHL president Clarence Campbell — lit the powder keg for a social and political movement in Quebec that culminated in the Quiet Revolution just over a decade later.

Recognizing that I still had a lot to learn, I jumped in with both feet. I even bought myself a Canadiens shirt, which my mom jokingly told me I wasn't allowed to wear in her house, so I could get into the spirit of things. I'm not sure whether it helped, but I quickly found myself caught up in the project. I was reading as much as I could about the Canadiens and watching old clips on YouTube. I even had the chance to talk to a few of the team's legends, which further sparked my passion for the project.

Hearing some of these tales directly from former players like Yvan Cournoyer and Larry Robinson made me appreciate the wider fabric of the history I was weaving. When I told my father-in-law whom I had spoken with on the phone that day, I could tell he was excited. These were some of the players he had idolized in his younger days, and if he was happy to hear that their perspectives would help inform some of these stories, then I knew other Habs fans would be too.

Throughout this journey, I have been fortunate to learn about this incredible franchise. While I have come away with a deeper understanding of the many recurring characters such as Richard, Jean Béliveau, and Ken Dryden, for example, what I really appreciated was learning about other figures throughout the club's history that I may have taken for granted because I worshipped another team.

I still remember feeling giddy when I discovered that Mario Tremblay's nickname as a player translated to "the Bionic Blueberry." As far as sobriquets go, it doesn't get much better than that. That may be old hat for you, but it was moments like that that reminded me why I got into studying hockey history in the first place.

I won't go as far as saying that writing *Habs 365* has made me a fan of the Montreal Canadiens, but it's definitely given me a greater appreciation and respect for the team. So before we go any further, I want to thank you for entrusting me with your favourite team's history. I don't take the responsibility lightly, and I hope that comes across in the pages that follow.

JANUARY 1

CANADIENS TAKE WINTER CLASSIC, 2016

It was only fitting that one of hockey's oldest and greatest rivalries returned to the game's humble beginnings: the outdoors. On January 1, 2016, the Boston Bruins hosted the Canadiens at Gillette Stadium in Foxborough, Massachusetts, for the Winter Classic. Some might have thought the Bruins would have an advantage playing on the hallowed ground that was home to the NFL's New England Patriots, a club that was poised to win the Super Bowl that season, but the Canadiens made them feel as though they were playing at the Montreal Forum.

Just over a minute into the matchup, David Desharnais scored to give the Habs the lead. In the second frame, the Canadiens were buoyed by goals from Paul Byron and Brendan Gallagher, who was back in the lineup after a month off mending two broken fingers. Although Boston's Adam McQuaid broke goaltender Mike Condon's shutout bid early in the final frame, Montreal added two more goals to win 5–1, the largest margin of victory at a Winter Classic since the tradition began nearly a decade earlier.

JANUARY 2

JOSÉ THÉODORE SCORES A GOAL, 2001

Every goalie dreams of scoring a goal. But José Théodore was the first to admit he wasn't even trying to score when he flipped the puck down the ice. On January 2, 2001, with nine seconds remaining in a game against the Islanders, the Canadiens goaltender found the back of the net, becoming the first netminder in franchise history to light the lamp. With New York's net empty, Théodore retrieved the puck from behind his crease and backhanded it. He thought an Islander would have intercepted the shot, but the puck found its way into the yawning cage, making it 4–0.

Théodore jumped for joy as he celebrated with his teammates, but even better than the goal was that he stopped all 32 shots he faced that night to record his first shutout of the season. While Théodore was the fourth goalie in NHL history to record a goal by shooting the puck into the opposing team's net, he was the first to accomplish the feat and earn a shutout in the same game, a distinction he holds to this day.

JANUARY 3

KEN DRYDEN EARNS 40TH
SHUTOUT, 1978

t doesn't matter if it's your first shutout or your 40th, anytime you turn aside every shot you face to backstop your team to a victory, it's an incredible feeling. Following a flawless performance against the St. Louis Blues on January 3, 1978, Canadiens goaltender Ken Dryden, who stopped 22 shots that night, reflected on the milestone. "It's games like tonight that are special," the always cerebral netminder told reporters. "Feelings like this are what makes hockey very special to me."

Although Dryden already had four Stanley Cups, three Vezina trophies, and a Conn Smythe on his resume, there was nothing like a perfect game to put things in perspective. He may never have imagined having all that hardware to his name while he was growing up and playing on his backyard rink with his older brother, Dave, who also went on to become an NHL goaltender, but a shutout is always special, whether you are tending twine in the big leagues or honing your skills on the ice under the stars.

LARS ELLER NOTCHES FOUR AGAINST THE JETS, 2012

t was a great night for the great Dane. On January 4, 2012, in a game against the Winnipeg Jets, Montreal's Lars Eller scored four goals and added an assist in a 7–3 rout to the delight of the home crowd at the Bell Centre. Following the matchup, he told reporters that "fans haven't gotten what they've paid for most of the year," but he made sure they got their money's worth that night.

After notching his first goal in the opening frame to make it 3–0, Eller potted two more early in the third period to record his first career hat trick. But the Danish forward wasn't done just yet. Just over the halfway mark of the final stanza, he was awarded a penalty shot. Although Eller hadn't had an opportunity in the shootout that season, he beat Jets goaltender Chris Mason with a spin-o-rama move, dazzling the Canadiens faithful to cap off a milestone evening. Eller would play four more seasons with Montreal, but that would be his only hat trick as a Hab.

JANUARY 5

FIRST CANADIENS GAME, 1910

A month after the Montreal Canadiens were founded as part of the newly formed National Hockey Association, the team played its first game on January 5, 1910. Taking on the Cobalt Silver Kings, a squad hailing from a Northern Ontario mining town that was known for its silver deposits, at the Jubilee Rink in Montreal, the Canadiens stormed out to a 3–1 lead in the first half of the game. It's worth noting that until the 1910–11 season, the NHA played two 30-minute frames before switching to three 20-minute periods.

But the Silver Kings rallied in the second half. They scored three quick goals to take the lead before the teams exchanged a few more goals to finish regulation tied 6–6. Shortly into overtime, George "Skinner" Poulin found the back of the net to give the Canadiens their first victory. The win, however, was short-lived. A few days later, the rival Canadian Hockey Association folded, and two of its teams were absorbed by the NHA. None of the results counted, and the bulging league officially restarted a couple of weeks later.

KJELL DAHLIN RECORDS FIRST CAREER HAT TRICK, 1986

K jell Dahlin continued to make his Calder case. The Swedish winger was drafted 82nd overall by Montreal in 1981 and got off to a hot start after joining the Canadiens for the 1985–86 season. Dahlin was named Rookie of the Month in October, and when he earned the honour again for December, he proved why just a few hours after getting the nod when he scored three goals, his first career hat trick, and an assist.

The offensive outburst in a 9–2 win against St. Louis gave Dahlin 22 goals and 47 points in 38 games, the most among all rookie players. He continued his torrid pace and finished the campaign with 71 points, making him the highest-scoring rookie, but he lost the Calder Trophy to blueliner Gary Suter, who finished just a few points behind him. Dahlin would've been the first member of the Canadiens to take home the award since Ken Dryden in 1972, but it wasn't meant to be. As of this writing, Dryden is still the last Hab to earn the Calder.

JANUARY 7

HOWIE MORENZ BAGS HAT TRICK IN ROUT, 1928

Howie Morenz was hockey's first superstar. Known as "the Stratford Streak" for his blistering speed, Morenz joined the Canadiens in the 1923–24 season after filling opponents' nets in the Ontario Hockey Association with Stratford. By his fourth season in Montreal, he had established himself as one of the league's premier goal scorers. In a game against the Maple Leafs on January 7, 1928, Morenz recorded his seventh career hat trick to power the Habs to a 9–1 victory.

Guided by Morenz's play, the Canadiens scored eight unanswered goals before Toronto finally got on the board with five minutes remaining. But here's the thing — nobody actually scored for Toronto. Leafs forward Bill Carson broke through Montreal's defence, and in a last-ditch effort, Herb Gardiner tossed his stick to keep him from scoring. According to the rules of the day, Carson was awarded a goal (the penalty shot would not be introduced until the 1934–35 season). A couple of games later, Morenz was at it again, recording another three-goal performance.

JANUARY 8

LARRY ROBINSON MAKES HIS DEBUT, 1973

The story goes that when Larry Robinson was called up for his first game with the Canadiens on January 8, 1973, his American Hockey League bench boss, Al MacNeil, told him that on his first shift he needed to hammer somebody. MacNeil had long advocated for Robinson to use his towering six-foot-four frame to play more physically and wanted to make sure his pupil made a good first impression. So Robinson heeded his coach's advice. The way Robinson remembers it, the first guy he came across on the ice was veteran Bobby Nevin. Robinson laid out the Minnesota winger, and that was that.

Nevin may have been the first player in the NHL to be flattened by one of Robinson's thundering bodychecks, but he certainly wasn't the last. Robinson never played another game in the minors and went on to become one of the most formidable defencemen in league history. He patrolled the Montreal blue line for nearly two decades, winning six Stanley Cups and picking up two Norris trophies and the Conn Smythe along the way.

BERT OLMSTEAD SCORES EIGHT POINTS AGAINST THE HAWKS, 1954

When Maurice Richard scored eight points in a game against the Detroit Red Wings on December 28, 1944, establishing an NHL record, Bert Olmstead was still playing junior hockey in Saskatchewan. But a decade later, as a member of the Canadiens, Olmstead took a page out of Richard's book in a game against the Chicago Black Hawks on January 9, 1954. Taking on his former team, he racked up eight points — four goals and four assists — to match Richard's performance and tie the league record.

Richard might have been 10 years older than when he originally accomplished the feat, but he was no slouch that game either. The 32-year-old recorded four assists and helped set up two of Olmstead's goals. The two had a history of setting each other up. When Olmstead was traded to the Canadiens in 1950, he started playing on the top line with the Rocket and Elmer Lach. Olmstead would stay the better part of a decade in Montreal and would later spend time flanking Jean Béliveau and Bernie "Boom Boom" Geoffrion.

BREAKING NEWSY, LALONDE SCORES SIX, 1920

Édouard "Newsy" Lalonde came by his nickname honestly. Growing up in Cornwall, Ontario, Lalonde worked in a newsprint plant when he wasn't honing his skills in the hockey rink. The moniker stuck, and by the time he made it to the Canadiens for the NHL's inaugural season, he was still known as Newsy. By his second campaign in the league, Lalonde had established himself as one of hockey's top snipers, scoring 23 goals in 17 games, the most in the league. The following season, he was once again vying for the goal-scoring title.

On January 10, 1920, in just the fifth game of the campaign, Lalonde scored six times against the Toronto St. Patricks to extend his league-leading total to 11 goals. Following his outburst against Toronto, there were just two games down the stretch in which Lalonde failed to score a goal. He finished the season with 37 goals in 23 games, but he was two tallies behind former teammate "Phantom Joe" Malone, who found the back of the net 39 times with Quebec.

TOE BLAKE'S CAREER-ENDING INJURY, 1948

Toe Blake hoped he would be back in a couple of months. In a game against the New York Rangers on January 11, 1948, the Canadiens veteran sustained a double fracture in his right ankle when he was checked into the boards by Rangers defenceman Bill Juzda. After evaluating the injury and discovering it was a clean break, Montreal was optimistic that its long-time captain would be back to finish out the campaign.

Although Blake remained with the team for the rest of the season, continuing to serve as its leader off the ice despite being in a cast, that January matchup would prove to be his last NHL game. When he was forced to hang up his skates, Blake had finished his Canadiens tenure with 529 points, the most in franchise history, and a trophy case that included three Stanley Cup rings, the Lady Byng, and the Hart. Blake's playing days were over, but he would return to the club as head coach and lead Montreal to a dynastic eight titles during his time behind the bench.

MIKE CAMMALLERI TRADED MID-GAME, 2012

Mike Cammalleri found out his services were no longer needed. Not before the game. Not after the game. Right in the middle of the game. During the second intermission against the Bruins on January 12, 2012, the Canadiens, down a goal with a period to play, traded him, along with goaltender Karri Rämö and a 2012 fifth-round pick, to the Calgary Flames in exchange for Rene Bourque, prospect Patrick Holland, and a second-round pick the following year.

The timing may have been curious, but it wasn't a complete surprise. A day earlier, following practice, Cammalleri voiced his frustration about Montreal's position at the bottom of the standings to reporters. "I can't accept that we will display a losing attitude as we're doing this year. We prepare for our games like losers. We play like losers. So it's no wonder why we lose," he said. So instead of returning to the ice with his teammates for the final frame, the disgruntled winger was on his way to the airport to join his new team out west.

JANUARY 13

CANADIENS ACQUIRE THE BIG M, 1971

Pete Mahovlich might have lost some teammates, but he gained his brother. On January 13, 1971, the Canadiens sent Bill Collins, Mickey Redmond, and Guy Charron, who was with the club's AHL affiliate in Nova Scotia, to the Detroit Red Wings for his older brother, Frank Mahovlich. Known as "the Big M" for being one of the biggest players of his day, Mahovlich initially found success in the NHL with the Maple Leafs, but following a tumultuous relationship with general manager and bench boss Punch Imlach that took a serious toll on his mental health, Mahovlich was traded to the Red Wings in 1968, where his younger brother, Pete, was playing (Pete would be traded to Montreal a year later).

Free from Imlach in Detroit, Frank rediscovered his love for the game, and after a few seasons there, he was initially reluctant about reporting to Montreal. But when Mahovlich met with the Canadiens brass, they quashed his trepidation by telling him he would be rooming with Pete on the road. The Mahovlich brothers would go on to win two championships together in Montreal.

JANUARY 14

CLEGHORN BROTHERS EACH
SCORE FOUR, 1922

The Cleghorn brothers, Sprague and Odie, started their professional hockey careers together in Montreal with the Wanderers of the National Hockey Association, but they found themselves squaring off when they joined the NHL in 1918. The elder Cleghorn, Sprague, one of the dirtiest players in the game, suited up for the Ottawa Senators and the Toronto St. Pats, while Odie patrolled the wing for the Canadiens. The pair, however, were reunited for the 1920–21 season, when Sprague was traded to Montreal.

Not long into their reunion, the Cleghorn brothers each had one of the best performances of their careers. On January 14, 1922, in a matchup against the Tigers, they scored four goals apiece, marking the first time in NHL history that a pair of brothers on the same team scored four goals in the same game. And, somehow, they nearly repeated the feat in their very next contest. Four days later, Odie found the back of the net four times against Ottawa, but Sprague was held to just two goals and an assist.

PATRICK ROY PICKS UP
FIRST SHUTOUT, 1986

P atrick Roy stopped every shot he faced when he made his first NHL appearance. Sure, it was only two shots when he relieved Doug Soetaert in a game against the Winnipeg Jets on February 23, 1985, but he did manage to secure the victory. And while it wasn't exactly a shutout, it was a preview of things to come. The following season, Roy, who turned 20 just before the campaign began, wrestled the starting job away from Soetaert. Although he was racking up wins, a shutout still eluded him.

But on January 15, 1986, in another matchup against the Jets, Roy turned aside all 19 shots he faced to record his first career NHL goose egg. It would be his only shutout in the regular season that year, but the young netminder added another in the Stanley Cup Final, backstopping the Canadiens to a championship title and earning the Conn Smythe as the most valuable player of the post-season. Roy would go on to earn 32 more shutouts for Montreal in the regular season and playoffs.

PHIL GOYETTE RECORDS FIRST HAT TRICK, 1960

Despite having two charley horses, one in each leg, Phil Goyette still managed to light the lamp three times in a game against the Boston Bruins on January 16, 1960, to record his first regular-season hat trick; two years earlier, he opened the 1958 playoffs with a three-goal performance against the Detroit Red Wings. A slick playmaking centre from Lachine, Quebec, Goyette joined the Canadiens for the 1956–57 season and managed to win the Stanley Cup in each of his first three campaigns with Montreal. Slotting in behind Jean Béliveau and Henri Richard on the depth chart, Goyette had to make the most of his opportunities.

Despite not scoring more than 10 goals in each of his first three campaigns, that three-goal effort against the Bruins brought his goal count up to 12 that year. He would finish the season with 21 tallies, a career high that he would later surpass with the New York Rangers and the St. Louis Blues. In the 1960 playoffs, Goyette and the Canadiens were once again crowned champions, winning their fourth straight title.

MICHEL THERRIEN FIRED, 2003

After winning just two of his last 12 games, Canadiens head coach Michel Therrien was relieved of his duties. Following a 4–1 loss on the road to the Flyers, Montreal general manager André Savard made the decision to part ways with his bench boss and informed him before morning practice on January 17, 2003. The club swapped Therrien with Claude Julien, who had been coaching the Canadiens' AHL affiliate in Hamilton for the past three seasons. It would not be the last time Therrien would be replaced by Julien in Montreal.

In 2012, Therrien returned to coach the Canadiens under GM Marc Bergevin. In the 2014–15 campaign, Therrien guided the team to a 50-win season, but the Canadiens were eliminated in the first round of the playoffs. Midway through the 2016–17 season, following struggles in January and early February, Bergevin fired Therrien and replaced him once again with Julien, who had been dismissed by the Boston Bruins just a week earlier. Following his second departure from Montreal, Therrien became an assistant coach with the Flyers.

WILLIE O'REE MAKES HISTORY AGAINST THE HABS, 1958

When Willie O'Ree answered the telephone, he was not expecting his coach, Joe Crozier, to be on the other end of the line. Crozier, O'Ree's bench boss with the Quebec Aces of the Quebec Hockey League, was calling to let his pupil know he would be joining the Boston Bruins for a pair of weekend games against the Montreal Canadiens. After hanging up the phone, O'Ree was a bundle of nerves. He hardly slept that night, but it didn't matter. He was going to the NHL.

When O'Ree skated onto the ice the next day, January 18, 1958, it marked an important moment in hockey history. He became the first Black player to suit up for an NHL game. It had been a long road to the big leagues for O'Ree, who had to conceal that he was blind in one eye, but he made it. He didn't get on the scoresheet that night against the Canadiens, but he told reporters after the game that it was "the greatest thrill of my life."

JANUARY 19

DIDIER PITRE RECORDS FIRST
NHL HAT TRICK, 1918

Didier Pitre was known as "the Cannonball" because he had one of the hardest shots in hockey. But Pitre had much more than a cannonading release — he was also an exceptional skater. Legend has it he could skate as fast backward as he could forward. As someone who only mastered backward skating as an adult, this is perhaps the more impressive fact. An original member of the Canadiens in the National Hockey Association, Pitre was an integral part of the Flying Frenchmen line that also featured Jack Laviolette and Newsy Lalonde. Although Pitre filled the back of the net, he wasn't exactly known for setting up his linemates. In the 1911–12 season, he racked up 27 goals in 18 games while recording zero assists.

After helping the Canadiens win the first Stanley Cup in franchise history in 1916, Pitre played six seasons for the team in the NHL, eventually picking up his first hat trick in the league on January 19, 1918. He would accomplish the feat four more times before hanging up his skates in 1923.

JANUARY 20

THE ROCKET RECORDS 23RD
CAREER HAT TRICK, 1955

After Maurice Richard recorded his 23rd career hat trick in a 6–2 victory over the Maple Leafs on January 20, 1955, some of the newspaper coverage remarked on how incredible the accomplishment was given his age. But here's the thing — he was only 33 years old, and yet a Canadian Press dispatch commented that "the ever-startling Maurice Richard … [was] still an explosive super-star when most athletes are past their peak." While Richard may have been considered old by hockey standards, he was still the best sniper in the game.

And if reporters were blown away by the greybeard Richard picking up three goals, they must have fallen off their chairs a few weeks later when he scored four times against the New York Rangers. He would finish the campaign with 38 goals, tied for the most in the league that year with teammate Bernie "Boom Boom" Geoffrion. Richard would reach the 30-goal mark two more times, then narrowly missed the 20-goal plateau in each of his final three seasons before retiring in 1960.

JOCELYN THIBAULT STONEWALLS
FORMER TEAMMATES, 1999

Jocelyn Thibault found himself in an impossible situation. As the other goalie in the infamous Patrick Roy trade to the Colorado Avalanche, he would always be measured against "Saint Patrick" in Montreal. No one could live up to those expectations. After playing the better part of three seasons with the Canadiens, Thibault was traded to the Chicago Blackhawks, along with Brad Brown, Dave Manson, and a fourth-round draft pick, for Jeff Hackett, Alain Nasreddine, and Eric Weinrich.

A couple of months later, on January 21, 1999, Thibault faced the Canadiens. He stopped all 33 shots he faced to record his 10th career shutout. While Thibault felt he had nothing to prove to his former team, his teammates understood the significance of the matchup and played their best in front of their goaltender, opening the scoring in the first period and adding two more tallies in the final frame to win 3–0. In the end, Thibault got the last laugh. "It's sweet to blank your old teammates, to shut them out," he told reporters following the game.

JANUARY 22

RED WINGS PLAY CANADIENS
IN JUNIOR UNIFORMS, 1966

The night before the Canadiens hosted the Detroit Red Wings on January 22, 1966, thieves broke into the Montreal Forum and made off with 50 Red Wings sweaters. The jerseys had been hanging in the visitors dressing room, and newspaper coverage estimated that each jersey was worth $20. Today, that many jerseys would be valued at well over $10,000. The Red Wings were not only out of pocket, they also needed uniforms for the game. With it unlikely that the police would find the marauders and the missing merchandise in time, Detroit had uniforms from its Ontario Hockey Association affiliate, the Hamilton Red Wings, shipped express to Montreal.

The Wings may have looked like a junior hockey team, but they certainly didn't play like one. Without a loss in the new year, Detroit continued that trend, defeating the Canadiens 3–0 to extend their unbeaten streak to eight games. Paul Henderson opened the scoring in the first period, and goaltender Roger Crozier took care of the rest, turning aside all 31 shots he faced to record his seventh career shutout.

HABS TRADE JEFF HACKETT, 2003

Jeff Hackett wasn't happy. After reigning Hart and Vezina winner José Théodore signed a three-year extension in the 2002 off-season, Hackett knew there was less room in the crease for him. He admirably stepped into the breach early in the 2002–03 campaign, but when Théodore struggled between the pipes, he still wanted out of Montreal. The disgruntled netminder was obliged on January 23, 2003, when the Canadiens sent him to the San Jose Sharks for Niklas Sundström, a former eighth overall pick, and a third-round draft pick. But Hackett wasn't in San Jose for very long. The Sharks immediately flipped him, along with Jeff Jillson, to the rival Bruins for Kyle McLaren and a fourth-round pick.

Meanwhile, in Sundström, Montreal got a veteran 40-point player who could also kill penalties. In his second game with the Canadiens, he scored a goal against the Blackhawks. Sundström spent the next two seasons in Montreal before returning to Sweden to finish his career with Modo, where, in his younger days, he played on a line with Peter Forsberg and Markus Näslund.

STEVE SHUTT SCORES FOUR TIMES, 1980

After joining a stacked Canadiens team as a 20-year-old, Steve Shutt developed into one of the most potent left wingers of his era. Playing on a line with Jacques Lemaire and Guy Lafleur for the 1976–77 campaign, Shutt scored 60 goals, a record for left wingers that held for three decades. Shutt consistently found ways to find the back of the net, but he was not known for scoring in bunches. By the 1979–80 season, he had bagged only a handful of hat tricks.

But when the Canadiens took on the Hartford Whalers on January 24, 1980, Shutt racked up four goals in a 7–2 victory. At the time, the Whalers were playing out of the Springfield Civic Center in Springfield, Massachusetts, while their arena in Hartford was being repaired following a roof collapse. While you would think Shutt might have been the only NHL player to light the lamp four times in that rink, just over a week later, the Whalers' Jordy Douglas matched the feat in what would be the team's final game in Springfield.

MARTIN RUČINSKY BAGS A HAT TRICK, 1996

After Martin Ručinsky scored his first career hat trick with the Canadiens on January 25, 1996, head coach Mario Tremblay told reporters he could easily be a 25-goal scorer in the league. The bench boss's words proved prophetic. Although the Czech winger had recorded only a handful of goals in his first 21 games since arriving as part of the package that sent Patrick Roy to the Avalanche, Ručinsky continued to find the back of the net following his three-goal performance.

In the next five games, Ručinsky picked up six more and would finish the campaign with 25 goals in 56 games for the Canadiens, proving his coach right. The following season, he scored 28 goals, the second most on the team behind only Mark Recchi. But a couple of years later in the 1998–99 campaign, Ručinsky led the Canadiens in goal-scoring despite recording only 17 tallies, marking the first time in nearly six decades that Montreal did not have a 20-goal scorer on the roster. The next season, however, Ručinsky bounced back to the 25-goal mark.

BOOM BOOM PLAYS FINAL
GAME OF THE SEASON, 1958

Bernie Geoffrion was poised to become the Canadiens' first 50-goal scorer since his teammate Maurice Richard accomplished the feat in 1945. After recording his 27th goal in just his 42nd game of the season against the Boston Bruins on January 26, 1958, it seemed as though the milestone was well within his grasp. But the next day during a scrimmage in practice, Geoffrion sustained a serious injury when he was checked hard by André Pronovost.

After writhing in pain on the ice, Geoffrion was rushed to hospital where it was discovered that the collision had punctured his bowel. The prognosis was so grave that a priest was summoned to be at Geoffrion's bedside while he underwent a procedure. Doctors feared he might not survive, but the operation was a success and Geoffrion made a full recovery. He was discharged a few weeks later and returned to the Canadiens just in time for the playoffs and to win his fourth Stanley Cup. Although the injury derailed his shot at hitting 50, Geoffrion, nicknamed "Boom Boom" for his pioneering slapshot, eventually hit the mark a few years later.

10K GOAL FOR CANADIENS, 2002

t didn't take Sergei Berezin very long to etch his name into the Canadiens' record books. Two days after he was acquired from the Phoenix Coyotes, on January 27, 2002, playing in his second game as a member of the Habitants, Berezin scored the club's 10,000th goal on home ice. It was the first time in NHL history that a team reached the milestone, and the newcomer couldn't help but feel the honour should have gone to someone else.

"I think it's a little unfair that I scored such an important goal," he told reporters following the game. "I've only been here since yesterday." Berezin hoped to hang on to the puck as a souvenir, but it was scooped up by the club's long-time public relations director, Donald Beauchamp, to be sent to the Hockey Hall of Fame. While Berezin joked he didn't mind having to go to the Hall to admire it, he was not so quick to give up his stick, since he had only a few on hand following the trade from Phoenix.

ALF SKINNER AND JOE HALL GET INTO ALTERCATION, 1918

Joe Hall earned the nickname "Bad Joe" from his violent play on the ice. But one night, on January 28, 1918, even he took it too far. In the final period of a game against Toronto, Hall levelled Arenas winger Alf Skinner. As Skinner crumpled to the ice, he swung his stick around and cracked Hall across the side of the face. Seeing red and with blood dripping from his face, Hall raised his stick and brought it down over his opponent's head like he was chopping a piece of wood.

While Hall was immediately ejected from the game, Skinner was reportedly still unconscious when he was helped off the ice. Not long after the players retired to their respective dressing rooms, the police arrived and placed both men under arrest for disorderly conduct. A few days later, Hall and Skinner appeared in court and were each handed a $15 fine and a suspended sentence. Hall continued his hard-hitting play, but it was the last time it landed him in front of a judge.

SNOWED-IN SABRES TIE CANADIENS, 1977

The Sabres were scheduled to be in Montreal on the evening of January 29, 1977, but there was just one problem. Several key members of the team were snowed in. After a winter storm hit Buffalo the night before, what many called the worst blizzard in decades, the next few days were spent digging out of the avalanche brought on by winds ripping off Lake Erie at upwards of 69 miles per hour, whipping up snow that choked the city. Among the thousands who couldn't leave their homes because their vehicles were buried were Sabres Rick Martin, Jim Lorentz, Brian Spencer, and Lee Fogolin.

With those four snowbound and unable to make the trek with their teammates to Montreal, where the Canadiens hadn't lost at home in 18 straight games, a lopsided match for the short-staffed Sabres seemed inevitable. But Buffalo battled. Despite trailing 3–2 with eight minutes in the final frame, the undermanned road warriors knotted up the score and managed to draw the Canadiens to a 3–3 tie at the Forum.

HABS LIMIT HURRICANES TO 10 SHOTS, 1999

D espite limiting their opponents to just 10 shots on net, the Canadiens were unable to pick up a victory against the Hurricanes on January 30, 1999. It was the fewest shots allowed in team history, breaking the record set more than four decades earlier when the Leafs were able to muster only 11 shots against Montreal. While Jeff Hackett still let three goals squeak through, at the other end of the ice, Artūrs Irbe stood on his head. The Latvian goaltender stopped 44 shots in a 3–1 victory.

Irbe had turned aside everything the Canadiens threw at him until Martin Ručinsky found the back of the net five minutes into the third period. Frédéric Chabot replaced Hackett for the final frame, but the French backup saw no action. The Canadiens denied the Hurricanes a single shot that session. It was the first time since March 8, 1984, that the club didn't allow a shot in a period. Funny enough, it was against the Hartford Whalers, a team that later relocated to Raleigh and became the Hurricanes.

JANUARY 31

JOHN SCOTT AN UNLIKELY ALL-STAR, 2016

t was one of the best moments in NHL All-Star Game history, and it almost didn't happen. On January 31, 2016, John Scott, a member of the Canadiens organization, was named MVP at the annual exhibition. Earlier in the month, the six-foot-eight enforcer, who was known more for his size than his skill, was the subject of a fan voting campaign to get him into the new three-on-three tournament that would feature the league's best players.

At the time, Scott was playing for the Coyotes, and when he was indeed named winner of the fan vote, the NHL was displeased. Less than two weeks later, in a move many believed was orchestrated to remove him from the All-Star Game, Scott was traded to Montreal and immediately sent down to the St. John's IceCaps in the American Hockey League. Despite being in the minors and the league's brass discouraging him from participating, he played in the game, and after being named most valuable player, Scott — all 260 pounds of him — was hoisted onto the shoulders of his teammates in celebration.

FEBRUARY 1

BOBBY ROUSSEAU SCORES FIVE, 1964

Bobby Rousseau led the charge against the Red Wings. On February 1, 1964, he racked up five goals in a 9–3 victory over Montreal's Motor City rivals. After scoring once in the opening period, Rousseau added two more in the middle frame before recording another pair of markers in the final stanza. It was the first five-goal performance from an NHL player in nearly a decade. The last time it happened it was Rousseau's teammate, Bernie "Boom Boom" Geoffrion, who tickled the twine five times in a game against the New York Rangers on February 19, 1955.

The Canadiens bombarded Detroit netminder Roger Crozier, who was supposed to have the night off but was a last-minute substitution for Terry Sawchuk, with 42 shots. In addition to Rousseau's five tallies, Yvan Cournoyer, playing in his fifth and final game that campaign in order to retain his amateur status, potted a pair. It was Cournoyer's last game with Montreal that year, but he would return the following season, becoming a fixture on the Habs for the next 15 years.

FEBRUARY 2

JOE MALONE SCORES FIVE MORE, 1918

It was just another night at the office for Joe Malone. After starting his NHL career with a five-goal performance, Malone, nicknamed "Phantom Joe" for his deceptiveness on the ice, continued to light the lamp. In the 11 games following his debut, he racked up 24 goals, which included another five-goal feat. When Montreal hosted the Toronto Arenas on February 2, 1918, Malone was at it again. After scoring twice in the first period, he completed the hat trick in the middle frame, his fifth three-goal performance of the campaign. He added two more in the final stanza as the Canadiens cruised to an 11–2 victory.

While Malone stole the show with his goal-scoring prowess, many of the spectators were waiting to see if there would be more fireworks between Joe Hall and the Arenas' Alf Skinner. A few games earlier in Toronto, the two had a violent altercation that ended with Hall bloodied and Skinner leaving the ice unconscious. But despite the home crowd at the Jubilee Rink chanting "get Skinner" and even throwing debris at him, there was no encore.

FEBRUARY 3

HABS ACQUIRE DALE WEISE, 2014

Before he was ever a Montreal Canadien, Dale Weise was "Dutch Gretzky." Although not known for his scoring prowess in the NHL, during the 2012–13 lockout, Weise played for the Tilburg Trappers in the Netherlands' top league, scoring 22 goals and 48 points in just 19 games. While it was difficult for him to live up to his moniker back in the big leagues, scoring just six goals over the next two seasons with the Canucks, Weise, who was six-foot-two and 210 pounds, also brought size and toughness to the lineup.

Looking to add some of that to the Canadiens, the club sent defenceman Raphael Díaz to Vancouver in exchange for Dutch Gretzky on February 3, 2014. Weise scored just three goals down the stretch, but he would reach double digits, for the first time in his career, in back-to-back seasons in Montreal, before he was traded to Chicago, along with Tomáš Fleischmann, for Phillip Danault and a second-round draft pick, on February 26, 2016, in what would turn out to be an incredibly shrewd move for the Canadiens.

FEBRUARY 4

GUY LAFLEUR RETURNS, 1989

t had been more than four years, but the Flower was back at the Forum in Montreal, where he had recorded six consecutive 50-goal seasons and won five Stanley Cups. But this time he was a member of the visiting team. On February 4, 1989, Guy Lafleur, who had spent his entire career with the Canadiens before initially hanging up his skates early in the 1984–85 campaign, was back in Montreal but with the New York Rangers. After taking a few years away from the game, Lafleur was lured out of retirement by the Blueshirts in 1988.

When the Rangers visited the Canadiens earlier that season, Lafleur was unable to play because of a fractured foot, but when they returned that cold night in February, he was back in the building where he became a legend. Although Lafleur was on the wrong bench, he received a standing ovation from the Montreal faithful. He didn't let them down. The Flower scored twice and assisted on another goal in a 7–5 loss to earn the game's second-star honours.

FEBRUARY 5

PATRICK ROY UPS THE ANTE, 1996

There was a lot of money on the board in the Avalanche's dressing room when the Canadiens came to town on February 5, 1996. And for good reason. Taking on his former team for the first time since he was traded to Colorado in December, Patrick Roy reached into his wallet to motivate his teammates to help secure the victory. According to reports, Roy put up $3,000, and Mike Keane, who was also part of the deal, threw down another $1,000.

Even without the money, there was no way Roy was losing that game. He made 37 saves in a 4–2 victory to record his 10th win since making his way to Denver. With 10 triumphs under his belt before the trade, he became the fourth goaltender in NHL history to win 10 or more games with two teams in one season. On the way off the ice, Roy flipped the puck at Mario Tremblay's feet, a little payback for when the Montreal bench boss hung him out to dry a couple of months earlier.

FEBRUARY 6

RAY GETLIFFE SCORES FIVE TIMES, 1943

With Toe Blake out of the lineup with a groin injury, Ray Getliffe was moved up to Montreal's top line to play with Elmer Lach and Joe Benoit. The shift worked out quite well for Getliffe, who started his NHL career seven years earlier with the Boston Bruins. On February 6, 1943, taking on his former team, he opened the scoring in the first period and then added four more goals and an assist to record six points, finishing just one point shy of the franchise record originally set by Joe Malone on January 12, 1918.

Getliffe finished with the most points by a Canadiens player in more than a decade, but Lach also wrote his name in the record books. He assisted on all of Getliffe's goals and picked up another helper on Benoit's second-period tally to set the Montreal benchmark for the most assists in a game, which stands to this day. Getliffe finished the season with 18 goals and 46 points in 50 games, both career highs to that point.

GEORGE HAINSWORTH BECOMES NHL'S ALL-TIME SHUTOUT LEADER, 1933

Heading into the 1932–33 NHL campaign, only Ottawa's Alec Connell had more shutouts than George Hainsworth. Known as "the Ottawa Fireman" because he also served on the nation's capital's fire department throughout his hockey career, Connell had recorded his 70th career shutout early in the season. Hainsworth, who was sitting only two behind him at the time, eventually had the opportunity to pass him on February 7, 1933, when the Canadiens hosted the Maple Leafs. The newspapers reported that Toronto severely outshot Montreal, but Hainsworth turned aside everything he faced to record his 71st shutout and surpass Connell for the all-time mark.

After finishing the season with 75 shutouts, Hainsworth, who had worn bleu, blanc, et rouge his entire career, was traded to the Leafs. But after three seasons in Toronto, he was released and finished his career back in Montreal, where he played four games in the 1936–37 season before hanging up his goalie pads. At the time of his retirement, Hainsworth had 94 shutouts, a record that stood for nearly three decades.

TREVOR LINDEN RECORDS
ONLY HABS HAT TRICK, 2000

t had been nearly four years since Trevor Linden had scored his last hat trick. But on February 8, 2000, Linden, who was now playing in Montreal since arriving by trade in the off-season, recorded three goals in a 5–4 overtime loss to the Edmonton Oilers. The hat trick marked his seventh point in as many games — an offensive outburst that was making up for a slow start followed by time off with an ankle injury — but Linden didn't care all too much about his three-goal performance.

Instead, he was more focused on the loss. "We don't see too many teams that play wide-open hockey like that, and when you consider the personnel we have, that's probably not the kind of game we want to play," he told reporters following the game. Perhaps Linden's words struck a chord. After dropping another game to the Capitals two nights later, the Canadiens then rattled off seven straight victories. But it wasn't enough to turn things around. The Habs missed the playoffs for the second straight year.

FEBRUARY 9

SCOTT GOMEZ FINALLY SCORES, 2012

"Did Scott Gomez score last night?" is what Canadiens fans had been asking themselves all season long. There was even a website, aptly called Did Scott Gomez Score Last Night? where fans could go to see if the Montreal forward, who hadn't scored a goal in more than a year, had broken his drought. Finally, on February 9, 2012, the Montreal faithful were able to rejoice when Gomez tipped in a shot in the third period against the New York Islanders to notch his first marker since February 5, 2011.

Gomez could sense the growing frustration with his play, but he told reporters he didn't get down on himself and just kept working. "It's certainly good to get a win, and of course it's great to finally score," he said. While the Canadiens paid a hefty price to get Gomez in 2009, giving up Ryan McDonagh as part of a six-player trade, he would score just one more goal for the Habs before he was bought out of the final two years on his contract.

FEBRUARY 10

HABS CARRY KRAUT LINE
OFF THE ICE, 1942

E ven against their archrivals, the Canadiens recognized that some things are bigger than the game. When Montreal travelled to Boston to take on the Bruins on February 10, 1942, it was much more than a matchup. It marked the last game that Boston's Milt Schmidt, Woody Dumart, and Bobby Bauer, who were collectively known as "the Kraut Line" because of their German heritage, would play that season. Like many NHL players during the Second World War, the trio enlisted to serve their country.

Not only were they putting their careers on hold, but they were also risking their lives. That potential sacrifice was not lost on their opponents and everyone in attendance that evening. After the trio combined for 11 points in an 8–1 victory, they were presented with gold identification bracelets, wristwatches, and their full season's salaries. But the greatest gift may have been the recognition they received from opponents. Joining forces with the Bruins, some of the Canadiens hoisted the three men on their shoulders and carried them off the ice.

HABS SNAP REVERSE RETRO CURSE, 2023

Mothball them. Burn them. Load them into a rocket and fire it into the sun. Habs fans were prepared to do whatever it took if it meant not seeing the team wear its 2022–23 Reverse Retro jerseys again. For eight games in the campaign, the Canadiens had sported special sweaters that were a throwback but a remix of the team's heritage as part of a league-wide initiative started the previous year. For this year's offering, Montreal went with a powder-blue look popularized by the defunct Montreal Expos from Major League Baseball. The jerseys were sharp, but they didn't translate to victories on the ice.

The first seven times they were worn, the Canadiens went 0-6-1 and were outscored 33–10 in those contests. But finally, on February 11, 2023, the club broke its Reverse Retro curse with a 4–3 shootout win against the Blues. Following the triumph, head coach Martin St-Louis said, "I don't know what next year brings but I hope it's not those jerseys." Well, at least they went out on a high note.

ROAD STREAK CONTINUES, 1975

The Habs were road warriors. It didn't matter where they played away from home, they were unbeatable. Heading into a game at Maple Leaf Gardens on February 12, 1975, the Canadiens were working on a 16-game unbeaten streak that stretched back to November 27, 1974. Over the course of that run, Montreal collected 10 victories and six ties.

Early in the matchup against Toronto, it certainly looked as though the Canadiens would extend the streak. Less than two minutes after puck drop, Steve Shutt opened the scoring. The Leafs' Inge Hammarström tied it up not long after, but blueliner Larry Robinson restored Montreal's advantage going into the first intermission. The Habs held the lead until late in the final stanza, when Hammarström scored his second of the night to force a tie. While it wasn't a victory, it nonetheless pushed Montreal's unbeaten road streak to an impressive 17 games. The Canadiens would add four more wins and two more draws on the road until they eventually faltered in Philadelphia, bringing the impressive run to a halt at 23 games.

FEBRUARY 13

HABS SNAP DETROIT LOSING STREAK, 1966

You know what they say, the fourteenth time's a charm. Maybe that's not entirely accurate, but we're going to go with it because it took the Canadiens 14 tries before they finally picked up another victory in Detroit. After recording a 5–2 win at Joe Louis Arena on February 16, 1964, it took nearly two years before the Habs left the Motor City in triumph. Over the course of that abysmal stretch, Montreal collected 10 losses and three ties in Detroit while being outscored 42–16 in those games.

But they finally snapped the skid on February 13, 1966. After Claude Provost opened the scoring just over a minute into the first period, he picked up another tally a few minutes later. The two teams exchanged goals to go into the final frame tied 3–3, but Gilles Tremblay found the back of the net just 35 seconds into the final stanza, and it held up as the game-winner. The Canadiens wouldn't lose another game in Detroit that season, including an overtime victory to secure Lord Stanley's mug.

FEBRUARY 14

KNUCKLES NILAN RACKS UP 39 PIMS, 1981

There was no love lost between Chris Nilan and the Washington Capitals on Valentine's Day in 1981. A hard-nosed player from Boston, Nilan was known as "Knuckles" because he wasn't afraid to chuck 'em. After making his debut for the Canadiens in the 1979–80 campaign, he quickly earned a reputation as a fierce competitor who would always stick up for his teammates. The next season, during that matchup against Washington, Nilan took exception to a hit Jim McTaggart made on Guy Lafleur, so he dropped the Capitals blueliner like a sack of potatoes. A brawl ensued, halting play for nearly 20 minutes.

When the dust settled, Nilan received 39 penalty minutes and a double misconduct for his role in the melee. After serving a one-game suspension for earning his third game misconduct of the year, the enforcer continued racking up penalty minutes and finished the season with 262, a club record at the time. Nilan later surpassed his own benchmark twice and collected 358 penalty minutes in 1984–85, a franchise record that stands to this day.

FEBRUARY 15

ROADRUNNER SCORES FIVE, 1975

G uy Lafleur was out with a broken finger, but the Canadiens still had plenty of firepower. Hosting Chicago on February 15, 1975, the Habs scored 12 times to trounce the Black Hawks by nine goals. After Guy Lapointe and Serge Savard each scored in the first period, Mario Tremblay bulged the twine early in the middle session but was later tossed from the game for headbutting Chicago's Randy Holt, a player who would later set the NHL record for the most penalty minutes in a single contest.

From there it was the Yvan Cournoyer show. Known as "the Roadrunner" for his blistering speed, Cournoyer found the back of the net five times, becoming the first Canadiens player to reach the milestone since Bobby Rousseau accomplished the feat 11 years earlier in a matchup against the Red Wings. But Cournoyer didn't stop at lighting the lamp — he also picked up two assists. When the final buzzer sounded, the Canadiens had a dozen goals and Cournoyer had seven points, the most by a Montreal player since Jean Béliveau in 1959.

FEBRUARY 16

HABS RAISE FLOWER'S NO.
10 TO THE RAFTERS, 1985

They don't do jersey retirements like they used to. Back in the day, when a player had his number raised to the rafters, he often stepped out onto the ice in full equipment. Now they are typically in suits, but there's something to be said for seeing players return to the ice in the uniforms they helped define. Granted, when Guy Lafleur had his No. 10 honoured on February 16, 1985, he was not that far removed from his last game with the Canadiens.

After recording only two goals in 19 games that season, Lafleur, who was not seeing eye to eye with former teammate-turned-coach Jacques Lemaire, decided to hang up his skates in November 1984. So even though it had been only a few months, it was still emotional to see him take one final skate around the ice at the Montreal Forum. It would be his last time sporting a Canadiens sweater, but the un-retired Lafleur would return to the Forum a few years later with the New York Rangers and then with the club's provincial rivals, the Quebec Nordiques.

THE BIG M HITS 1K, 1973

Bobby Clarke stole the show. When the Canadiens hosted the Philadelphia Flyers on February 17, 1973, Frank Mahovlich was on the verge of making history. The Big M was just two points shy of reaching the 1,000-point mark, which would make him the eighth player in NHL history to achieve the milestone and just the second player to accomplish the feat in a Canadiens sweater. But after Clarke opened the scoring in the first period, the Flyers added two goals to take a 3–0 lead.

Early in the second frame, Serge Savard got the Canadiens on the board, with Mahovlich assisting on the tally to move one point closer. The two teams continued exchanging goals, including another from Clarke, and Philadelphia went into the final stanza ahead 5–3. Mahovlich assisted on Steve Shutt's second of the period to tie it up 6–6 and reach the vaunted landmark, but Clarke scored the eventual game-winner six minutes later to complete the hat trick, his first in the NHL, pushing the Big M out of the headlines.

GEORGE VÉZINA RECORDS FIRST NHL SHUTOUT, 1918

Georges Vézina was unflappable. He was so calm under pressure that the Chicoutimi, Quebec, native was dubbed "the Chicoutimi Cucumber" because he was cool as a ... well, you know. Legend has it that when the Canadiens were still part of the National Hockey Association, they travelled to his hometown to take on one of the local teams. The young Vézina just happened to be the netminder. But even though he was stacking up against a squad of professional players, he just focused on his game and backstopped his club to victory.

The Canadiens were reportedly so impressed by his play that they offered him a roster spot. Vézina initially declined, but he eventually joined the Habs for the 1910–11 season and then made his way to the NHL when the team joined the upstart league in 1917. Toward the end of the inaugural campaign, on February 18, 1918, Vézina stayed cool and did something none of his colleagues had been able to do up to that point: he stopped every shot he faced to record the first shutout in NHL history.

HABS MOUNT EPIC COMEBACK, 2008

t was the biggest comeback in franchise history. Just over five minutes into the second period of a game against the New York Rangers on February 19, 2008, the Canadiens were down 5–0. After the Blueshirts chased rookie Carey Price from his net with three goals in the opening frame, Cristobal Huet took over, but he didn't fare much better, allowing two goals of his own early in the middle session. But just before the halfway mark of that frame, Michael Ryder put the Habs on the board.

Just over a few minutes later, Ryder found the back of the net again. Although the Canadiens were still down by three, the game suddenly got a lot more interesting. Alex Kovalev scored not long into the final frame, and then Mark Streit lit the lamp nine seconds later to move the Canadiens within one. With less than five minutes remaining, Kovalev potted another to recover from a five-goal deficit and force overtime. The extra session solved nothing, but the Habs won it in a shootout, capping off an improbable comeback.

JEAN BÉLIVEAU HITS 1,200 POINTS, 1971

J ean Béliveau hadn't talked about retiring, but many speculated that with "le Gros Bill" turning 40 following the 1970–71 season, he would soon be hanging up his skates. But that was a decision to be made in the off-season. Until then, Béliveau had a job to do. Besides, while he may have been Montreal's elder statesman, he still was in the midst of one of his most productive campaigns in the past decade. Heading into a game against the Black Hawks on February 20, 1971, he had 54 points in 48 games and was just three points back from reaching the 1,200-point mark.

With Prime Minister Pierre Elliott Trudeau in attendance at the Forum that evening, Béliveau continued his swan song. In the opening period, he set up rookie Phil Roberto for two goals and then, in the middle frame — passing the torch figuratively and the puck literally — Béliveau helped the youngster complete the hat trick and reach his own milestone, becoming just the second player in NHL history to rack up 1,200 career points.

FIRST HAT TRICK FOR BRENDAN GALLAGHER, 2019

The Montreal faithful were trying to will Brendan Gallagher to complete the hat trick. After the scrappy winger scored twice in the first period against the Philadelphia Flyers on February 21, 2019, the fans were cheering him on for one more. In 466 career NHL games up to that point, he had never scored three goals in a game. Gallagher was a proven goal scorer and had 10 multi-goal efforts under his belt, but he had yet to register a three-goal performance. He went after the puck with a dogged determination night in and night out, but the bounces just hadn't gone his way.

But with plenty of game left to play against the Flyers, the Bell Centre crowd wanted to make sure he finally got one. When Gallagher was sitting in the penalty box for tripping early in the second period, Habs fans yelled at him to get it done. Not long after exiting the sin bin, he made good on it, recording his first NHL hat trick in his seventh season with the Canadiens. The arena erupted, and his teammates rejoiced.

TOE BLAKE SCORES HIS FIRST IN THE NHL, 1936

Some nicknames just stick. When Hector Blake was growing up in Victoria Mines, just outside of Sudbury, Ontario, where I am writing these pages, his baby sister Margaret couldn't pronounce his name properly. What came out of her mouth sounded more like "Hec-toe," and before long everyone just started calling him "Toe." The moniker followed him to hockey's professional ranks, and years later he was still known as "Toe" to his teammates.

Blake made his NHL debut for the Montreal Maroons in the 1934–35 season, appearing in just eight games. But the following year, he was traded to the crosstown Canadiens, along with Bill Miller and the rights to Ken Grivel, in February 1936 for Lorne Chabot. On February 22, in his fifth game with the bleu, blanc, et rouge, Blake scored the lone goal, his first NHL tally, in a 1–0 victory against the New York Americans. It would be the first of many for Toe with the Canadiens. He would go on to score 234 more for Montreal over the next decade.

HABS RETIRE BOB GAINEY'S NO. 23, 2008

L egendary Soviet coach Viktor Tikhonov considered Bob Gainey to be the most complete hockey player in the world. He was so skilled on both sides of the puck that the NHL basically introduced an award, the Frank J. Selke Trophy, to honour his defensive abilities as a forward. Gainey was the inaugural winner of the Selke in 1978 and won it three more times consecutively in the seasons that followed. But before Gainey's notable two-way play added to his personal trophy collection, his defensive instincts made him a cornerstone of the Canadiens dynasty in the 1970s and helped the club capture four straight championships from 1976 through 1979.

Gainey was inducted into the Hockey Hall of Fame a few years after he hung up his skates in 1989, but one of his greatest honours was when the Canadiens raised his No. 23 to the rafters, fittingly, on February 23, 2008. Like Lafleur before him, when Gainey arrived for the ceremony, he did so in full gear and uniform, taking a lap around the ice to the delight of the Montreal faithful.

FEBRUARY 24

HABS FIRE 61 SHOTS ON PENS, 1990

Frank Pietrangelo should have called in sick. With Mario Lemieux out of the lineup, the Penguins knew they would be missing some key firepower in Montreal, but they did not expect the offensive onslaught the Canadiens threw their way. That evening, on February 24, 1990, the Habs fired 61 shots on Pietrangelo. And while the Pittsburgh netminder valiantly stopped 50 of them, despite getting hung out to dry by his club on several breakaway opportunities, the Penguins were trounced 11–1 at the Forum.

Montreal's 61-shot barrage established a club record for the most shots in a game, eclipsing the previous mark of 59 set on October 12, 1963, in a game against the New York Rangers. Those 61 shots in regulation weren't that far off the club's playoff record for most shots in a matchup. During the third game in the 1967 Stanley Cup Final against the Maple Leafs, the Canadiens rifled 63 shots on Toronto goalie Johnny Bower, but that included nearly 30 minutes of overtime. Bower stopped all but two in a 3–2 victory.

FEBRUARY 25

UNBEATEN STREAK HALTED AT 28 GAMES, 1978

As the saying goes, all good things must come to an end, including unbeaten streaks. After losing to the Pittsburgh Penguins on December 17, 1977, the Canadiens went 28 games without a defeat. The impressive run included an eight-game winning streak and a seven-game winning streak. All told, during that span, the Canadiens racked up 23 victories and five ties. On paper it seemed as though the streak might have continued when Montreal hosted the New York Rangers on February 25, 1978. For that game, the Blueshirts went with Swedish goaltender Hardy Åström between the pipes.

Åström had just been recalled from the minors and was making his big-league debut, becoming just the second European goalie to suit up in the NHL. Although the Canadiens hoped he might have had some jitters backstopping the Rangers, he later said he wasn't nervous because he had represented Sweden in big games on the international stage, including the 1976 Canada Cup. Sure enough, Åström stopped all but three shots he faced in a 6–3 victory, halting Montreal's streak.

DOUG HARVEY SETS SINGLE-SEASON ASSIST RECORD, 1955

B efore there was Bobby Orr, there was Doug Harvey. After making his debut for the Canadiens in 1947, Harvey quickly established himself as one of the best blueliners in the game. By the end of his eighth campaign in Montreal, he took home his first Norris Trophy as the league's top defenceman. He would earn the trophy six more times over the course of his Hall of Fame career, a feat that would be surpassed only by Orr. Known for taking his time and making the best play possible, Harvey always made sure he moved the puck up the ice and got it to his teammates.

When the Canadiens hosted the Bruins on February 26, 1955, Harvey was sitting at 40 assists and needed just one more helper to establish a new single-season record for defencemen. In the opening period, he set up Maurice Richard to record the milestone assist, surpassing the mark set by Toronto's Babe Pratt in 1943–44. Stat corrections now credit Pratt with 41 assists that year, but no matter — Harvey finished with 43.

OTTAWA DEFEATS MONTREAL
IN QUEBEC, 1918

With poor attendance at the Canadiens' Jubilee Rink in Montreal, general manager George Kennedy had an idea: play somewhere else. With the Habs scheduled to play their final home game of the season against the Ottawa Senators on February 27, 1918, the GM, who was also responsible for the updated crest the team was wearing that season that would forever be linked to the franchise, requested the league transfer the matchup to another location.

Provided that Kennedy's club covered the additional travel costs for Ottawa, the NHL agreed and the game was played in Quebec City, the league's first neutral-site game. The change in venue didn't help the Canadiens, however. Despite opening the scoring, they lost 3–1. While Kennedy's plan didn't pay off, nearly eight decades later, the NHL used neutral-site games as a way to test the water for future expansion plans. During the 1992–93 and 1993–94 campaigns, the league held 50 neutral-site games in locations around the United States from Sacramento to Milwaukee and in Canada from Saskatoon to Halifax.

CLAUDE LAROSE POTS FOUR, 1974

laude Larose was not what you would call a goal scorer. Although he reached the 20-goal mark once during his first stint with the Canadiens, and again when he returned in 1970, the winger was not exactly known for filling the back of the net. But when the Habs took on the Penguins on February 28, 1974, Larose picked up four goals in a 7–1 rout.

Larose, an NHL veteran of more than a decade, had missed most of the season while recovering from a broken leg suffered in the final game of the 1972–73 campaign. He had scored only three goals in the first 24 games since returning to the lineup, but he picked up a hat trick on February 26, his first in nearly seven years. In Montreal's next matchup, two days later, he exploded for four. Following the game, he was just as dumbfounded as the fans. "I never thought when I had three goals I would get four," he told reporters. In the next contest, Larose potted another two to keep his hot streak going.

FEBRUARY 29

HENRI RICHARD'S BIRTHDAY, 1936

Many referred to Henri Richard as "the Pocket Rocket" because he was the little brother of Maurice "Rocket" Richard, but as you might already know, the younger Richard did not necessarily care for the moniker. My father-in-law, Maurice, who idolized the Rocket growing up, had the chance to meet Henri at an autograph-signing session. When Maurice asked him to sign a photo as "the Pocket Rocket," he obliged the request but confessed he never cared for that nickname.

And why would he? He may have been smaller than his older brother, and would always be compared to Maurice, but Henri carved out a Hall of Fame career that stood for itself. Born in Montreal on February 29, 1936, Henri was a standout in junior. He wasn't initially expected to crack the Canadiens roster out of training camp in 1955, but he did and became a fixture on the team for the next two decades, winning 11 Stanley Cup championships, an NHL record — and three more than his big brother.

MARCH 1

NEWSY LALONDE SCORES FIVE, 1919

Newsy Lalonde put his club on his back. In the third game of Montreal's matchup against the Ottawa Senators for the NHL title, on March 1, 1919, Lalonde scored five of the Canadiens' six goals to power his team to a 6–3 victory and a commanding 3–0 series lead. After opening the scoring just over halfway through the first frame, Lalonde added another a few minutes before intermission. He led the charge again in the second stanza, completing the hat trick just a couple of minutes into the session, before adding another marker with less than six minutes remaining to make it 5–2.

Ottawa added a second tally in the third to close the deficit to two, but Lalonde restored Montreal's three-goal lead with his fifth and final goal of the night late in the frame. Two days later, he was at it again, scoring two of Montreal's three goals in a 6–3 loss to the Senators. By the time the Canadiens closed out the series in five games, Lalonde had racked up an incredible 11 goals.

MARCH 2

HABS ACQUIRE ALEX KOVALEV, 2004

t was a fresh start for Alex Kovalev. On March 2, 2004, the New York Rangers traded the mercurial Russian winger to the Canadiens for prospect Jozef Balej and a second-round draft pick later that year. The move wasn't a total shock for Kovalev. Playing in just his first full season on Broadway since the Pittsburgh Penguins sent him there a year earlier, things just didn't click for him in his second tour of duty in the Big Apple. Originally drafted 15th overall by the Rangers in 1991, Kovalev won a Cup with New York but was also remembered for the time head coach Mike Keenan left him out on the ice for a five-minute shift as punishment.

Kovalev would pick up only a few points in a dozen games down the stretch for the Canadiens, but he was a clutch performer in the playoffs, scoring six goals and 10 points in 11 games. Following the NHL's 2004–05 lockout, the team signed Kovalev to a four-year, $18 million contract. Over the next four seasons in Montreal, he would be a part of some memorable moments.

MARCH 3

HABS TROUNCE BULLDOGS 16–3, 1920

The Canadiens really put the scorekeeper to work in a game against the Quebec Bulldogs on March 3, 1920. Before the first period came to a close, they had put four past goaltender Frank Brophy, with three of those coming from "the Cannonball," Didier Pitre. After the Canadiens added two more to their lead in the first half of the second frame, the Bulldogs finally got on the board. But just 40 seconds later, the Habs scored five straight in just over five minutes to head into the second intermission with a commanding 11–1 advantage.

The club's seven-goal outburst that session matched the league record for the most goals in a period by a single team. The Canadiens, however, weren't done yet. In the final stanza, they added five more goals to easily win 16–3, establishing a franchise record for goals in a game that still stands. When the dust settled, Pitre, Newsy Lalonde, Odie Cleghorn, and Harry Cameron had each collected hat tricks, as the scorekeeper busily filled out the game sheet.

MARCH 4

THE FLOWER HITS 1K, 1981

After being held off the scoresheet for a few games, Guy Lafleur registered a milestone night against the Winnipeg Jets. The slump wouldn't have been notable for Lafleur, except he was closing in on the vaunted 1,000-point mark, so some pressure was starting to build. The Flower would have likely reached it earlier in the season had he not missed so many games with injuries (which also prevented him from reaching the 100-point mark for the seventh straight season).

When the Canadiens hosted the Jets on March 4, 1981, Lafleur broke out of his four-game rut early, assisting on Pierre Larouche's 20th goal of the campaign four minutes into the game. Just before the halfway mark of the frame, Lafleur also scored his 20th tally, moving within one point of 1,000. After the Canadiens scored seven straight goals, he potted his second of the night 54 seconds into the final session to hit 1,000. Accomplishing the feat in just 720 games, Lafleur became the fastest player in NHL history to reach the milestone.

MARCH 5

ROGIE VACHON GETS
FIRST SHUTOUT, 1967

With the Gumper on the shelf, the Canadiens looked to their goaltender of the future. While veteran netminder Gump Worsley recovered from an injury, the club called up 21-year-old Rogie Vachon from the minor leagues in Houston to join Charlie Hodge in the crease. A few weeks after making his NHL debut, on March 5, 1967, Vachon turned aside all the shots he faced from the New York Rangers to record his first career shutout. Even after Worsley returned from injury, the rookie held the net, going 11-3-5 down the stretch.

Vachon continued to play above his age in the playoffs, backstopping the Habs to the Stanley Cup Final before coming up short to a greybeard Maple Leafs team that had already stunned the hockey world by upsetting the top-seeded Chicago Black Hawks in the first round. The next season, Vachon and the Gumper split the duties between the pipes to earn the Vezina as the league's top goaltending tandem. Worsley took on the lion's share of the work in the post-season, but Vachon won his first of three championships with the Canadiens.

MARCH 6

BILL DURNAN SETS SHUTOUT RECORD, 1949

Nothing was getting by Bill Durnan. Nothing. When the final buzzer sounded on March 6, 1949, Durnan had turned aside every shot he faced for the fourth straight game. Over those contests, Durnan, who was the last goalie in the NHL to wear the "C" on his jersey (he held the captaincy after Toe Blake retired), kept the puck out of his net for a combined 283 minutes and 45 seconds, setting a modern record for the longest shutout streak. It just so happened that the record he surpassed belonged to the goalie at the other end of the ice, Frank Brimsek, a.k.a. "Mr. Zero." During the 1938–39 campaign with the Boston Bruins, Brimsek was flawless for 231 minutes and 54 seconds.

After topping Mr. Zero that game, Durnan would extend his streak to 309 minutes and 21 seconds before allowing two goals in a game against the Black Hawks. The record held until Brian Boucher of the Phoenix Coyotes surpassed it in 2004. Following his incredible performance in 1948–49, Durnan earned his fifth Vezina trophy as the league's top netminder.

MARCH 7

GERRY MCNEIL PICKS UP
10TH SHUTOUT, 1953

The Black Hawks couldn't solve Gerry McNeil. But then again, few teams could in the 1952–53 campaign. On March 7, McNeil stopped everything Chicago threw his way to record his 10th shutout of the season, matching a franchise record for the most in the modern era. He would finish the year with 10 shutouts, sharing the league lead with Toronto's Harry "Apple Cheeks" Lumley. McNeil's flawless performances couldn't have come at a better time.

After finishing the previous season with the second-most goals for in the NHL, the next year the Habs scored the third fewest in the six-team circuit. With the team's offence sputtering, McNeil was relied upon to keep the pucks out of the net. Even when he wasn't perfect, he still found ways to stymie his opponents. In the last game of the season against Detroit, Gordie Howe was sitting at 49 goals and seemed poised to join Maurice Richard in the 50-goal club. But McNeil stopped every shot Howe could muster, and that was as close to the milestone the Red Wings legend would ever get.

MARCH 8

ZDENO CHARA SIDELINES
MAX PACIORETTY, 2011

The Bell Centre faithful held its collective breath. With time winding down in the second period in a game against the Bruins on March 8, 2011, Boston captain Zdeno Chara drove Max Pacioretty into the stanchion that separated the two benches. He crumpled to the ice, and Habs fans erupted into a chorus of boos. But as Pacioretty lay motionless, the gravity of the situation took hold. The winger was eventually taken off the ice on a stretcher while his teammates looked on helplessly from the bench. Following examination at the hospital, it was revealed that Pacioretty had a severe concussion and a non-displaced fracture of his fourth cervical vertebra. Quite simply, he broke his neck.

Outrage soon followed in the hockey world and beyond. Montreal police opened a criminal investigation, and Air Canada threatened to pull its sponsorship from the league following the violent incident. Pacioretty missed the rest of the campaign, but he made a full recovery and returned the following season, scoring 33 goals and 65 points, both career benchmarks.

LYLE ODELEIN BAGS A HAT TRICK, 1994

Lyle Odelein was red-hot. The defensive defenceman, who was not exactly known for his scoring prowess, continued to be a revelation on the Canadiens' power play, proving he had some skill to his game. On March 9, 1994, Odelein scored three power-play goals in a 7–2 victory over the St. Louis Blues, becoming the first Montreal blueliner to record a regular-season hat trick since Larry Robinson in 1985. A month earlier, in a game against the Hartford Whalers, Odelein collected five assists, matching a franchise record for the most helpers in a game by a defenceman.

Just two seasons earlier, Odelein finished with one goal and seven assists in 71 games, but after head coach Jacques Demers started regularly deploying him on the power play, he began piling up the points. Following his hat trick against the Blues, Odelein had five goals and 18 points in his previous 16 games. He finished the campaign with 11 goals and 40 points, both career highs that would go unmatched.

MARCH 10

BLAKE GEOFFRION SCORES FOR MONTREAL, 2012

I am not a spiritual person, but I believe in the hockey gods. When Blake Geoffrion was traded to the Canadiens on February 17, 2012, he could no longer wear No. 5 because, of course, that number belonged to his grandfather Bernie Geoffrion and was retired by the club the year Blake was drafted to the NHL. But Blake's Canadiens pedigree went beyond Boom Boom. His great grandfather was Howie Morenz, who famously wore No. 7 until his tragic death in 1937. So to pay homage to both his grandfather and great-grandfather, Blake donned No. 57.

In his first five games with the Canadiens, Geoffrion was held off the scoresheet, but when the team travelled to Vancouver to take on the Canucks on March 10, 2012, he scored his first goal in a Canadiens sweater. It was his first NHL tally in nearly a year, and it happened the day before the 75th anniversary of Morenz's funeral, which was held at the Forum. Geoffrion scored one more goal as a member of the Canadiens.

MARCH 11

LAST GAME AT THE FORUM, 1996

t was the end of an era. The final mass at the Cathedral on Atwater. On March 11, 1996, the Canadiens played their last game at the Montreal Forum. Opened more than seven decades earlier, the Forum was one of the most iconic buildings in hockey and was the backdrop to 12 Stanley Cup celebrations. But it was home to much more than championships: It was where players such as Maurice Richard and Jean Béliveau became legends. It was also where infamous moments in hockey history such as the Richard Riot and the Good Friday Massacre occurred.

So when it was time to say goodbye, the Canadiens recruited their former leaders to pass a torch, a nod to the club's motto "To you from failing hands we throw the torch. Be yours to hold it high," in the hopes of continuing the team's winning tradition at its new home. Every captain received their fair share of applause, but the Rocket brought everyone to their feet, receiving nearly a 10-minute standing ovation that became the most enduring image from the ceremony.

MARCH 12

GUMPER GETS EGGED, 1967

The last thing Lorne "Gump" Worsley expected he would need to stop was an egg. But during a game against the New York Rangers on March 12, 1967, a fan snuck a bag of eggs into Madison Square Garden and, early in the first period, chucked one at the Gumper, hitting him in the right temple. The impact of the shot dazed Worsley and forced him to leave the game.

Worsley was a tough customer and was no stranger to punishment in the net. He once took a cannonading slapshot from Bobby Hull that hit him square in the head and knocked him unconscious, but he never thought he would need to worry about blocking projectiles from the stands. Following the game, he told reporters he didn't even realize it was an egg until he felt the yolk run down the side of his head. Worsley opted not to press charges, but he sustained a concussion that kept him out of the lineup for six weeks. Lucky for the Gumper the egg wasn't hard-boiled.

MARCH 13

MATS NÄSLUND HITS 100, 1986

The Canadiens' century club is pretty exclusive. Prior to 1985–86, it had only three members: Guy Lafleur, Pete Mahovlich, and Steve Shutt. Lafleur, of course, was the first Hab to accomplish the feat, and he did it for five consecutive years. But on March 13, 1986, Montreal's limited membership added to its ranks. In a game against the Bruins, Mats Näslund, who was known as "le Petit Viking" because he was Swedish and small in stature, reached the 100-point mark for the first time in his career.

Just over the halfway mark of the first period, the swift Swede assisted on Petr Svoboda's first of the season to reach the milestone. Näslund added a goal later in the contest, his 40th of the season, but the Canadiens fell 3–2. He would finish the year with 110. In the post-season, he continued to lead the team in scoring, collecting 19 points in 20 games as the Canadiens captured their 24th Stanley Cup. As of this writing, Näslund remains the last member of the bleu, blanc, et rouge to hit 100.

MARCH 14

ERIK COLE HIGH-FIVES REF, 2012

igh-five! After putting the puck past Ottawa netminder Ben Bishop on March 14, 2012, Erik Cole was all alone behind the net. Not wanting to waste the moment, he took matters into his own hands. As he skated by referee Greg Kimmerly, he extended his arm and gave the official a high-five while he was signalling it was a good goal. "I wanted to celebrate with somebody, and he was the only one around," the left winger explained. Cole did eventually get to revel with his teammates on the side wall, but there was no topping the initial celebration.

Although Kimmerly did appear to give Cole a discerning glance following the gesture, Cole had every reason to celebrate. It was his 27th tally of the season, and he was on pace for a banner year in goals. Cole had reached the 30-goal mark once before, but that was six years ago as a member of the Carolina Hurricanes. He added eight more down the stretch to finish with a team-leading 35, a career high.

DICK IRVIN ROTATES GOALIES, 1941

Dick Irvin was ahead of his time. Looking to find an edge in a game against the New York Americans on March 15, 1941, the Canadiens bench boss alternated his goaltenders, Bert Gardiner and Paul Bibeault, in what the newspapers reported at seven-minute intervals. Although it remains unclear just how closely Irvin stuck to the rotation, having the pair split the crease worked out as the Habs blanked the cellar-dwelling Americans 6–0. The idea apparently came to Irvin earlier in the season following a loss to the Rangers in which he lamented not having an extra goalie.

The approach was unconventional, but Irvin refined his strategy in the coming years, particularly in the 1955 Stanley Cup Playoffs. In the team's opening series against the Boston Bruins, Irvin had both his netminders, Jacques Plante and Charlie Hodge, play parts of the first three games. Plante would eventually take the reins the rest of the way, but Irvin's method was nothing if not innovative. Sharing the net in a game would not become commonplace, but platooning goaltenders became an NHL standard.

FIRST GAME AT MOLSON CENTRE, 1996

t was the start of a new chapter. Less than a week after bidding adieu to the Forum, the Canadiens moved into their new home, the Molson Centre, on March 16, 1996. But before taking on the New York Rangers, the club needed to christen the $230 million state-of-the-art building with a little bit of history. Before the game began, the team raised the retired numbers of its most iconic players to the rafters, ensuring that the franchise's legends would continue to watch over the club.

Much like the farewell ceremony at the Forum, Maurice Richard received the longest standing ovation from the Montreal faithful. The former fiery winger was so moved by the applause that he was brought to tears. Following the banner-raising, the current players were called out onto the ice. Captain Pierre Turgeon, who carried the flame from the Forum, was the last in the procession, holding the torch high to ignite the next saga. After Vincent Damphousse scored the first goal in the new building, Turgeon scored the last in a 4–2 victory.

MARCH 17

THE RICHARD RIOT, 1955

Clarence Campbell was public enemy number one in Montreal. Following an incident in which Maurice Richard landed a punch on linesman Cliff Thompson during a skirmish in a game against the Bruins, the NHL president suspended the winger for the rest of the regular season and the playoffs. Canadiens fans were rightfully outraged by the suspension. For many, it was proof that Campbell treated Richard, a proud French Canadian, more harshly than his English counterparts.

Amid that tense backdrop, just a day after handing down his decision, Campbell, against his better judgment, attended Montreal's next game on March 17, 1955. It didn't take long for things to turn ugly. Expressing their frustration, fans hurled everything from tomatoes to pennies at Campbell before a tear gas cannister erupted, halting the game and spilling mayhem out into the streets. When the dust settled, damage had been done across more than 15 blocks, and more than 100 people were arrested. For some, the Richard Riot lit the powder keg for Quebec's Quiet Revolution, which would ignite in the 1960s.

MARCH 18

THE ROCKET REACHES 50, 1945

Maurice Richard did something nobody else had done before. In the 50th and final game of the campaign, on March 18, 1945, he collected his 50th goal of the season, becoming the first player in NHL history to reach the benchmark. The Bruins hoped Richard wouldn't accomplish the feat on their watch at the Boston Garden, and they nearly succeeded in thwarting the record-setting goal, but he lit the lamp in the last few minutes of the final stanza.

A night earlier, at home against the Black Hawks, the Forum erupted when fans thought Richard had tallied the milestone marker, only to have referee King Clancy disallow it. Montreal fans weren't able to witness Richard write his name in the league's record books, but his accomplishment inspired a province and a generation of players. Although future teammate Bernie Geoffrion reached the 50-goal mark in 1961, it took nearly four decades before another player scored 50 goals in 50 games. Fittingly, it would be Mike Bossy, who grew up in Montreal and idolized Richard.

BOOM BOOM SURPASSES ROCKET FOR ART ROSS LEAD, 1955

Bernie Geoffrion was stuck between a rock and a hard place. When his teammate Maurice Richard was suspended for the rest of the season and the playoffs, he was two points behind him for the lead league. With a pair of games left on the schedule, many Habs fans did not want to see Geoffrion surpass the Rocket. Richard had been in the NHL for more than a decade but had never finished with the most points to earn the Art Ross Trophy.

So when the Canadiens hosted the Rangers for their penultimate game on March 19, 1955, many fans hoped Geoffrion would be held off the scoresheet, but he ended up scoring a goal and collecting two assists to surpass Richard with 75 points. Geoffrion would go on to win the scoring title, leaving much of the Montreal faithful in an uproar. Richard never held a grudge against Geoffrion, but some of the fans never forgave him for winning the trophy they felt should have been Richard's that year.

KOVALEV'S SPIN-O-RAMA, 2008

Alex Kovalev put Zdeno Chara in a spin cycle. Skating into the Bruins' zone in a game on March 20, 2008, Kovalev saw Chara closing in on him just above the left faceoff circle. But Kovalev did a spin-o-rama, much to the delight of play-by-play announcer Chris Cuthbert and the home crowd, to elude the hulking defenceman, who had just returned to action after missing five games with an injury. After catching Chara flat-footed with his evasive manoeuvre, Kovalev advanced across the circle toward the net and uncorked a backhand shot that trickled through the pads of goaltender Tim Thomas and into the back of the net.

Sure, the spin move was the showstopper, but it was almost more impressive that Kovalev's backhander beat Thomas from that distance. Perhaps Thomas was so awestruck by the play that he didn't see it coming, but it's definitely one he would like back. Kovalev scored 35 goals for the Canadiens that regular season, the most since his time with the Penguins, but few were as memorable as that spin-o-rama backhander.

THE BIG M SCORES 500TH CAREER GOAL, 1973

t might not have been how Frank Mahovlich envisioned his 500th goal in his mind, but he took it just the same. Early in the third period in a game against the Vancouver Canucks, on March 21, 1973, Mahovlich took a pass from Henri Richard. But instead of rifling it toward the net, Mahovlich whiffed on the shot but got enough of the puck that it trickled toward the cage. Somehow it made it past Canucks goalie Dunc Wilson, and the Big M became just the fifth player in NHL history to record 500 career goals, joining Gordie Howe, Bobby Hull, Maurice Richard, and Jean Béliveau.

Mahovlich later reflected that he couldn't believe it went in. Ditto for Wilson. Following the game, the Vancouver netminder told reporters he would rather not have made history on that shot. Earlier in the match, he stopped the Big M on a breakaway, and while that would have been a more fitting way to give up a milestone goal, the hockey gods can be a fickle bunch.

MARCH 22

DICKIE MOORE SETS SINGLE-SEASON POINT RECORD, 1959

Dickie Moore was a gentleman off the ice but one of the game's most fierce competitors on it. His strong play on both sides of the puck earned him the nickname "Digging Dickie" for his dogged determination in the corners. And he was one tough customer. After overcoming injuries as a boy growing up in Montreal, including being struck by a car and a dog bite to the face — he nearly lost a lip — Moore battled back from injuries in the NHL that would have kept lesser players on the shelf. But there was much more to Moore's game than his fierce tenacity. He was also offensively gifted.

During the 1957–58 campaign, he racked up 84 points despite playing the final stretch of the season in a cast to mend a broken wrist, somehow not even missing a shift. The next year, in the final game of the season, on March 22, 1959, Moore made history when he recorded a goal and assist to finish with 96 points, the most by a player in a single season.

MARCH 23

RICHARD SCORES FIVE GOALS AGAINST LEAFS, 1944

The third star of the game: Maurice Richard. The second star of the game: Maurice Richard. And, finally, the first star of the game: Maurice Richard. On March 23, 1944, in a playoff matchup against the Leafs, Richard earned all of the "three stars of the game" after an incredible five-goal performance. Since Imperial Oil began the promotion for its Three Star brand of gasoline eight years earlier, no NHL player had collected all three stars.

But if anyone earned all the accolades that evening, it was definitely Richard. Not only had he matched the league record for the most playoff goals in a game, originally set in 1919 by Newsy Lalonde, but he scored all of Montreal's goals in a 5–1 victory. Richard would bag two more goals against Toronto in the last game of the series, before notching five goals in the Stanley Cup Final to secure his first championship. Nine months later, he would find the back of the net five more times in a game that entered hockey lore. Stay tuned.

MARCH 24

GUY CARBONNEAU SCORES FIFTH SHORT-HANDED GOAL, 1983

Guy Carbonneau had no idea Minnesota's net was empty. With just over a minute remaining in a game against the North Stars on March 24, 1983, the Canadiens were killing a penalty. Down by a pair of goals, Minnesota pulled goaltender Don Beaupre for the extra attacker. But when defenceman Brad Maxwell fumbled the puck deep in the Montreal zone, Carbonneau jumped on the loose biscuit and started skating down the ice. It was only when he heard one of his teammates hollering from the bench that the net was empty that he looked up and saw the yawning cage.

A bourgeoning penalty-killing specialist, Carbonneau, who was playing in his rookie campaign, took his time and put the puck in the back of the net for his fifth short-handed goal of the season, establishing a new team record. The only player who finished with more short-handed tallies that year was Wayne Gretzky. The next season, Carbonneau extended his own benchmark to eight shorties, a record that still holds at the time of this writing.

MARCH 25

KOVALEV ELBOWS TUCKER, 2006

Alex Kovalev took matters into his own hands or, more accurately, his elbow. With time winding down in a game against the Maple Leafs on March 25, 2006, Kovalev narrowly avoided a full elbow to the face from Toronto's Darcy Tucker. Kovalev clearly got clipped by the pesky Leafs forward, but it could have been much worse. But when no call came, Kovalev continued skating. He managed to regain control of the puck and circled the Toronto zone.

When he saw Tucker coming at him again, he gave him a taste of his own medicine, driving his left elbow into Tucker's head. The thunderous hit drew a raucous ovation from the Montreal faithful as a melee ensued and the two fought against the boards. Kovalev received two majors, for elbowing and fighting, along with a game misconduct to end his night. Although he faced fines and suspension from the league for his actions, he didn't care. He later told reporters he was simply protecting himself after the officials seemingly refused to do their jobs.

MARCH 26

PIERRE LAROUCHE'S HATTY, 1981

Pierre Larouche hadn't scored a goal in nine games. For a two-time 50-goal scorer like Larouche, that was a big drought. And while he was certainly feeling the pressure to find the back of the net, the centre tried not to let it bother him too much. Instead, when he wasn't on the ice, he went back and reviewed game film. He later told reporters that the tape helped him see that he wasn't getting as close to the net as he normally would. "I was staying back, and that's not my style," he said.

So when the Canadiens hosted the Calgary Flames on March 26, 1981, Larouche put his observation to the test. Just over seven minutes into the first period, he scored Montreal's opening goal to snap his skid. He would add two more to complete the hat trick, his third of the season. He also added an assist on linemate Mark Napier's second-period goal for good measure. The Canadiens cruised to an 8–2 victory to extend their home unbeaten streak to 24 games.

MARCH 27

CHRIS CHELIOS HITS 20, 1988

Late in the second period of a game against the Whalers, on March 27, 1988, Canadiens blueliner Chris Chelios rifled a shot at goaltender Richard Brodeur. The Hartford netminder initially stopped the puck, but the rebound came right back to Chelios and he was able to put it in the back of the net. The tally was his 20th of the season, marking the first time a Canadiens defenceman reached that benchmark since Guy Lapointe did it in 1975.

Chelios wouldn't rack up any more goals that season, but the next year he collected 73 points and won his first Norris as the league's top defenceman. But after just another season with the Canadiens, he was traded to Chicago, where he would add two more Norris trophies to his collection. He spent nearly a decade in the Windy City, along with another in Detroit, before finally hanging up his skates at the age of 48. A big reason for Chelios's longevity was his commitment to fitness; he was notorious for riding a stationary bike in the sauna.

MARCH 28

GUS RIVERS ENDS LONGEST
GAME IN NHL HISTORY, 1930

Gus Rivers couldn't have found a better time to score. The Winnipeg, Manitoba, native had scored only one goal in 19 games during the regular season, but it takes just one to end overtime. On March 28, 1930, after three extra sessions failed to break a 1–1 deadlock between the Canadiens and the New York Rangers, Rivers scored just under nine minutes into the fourth overtime period to give the Habs a 2–1 victory and end the longest game in NHL history up to that point.

While much of the crowd at the Forum might have been starting to nod off, Rivers brought them out of their seats with his sudden-death heroics. That would prove to be the only goal he'd score that post-season, but that's all they'd need from him. Two days later, the Canadiens shut out the Rangers to punch their ticket to the Final. Taking on the defending-champion Bruins for the rights to Lord Stanley's mug, Montreal swept a powerhouse Boston squad that finished the regular season with just five losses.

MARCH 29

SERIES NOT COMPLETED, 1919

After the Canadiens and Seattle Metropolitans, of the Pacific Coast Hockey Association, duelled to a 0–0 deadlock after two periods of overtime, the game ended as a scoreless draw. That set the stage for a pivotal game on March 29, 1919, at Seattle's Ice Arena. Down 2–1 in the series, Montreal needed a victory to keep its Stanley Cup dreams alive. The Habs couldn't find the back of the net a few nights earlier, but they managed to get four by the Metropolitans to even the series and force a deciding fifth game.

But just five hours before the finale on April 1, it was announced the series would be cancelled. Five Canadiens players and manager George Kennedy were bedridden with fevers from the Spanish flu pandemic that was gripping the globe. A few days later, Montreal's Joe Hall, one of the toughest players in hockey, succumbed to the virus. In the end, both teams had their names engraved on the trophy accompanied by the ominous words "Series Not Completed," a grim reminder of what the league had lost.

MARCH 30

HABS WIN FIRST STANLEY CUP, 1916

I t was winner takes all for the rights to Lord Stanley's mug. After splitting the first four games of the championship, the Canadiens took on the Portland Rosebuds on March 30, 1916, to determine who would take home hockey's holy grail. The entire series was played at the Forum in Montreal, but the games alternated the rules of the National Hockey Association and the Pacific Coast Hockey Association. Some of the key differences were that the high-flying West Coast circuit used an extra player, known as a rover, and allowed limited forward passing.

For the pivotal game, the Habs held the advantage under NHA regulations. The Canadiens opened the scoring just over halfway through the first period. It looked as though it might be all they would need, but Portland knotted up the score with eight minutes remaining in regulation. With overtime looming, Samuel George "Goldie" Prodgers, who was used sparingly by the Canadiens that season, scored with just four minutes remaining. Montreal held the lead to win the first Stanley Cup in franchise history.

MARCH 31

HOWIE MORENZ WINS BATTLE OF MONTREAL IN OT, 1927

Every goal counted in the first-ever NHL Battle of Montreal. In the opening round of the 1927 Stanley Cup Playoffs, the Canadiens squared off against their city rivals, the Maroons, in a two-game, total-goals series. The format was exactly how it sounds. Whoever scored the most goals over two games won the series. Although the Canadiens finished with the most goals in the Canadian Division, the Maroons were the defending champions and were not going down without a fight.

After the first game ended in a 1–1 draw, the pivotal matchup was set for March 31, 1927. When regulation ended in a scoreless deadlock, it truly became a next goal wins scenario. Not long after the halfway mark of the extra session, Howie Morenz, a.k.a. "the Stratford Streak," put the puck past goaltender Clint Benedict to seal the series. The Canadiens got lucky despite their anemic offence, but they were no match in the next round for the Ottawa Senators, who outscored them 5–1 to go to the Final, where they would win their fourth and final Stanley Cup.

MARK RECCHI SCORES 250, 1996

Before Mark Recchi became a doctor, he was a Montreal Canadien. He never actually became Dr. Recchi, but there's a pretty good story there. When he was playing with the Bruins in the twilight of his NHL career, Recchi suggested the Canadiens exaggerated the severity of Max Pacioretty's injuries in an effort to exact a suspension against his teammate Zdeno Chara. As you will recall, Chara drove Pacioretty into the stanchion, resulting in a severe concussion and fractured vertebra.

While much of the hockey world dismissed this theory, it lived on as a meme, and at least once Sportsnet featured Recchi's name on a broadcast as Dr. Recchi. We will never know how he would have fared as an MD, but he did pretty well as a Canadien. After he was traded to Montreal from Philadelphia in 1995, he played five seasons for the Habs, including two back-to-back 30-goal campaigns. In his first full year in Montreal, Recchi reached a milestone. On April 1, 1996, in a game against Buffalo, he scored his 250th career goal.

APRIL 2

FLOWER HITS 50, 1980

Jim Korn found out the hard way it's best not to hit the Flower. During a game against the Canadiens on April 2, 1980, the Red Wings defenceman struck Guy Lafleur. Lafleur later said it was a fair play, but he felt it changed the course of the game. "I don't know if it woke the whole team up — but it woke me up," he told reporters. He would go on to score his 49th goal of the season to give Montreal a 4–2 lead. Just over five minutes into the final frame, Lafleur hit the 50-goal plateau for the sixth straight season, becoming the first player in NHL history to accomplish the feat.

Lafleur and the Habs were in enemy territory at the newly minted Joe Louis Arena, but he still received a rousing standing ovation from the home crowd. Later that evening, Wayne Gretzky also punched his ticket to the 50-goal club for the first time in his NHL career. He would, of course, reach the mark in eight consecutive seasons, surpassing Lafleur's incredible feat.

APRIL 3

HABS WIN CUP, 1930

The Boston Bruins may have been the defending champs, but they were no match for the Canadiens. On April 3, 1930, the two clubs squared off for the second game in a best-of-three series for the Stanley Cup. After the Habs took the first matchup 3–0, the Bruins were on the ropes. Although Boston's season was on the line, they sure didn't play like it. According to newspaper reports, the Canadiens outskated and outplayed the Bruins for the first two periods. After opening the scoring nine minutes into the contest, the Habs added to their lead and were up 3–0 early in the second session.

Eddie Shore got the Bruins on the board just after the halfway mark of that period, but Howie Morenz scored five minutes later to restore the Canadiens' three-goal lead. The Bruins added two more in the final stanza, but it was too little too late. When the final buzzer sounded, Boston had lost two games in a row for the first time that year, while Montreal won its first championship in six years.

MICHEL "BUNNY" LAROCQUE WINS VEZINA, 1977

E ver since he was a boy, nobody called Michel Larocque by his first name. Rather, he was known as "Bunny." The sweet sobriquet was given to him by his mother and it stuck around, even as he broke into the big leagues with the Canadiens. Drafted sixth overall by Montreal in 1972, Larocque made his debut the following year, sharing the crease with Wayne Thomas and Michel Plasse, who each saw more action that season with starter Ken Dryden in the midst of a contract dispute and clerking at a law firm.

When Dryden returned to the ice for the 1974–75 season, he and Larocque would form a formidable tandem. Together they would win three straight Vezina trophies for the best goals-against average in the league. They shared the hardware for the first time on April 4, 1977, after finishing the season with a combined 2.14 GAA. Dryden had won it the season before, but Larocque wasn't officially a co-winner because he was a few games shy of the 25-game minimum required for the Vezina back in the day.

APRIL 5

HABS TROUNCE CAPS 10–2, 1975

The Capitals didn't stand a chance. Heading into the penultimate game of their inaugural season in the NHL, they had won only seven games. Just one of those victories had come on the road, which led to the team jubilantly celebrating with a garbage can that the club called "the Stanley Can," because after so much futility as visitors, it felt like they had won the championship. Just over a week after that triumph, Washington travelled to Montreal for a matchup on April 5, 1972.

The Capitals had won only seven games in 78 outings, while the Canadiens had lost only eight times at the Forum and were tops in the Norris Division. Sometimes a matchup may not appear as lopsided on the ice as it does on paper, but that certainly wasn't the case that night. The Habs outshot the Capitals 45 to 18 and easily cruised to a 10–2 victory. Jacques Lemaire and Serge Savard each scored two goals, while Glen Sather, who had only six assists in 61 games, nearly doubled his season total, collecting four helpers.

APRIL 6

PAUL MASNICK SCORES
IN DOUBLE OT, 1952

Paul Masnick's season with the Cincinnati Mohawks of the AHL may have been over, but there was still more hockey to be played. The day after his team was eliminated from the post-season, Masnick was in Boston on April 6, 1952, to join the Canadiens for the sixth game of their semifinal series against the Bruins. Down 3–2 in the series, the Habs needed a victory to force a decisive seventh game.

While the Regina native had played 43 games for Montreal a year earlier, his last NHL action was more than three months ago, before he was sent back to the American Hockey League. The Bruins jumped out to an early 2–0 lead in the first period, but the Canadiens eventually knotted up the score to force overtime. When the first extra session solved nothing, they went to double OT at the Boston Garden. Less than eight minutes into the frame, an unlikely hero emerged. Masnick, who was in the minors the day before, cashed in a Doug Harvey rebound to keep Montreal's season alive.

APRIL 7

BOOM BOOM NETS STANLEY CUP FINAL HAT TRICK, 1955

The last time the Red Wings played at the Montreal Forum, the game was cancelled following a protest against NHL president Clarence Campbell's decision to suspend Maurice Richard for the remainder of the campaign and playoffs. When the Canadiens hosted their Motor City rivals on April 7, 1955, for the third game of the Stanley Cup Final, Richard was, of course, not in the lineup. Missing a key piece of their firepower and down two games to none, the rest of the team needed to step up.

Bernie Geoffrion, who won the scoring title in Richard's absence, to the chagrin of much of the fan base, scored two goals in the opening frame and then completed the hat trick in the second period to lead the Habs to a 4–2 win to get back in the series. The victory also snapped Detroit's 15-game winning streak, which extended back to the tail end of the regular season. The Canadiens would push the series to seven games, but they came up a win shy of their eighth championship.

MAURICE RICHARD AND "SUGAR" JIM HENRY, 1952

t is one of the most iconic images in hockey history. With a bandage above his left eye and blood still running down his face, Maurice Richard is shaking hands with Bruins goaltender "Sugar" Jim Henry, who is sporting a black eye, an occupational hazard of tending the twine without a mask. The snapshot, taken at the conclusion of a hard-fought Game 7 on April 8, 1952, captures two warriors who left it all on the ice. And after the battle was over, with both players sacrificing their bodies for the emblems on their sweaters, they shook hands like gentlemen.

But before that moment was immortalized, there's an even better story. During the second period, Richard was knocked out cold following a dust-up with Boston's Leo Labine. While the home crowd at the Forum held its collective breath, Richard got stitches for a deep gash above his left eye and then returned to the bench. In the final frame, with blood still streaking down his face, he scored the game-winner against Henry that would send Montreal to the Stanley Cup Final.

APRIL 9

SAKU KOIVU MAKES EMOTIONAL RETURN, 2002

As Saku Koivu emerged onto the ice, the sellout crowd at the Molson Centre rose to their feet. For the next eight minutes, they stood and celebrated the return of their captain. Koivu, who had missed the entire season while battling cancer, reclaimed his spot in the lineup and in the hearts of the Montreal faithful. As the raucous cheers continued while the crowd chanted "Saku! Saku! Saku!" public address announcer Michel Lacroix tried to interrupt the triumphant applause to start the game, not once but three times, and with every effort he was drowned out by the passionate supporters.

While Maurice Richard received a nine-minute standing ovation at the farewell ceremony for the Forum, this reception was practically unparalleled in the long and storied history of the franchise. Koivu didn't get on the scoresheet in his first game in more than a year, but he played eight minutes in a 4–3 victory that clinched the Canadiens a playoff spot for the first time in four years. The next game, he would pick up two assists.

CANADIENS WIN STANLEY CUP, 1956

Montreal's Stanley Cup was all but secured, so Émile Bouchard came over the boards. With time winding down in the game, the captain stepped out onto the ice for a swan song. He hadn't played for a few weeks, but Bouchard was dressed and waiting on the bench to take his final strides in a Canadiens sweater. He had been with the Canadiens for 15 seasons and had already collected three championships during his tenure.

After playing in a game against the New York Rangers on February 18, 1956, Bouchard, who had missed stretches of the campaign due to injuries, didn't see action for the rest of the regular season. He suited up for a playoff game against the Blueshirts a month later but didn't make another appearance until April 10, when Montreal was seconds away from clinching its third title in five years. After capturing his fourth championship, Bouchard hung up his skates but his impact on the club would continue. When Jean Béliveau became captain in 1961, he said it was Bouchard's example he followed.

APRIL 11

ROADRUNNER SCORES HAT TRICK, 1974

Yvan Cournoyer did what he did best: skating circles around opponents. In a playoff game against the New York Rangers, on April 11, 1974, Cournoyer picked up three goals on three separate breakaways in a lopsided 11–4 victory. While Cournoyer was modest in his post-game assessment, suggesting he got lucky with the number of breakaways, the truth is that when you skated as effortlessly as Cournoyer, those openings were just routine.

Known as "the Roadrunner," it was rather fitting that his second career playoff hat trick, a combination of his skating and penchant for finding the back of the net, came against the Rangers. Years earlier in his career, following a matchup in New York, Cournoyer remembered a reporter referring to him as the Roadrunner in his write-up. When Cournoyer returned to the Big Apple a few weeks later, he found the writer and said, "Do you know what you did to me? You called me the Roadrunner. Now I have to skate fast the rest of my career." And skate fast he did.

APRIL 12

HABS SWEEP BRUINS, 1987

The Bruins just couldn't catch a break. After defeating the Canadiens in the playoffs in 1943, they simply didn't have an answer for Montreal in the post-season for more than four decades. They would go on to lose to the Habs in 17 consecutive series over that span. So when they squared off again in the 1987 Stanley Cup Playoffs, it didn't look promising for the Bruins. Moreover, aside from the long-standing historical futility, the Canadiens had been Boston's tormentors quite recently, eliminating them in the first round in each of the previous three years.

The Habs opened the series with three straight victories, but the Bruins were on the verge of elimination and having their playoff dreams dashed yet again at the hands of their archrivals. Although the Bruins had a 2–1 lead early in the second period on April 12, 1987, Montreal scored three goals to complete the sweep and eliminate Boston for the 18th straight time. The last time the Bruins triumphed over the Habs in the post-season, the league was still a six-team circuit.

APRIL 13

ALEX KOVALEV SLASH, 2004

"Double overtime, you stop playing?" Canadiens defenceman Sheldon Souray didn't mince his words in response to an incident involving teammate Alex Kovalev. During the second extra frame against the Bruins on April 13, 2004, Kovalev was slashed by Travis Green. While it seemed pretty harmless, Kovalev shook his right hand as though he were in pain and lost sight of the play at the most critical moment. As Souray went to retrieve the loose puck, he collided with Kovalev, who was still focused on trying to draw a call.

The confusion allowed Bruins winger Glen Murray to take advantage of the situation. With a clear lane to José Théodore, Murray beat the Canadiens' netminder to clinch a 4–3 victory and give Boston a commanding 3–1 series lead. The enigmatic Kovalev later maintained he had lost the feeling in his hand, but Habs fans weren't interested in hearing any of his excuses. Kovalev did manage to make up for the gaffe. He scored the game-winner in the next contest and played a critical role in forcing a decisive seventh game.

APRIL 14

CANADIENS CHAMPIONSHIPS, 1931 AND 1960

When you have won as many Stanley Cups as the Montreal Canadiens, 24 by last count, you're bound to have more than a few title anniversaries that overlap. Case in point: April 14. On that day in 1931, the Habs blanked the Black Hawks 2–0 to secure their second straight Stanley Cup. The Canadiens were bruised and battered from a semifinal matchup against the Bruins that went the distance, but they still found a way to battle. George Hainsworth stopped every shot that came his way, and rookie Johnny Gagnon scored the championship-clinching goal.

Exactly 29 years later, the Canadiens did it again. Once again they shut out their opponents, defeating the Maple Leafs 4–0 to complete the sweep to win their fifth consecutive championship, a feat that will likely never be repeated. Following the game, head coach Toe Blake was asked what comes next after a fifth straight title. He responded that he liked odd numbers and that "after six comes seven." Blake would get to another odd number, but he would have to wait another six years.

APRIL 15

FIRST OCTOPUS CHUCKED AGAINST CANADIENS, 1952

NHL ice surfaces had been littered by newspapers, hats, programs, and even condoms over the years, but this was a first. Early in the fourth game of the Stanley Cup Final in Detroit, referee Bill Chadwick had to halt play because an octopus had been thrown onto the sheet. The game continued, and the Red Wings went on to defeat the Canadiens 3–0 to complete the sweep and hoist Lord Stanley's mug. The flying cephalopod was just a footnote in that game, but it would hold greater meaning in the coming years.

It turns out the mollusk-tossers were brothers Jerry and Pete Cusimano, who owned a local fish market in Detroit. The pair believed the octopus made for a natural good luck charm because its eight tentacles symbolized the number of wins needed to secure a championship in that era. So on April 15, 1952, they put their theory to the test. The rest, as they say, is history. A tradition was born, and throwing octopuses became synonymous with Detroit hockey in the decades that followed.

APRIL 16

MORE CANADIENS CUPS, 1953 AND 1957

All right, now the Canadiens are just showing off. April 16 was also a double championship anniversary day. The first was in 1953. When the Stanley Cup Final began that year against Boston, Jacques Plante was between the pipes, but after Plante allowed four goals in the opening matchup, Gerry McNeil took over in the crease. McNeil and Plante split the previous series against the Black Hawks, but head coach Toe Blake's gambit paid off. McNeil posted two shutouts in the final three games of the series, including the championship-clinching game, in which Elmer Lach scored the only goal just over a minute into overtime to break a scoreless deadlock.

Exactly four years later, once again facing off against the Bruins, the defending-champion Canadiens were searching for their second straight title. After Maurice Richard opened the series with four goals, Plante limited Boston to just four goals in the first four games. Holding a commanding 3–1 series lead heading back to Montreal on April 16, the Habs vanquished their archrivals to secure their sixth Stanley Cup on home ice in the NHL era.

ALEX KOVALEV SCORES HELMETLESS GOAL, 2008

N o matter what level you play at, there's nothing quite like scoring a goal without a bucket. Playing outside in the cold winter air, with the wind blowing through your hair, makes anybody feel like an NHLer. The league made helmets mandatory for incoming players starting in the 1979–80 season, but a number of players continued to play without a helmet. Chief among them was Craig MacTavish, who holds the distinction of being the last helmetless NHL player to score a goal.

After MacTavish hung up his skates, the only time players bulged the twine without head protection was by accident. So whenever it happened, it made any goal look like a highlight reel effort. When Alex Kovalev did it on April 17, 2008, you couldn't help but think of Guy Lafleur — "le Demon Blond" — racing down the ice. After losing his helmet in a dust-up with Zdeno Chara, Kovalev kept the play alive and scored a nifty backhander. And while the Bruins scored five straight to take that game, the only memory that matters is Kovalev's windswept locks.

MARCEL BONIN CLINCHES CHAMPIONSHIP, 1959

t must have been the gloves. After Montreal's Maurice Richard missed much of the 1958–59 campaign with injuries, legend has it that Marcel Bonin donned the Rocket's gloves when he wasn't available for the playoffs. Bonin, who was known as "l'Ours de Joliette" because he reportedly once wrestled a bear, a story so wild it just had to be included in this book, finished the regular season with 13 goals in 47 games, so there must have been some magic in Richard's mitts.

In Montreal's opening series against the Chicago Black Hawks, Bonin scored an incredible seven goals in five games to lead the Canadiens to the Stanley Cup Final. Richard returned for a handful of games in the championship matchup against the Maple Leafs, but Bonin continued to harness the Rocket's scoring prowess. It was only fitting that, on April 18, 1959, with the Canadiens on the verge of winning their fourth straight title, it was Bonin who scored the championship-clinching goal in the second period. He finished the postseason with a league-leading 10 goals in 11 games.

APRIL 19

CANADIENS MOUNT SERIES COMEBACK, 2004

t didn't look good for the Canadiens. After going down 3–1 in their opening-round series to the Bruins, their playoff dreams were turning into a nightmare. Never before in the storied history of the franchise had Montreal recovered from a 3–1 deficit in a best-of-seven series. But as they say, "never say never" and "records are meant to be broken." The history was not on their side, but the team did not quit.

The Habs rattled off two straight victories to set up a decisive winner-takes-all game in Boston on April 19, 2004. The two clubs appeared destined for overtime until Montreal's Richard Zednik broke a scoreless deadlock just over the halfway mark of the third frame. It would be all they'd need. Zednik would add an empty-net goal in the dying seconds, and José Théodore stopped all 32 shots that came his way to pick up his first career playoff shutout and become just the fourth goaltender in NHL history to earn a Game 7 shutout on the road.

GOOD FRIDAY MASSACRE, 1984

No other event came to symbolize the Battle of Quebec rivalry like the Good Friday Massacre. Played on April 20, 1984 — Good Friday, of course — the Canadiens squared off against their provincial rivals, the Quebec Nordiques. The rivalry between the two clubs had intensified following a divisional realignment a few years earlier, but no one was prepared for what would happen that night at the Forum. Near the end of the second period, a skirmish led to a bench-clearing brawl. Although the officials had tossed 11 players before intermission, this had not been communicated clearly to all the offenders.

When both teams returned to the ice to warm up for the third period, some of the players learned their fate from the public address announcer and, with nothing else to lose, started another brawl before being shown the gate. All told, 252 penalty minutes were handed out, the third most in a playoff game in NHL history. Legendary *Hockey Night in Canada* play-by-play man Bob Cole referred to it as the "brawl to end all brawls."

CAREY PRICE SHUTS OUT
BRUINS IN GAME 7, 2008

The Canadiens have been spoiled with goaltenders. From Georges Vézina to Jacques Plante and Ken Dryden to Patrick Roy, the franchise had been blessed with talent between the pipes. And then Carey Price seemed destined to join that list. Drafted fifth overall by Montreal in 2005, he made his NHL debut in the 2007–08 campaign, but it was his performance in the post-season that year that provided a glimpse into the greatness that would come.

Price opened his playoff career with a victory and a shutout a few games later, but he also had his share of struggles in the Canadiens' first-round series against the Boston Bruins, giving up five goals in two straight games, as the Bruins overcame a 3–1 deficit. But Price shut the door when it mattered most: Game 7. On April 21, 2008, the rookie goaltender stopped all 25 shots he faced to record his second playoff shutout. Throughout the game, the Montreal faithful lauded him by chanting "Carey! Carey! Carey!" a chorus that would come to define his tenure in Montreal.

APRIL 22

STEVE SHUTT RECORDS HAT TRICK, 1980

D espite netting his first career playoff hat trick to lead the Canadiens to a 6–2 victory, Steve Shutt wasn't happy with the team's performance. Following the game on April 22, 1980, he told reporters, "We didn't play as well tonight as we did in Minnesota." The Canadiens had taken the two games on the road at the Met Center handily, with Shutt recording the game-winner in the last matchup before returning to Montreal. The Habs were up 3–2 in the series following Shutt's three-goal effort, but he didn't feel there was much the team should be happy about.

"At times tonight we were a little sloppy," he said. "We made mistakes." Shutt's words would prove to be a harbinger of things to come. When the Habs went back to Minnesota to try to close out the series, they allowed five straight goals in the second period as the North Stars forced a seventh game against the four-time defending champions. There would be no fifth consecutive title as Minnesota defeated Montreal in the decisive matchup, handing the team its first playoff series loss since 1975.

APRIL 23

NORDIQUES TOP HABS 7–6 IN OT, 1985

Anybody but Dale Hunter. With less than two minutes remaining in overtime, on April 23, 1985, Hunter caught a pass from Michel Goulet, who had already recorded a hat trick that game, and wired the puck past Canadiens goaltender Steve Penney to complete a wild 7–6 victory over Montreal and give Quebec a 2–1 series lead. Hunter, of course, was no stranger to haunting the Habs. A few years earlier, he recorded the series-winner in overtime to take the first playoff Battle of Quebec.

Montreal had eliminated Quebec in six games the previous season, and Hunter and the Nordiques were out for revenge. Before his heroics in sudden death, the provincial rivals had combined for 12 goals, including five in the final frame, and traded 140 penalty minutes in a chippy affair. It was one of the biggest goals of Hunter's career, but the Nordiques' biggest goal was yet to come. Just over a week later, much to the chagrin of the Montreal faithful at the Forum, Peter Stastny scored the Game 7 overtime winner to send Quebec to the conference final.

JEAN BÉLIVEAU SCORES IN OVERTIME, 1969

You might be surprised to learn that Jean Béliveau scored only one overtime goal in his illustrious career. But during his tenure in the NHL, the league did not have regular-season overtime. It was scrapped during the Second World War and was not reintroduced for more than a decade after Béliveau retired. The only time "le Gros Bill" could tickle the twine in OT was during the playoffs. And despite racking up 68 post-season goals from 1954 to 1968, the most on the Canadiens during that span by a country mile, none were in sudden death.

But in the 1969 Stanley Cup Playoffs, the stars finally aligned for Béliveau. On April 24, 1969, just over halfway into the second overtime against Boston, Béliveau called for a pass from Claude Provost and then put the puck into the back of the net, picking up his first career overtime goal and sending Montreal to the Cup Final for the fifth straight year. Béliveau played in two more post-seasons before hanging up his skates, but it proved it be his only OT goal.

APRIL 25

PATRICK ROY STUNS BRUINS, 1994

B ruins coach Brian Sutter learned the hard way not to underestimate Patrick Roy. Before the fifth game of their playoff series against the Canadiens, on April 25, 1994, the Boston bench boss said, "Roy is going to have to be good because we are going to better." Famous last words. Not only was the Montreal goalie good, he was even better than the Bruins could have imagined. Although he was still recovering from appendicitis that saw him miss the third game of the series while he was in the hospital, Roy returned for the fourth matchup at the Forum and picked up a victory.

The next game, still on antibiotics to kick the infection, Roy turned in another incredible performance. Despite being outshot 61 to 36 by the Bruins, Roy put his team on his back, stopping all but one shot he faced, leading the Canadiens to a 2–1 overtime victory to take a 3–2 series lead. It also marked the 11th straight overtime win for the defending Stanley Cup champions, an incredible run for the Habs and their netminder.

APRIL 26

JAROSLAV HALÁK HAS
RECORD-BREAKING NIGHT, 2010

With the Canadiens on the brink of elimination, Jaroslav Halák proved once again that, during the spring of 2010, he was the best goalie on the planet. After stopping all but one shot he faced a few nights earlier on the road in Washington to keep Montreal's dreams alive, he put on a performance for the ages at the Bell Centre on April 26. Although Mike Cammalleri scored two goals in the opening period, Halák was flawless in the first frame, turning aside 18 shots. He was perfect yet again in the second session, making another 14 saves.

Montreal added to its lead early in the final stanza, but the Capitals finally got on the board with less than five minutes remaining. Halák, however, continued his otherworldly play between the pipes, making another 21 saves to close out the contest with 53 in regulation, an NHL record for the most stops by a goaltender in a non-overtime playoff victory in the modern expansion era. Two nights later in Game 7, Halák ... well, you'll just have to read on.

APRIL 27

JEAN BÉLIVEAU SETS PLAYOFF ASSIST RECORD, 1971

Just a few months shy of his 40th birthday, Jean Béliveau proved he was still one of hockey's most outstanding playmakers. On April 27, 1971, in a playoff game against the Minnesota North Stars, Béliveau assisted on three of Montreal's five third-period goals, guiding the team to a 6–1 victory and a 3–2 lead in the semifinal series.

The three helpers brought his career playoff assist total to 94, surpassing Gordie Howe's mark to establish a new NHL record. Through 12 playoff games so far that run, Béliveau had racked up 13 assists and was just two shy of equalling Stan Mikita's benchmark for the most assists in a single postseason. Béliveau, of course, would pick up four more helpers in the Cup Final to set a new record. After collecting his 10th and final championship, he hung up his skates. While Bobby Orr made short work of Béliveau's single playoff assist record the next year, his career playoff assist benchmark held for 13 years until Denis Potvin and Bryan Trottier both surpassed it in the 1984 Stanley Cup Playoffs.

JAROSLAV HALÁK STUNS CAPS, 2010

J aroslav Halák did it again. Just two days after setting an NHL record for the most saves in a non-overtime playoff game in the modern expansion era, the goalie continued to stun the Capitals. On April 28, 2010, squaring off in a do-or-die Game 7 on the road at the Verizon Center, Halák stopped 41 of 42 shots he faced, backstopping the Canadiens to a 2–1 victory to knock off the Presidents' Trophy winners.

Not only had the Habs busted the brackets of many who expected Washington to make a deep playoff run, they became just the ninth No. 8 team to eliminate a No. 1 team since the league adopted its current playoff format nearly two decades earlier, and just the first eighth seed to pull it off despite being down 3–1 in the series. Following the game, Halák reflected on what the club accomplished. "No one gave us a chance to win, not even one game," he said. Well, Halák and the Habs certainly proved the doubters wrong. And they were just getting started.

CLAUDE LEMIEUX SCORES IN OT, 1986

Guy Carbonneau's words of wisdom must have been ringing in Claude Lemieux's ears. During the decisive seventh game against the Hartford Whalers on April 29, 1986, the Montreal rookie was getting cross-checked in overtime. Every ounce of the young winger's being would've wanted to exact retribution, but he knew that's exactly what his opponents wanted and what Carbonneau had warned him about.

Ahead of the matchup, Carbonneau told him to forget about the other team and worry about his own game. So Lemieux did just that. Instead of looking for revenge, he called game. Just six minutes into the extra session, Lemieux backhanded the puck over Mike Liut's glove and just under the crossbar to give the Canadiens a 2–1 victory in Game 7. Lemieux, who had been called up from the minors just before the season's end, became the first rookie in NHL history to score an overtime goal in a seventh game. He continued to play like a poised veteran that post-season, collecting two more game-winning goals as the Habs went on to win the Stanley Cup.

APRIL 30

MARIO TREMBLAY RESIGNS, 1997

Mario Tremblay knew it was the right thing to do for himself and his family, but it didn't make it any easier. On April 30, 1997, standing beside Réjean Houle, GM of the Canadiens, Tremblay announced he was resigning as head coach of the club at an emotional press conference. After the Habs were eliminated a couple of nights earlier by the Devils, Tremblay said he went home to his wife and two daughters and couldn't see any happiness in their eyes.

Tremblay, who presided over Patrick Roy's final game with the Canadiens, had endured plenty of criticism during his brief tenure behind the bench in Montreal, and it was taking a toll on his family. "I have to do something to put a smile on their faces," he told reporters, fighting back tears. While Tremblay bled bleu, blanc, et rouge, having won four Stanley Cups with the team as a player, and loved his time as coach, hockey is just a game and family always comes first. Following his departure, the Canadiens named Alain Vigneault head coach.

MONTREAL WINS 13TH STANLEY CUP, 1965

The Montreal faithful had not forgotten. When NHL president Clarence Campbell presented the Stanley Cup to the Canadiens at the Forum on May 1, 1965, the fans let him have it. It had been a decade since Campbell suspended Maurice Richard for the remainder of the season and the playoffs, but Habs supporters had not forgiven him. And while the Canadiens had collected five straight championships following Richard's reinstatement, it didn't matter. To them, Campbell would always be remembered as the figure who robbed the Rocket of his shot at the Art Ross Trophy.

Nevertheless, as the heckling subsided and Campbell presented the silver chalice to captain Jean Béliveau, the fans basked in their sixth title in the past decade. Béliveau would also be named the inaugural winner of the Conn Smythe Trophy as the most valuable player in the playoffs, an easy choice after he racked up 10 points in the Final. He opened the scoring just 14 seconds into the game, and the Canadiens added three more in the first period to put the match out of reach for the Black Hawks.

NORDIQUES TAKE BATTLE OF QUEBEC IN GAME 7 OT, 1985

For the first time ever, the Battle of Quebec would be decided in a do-or-die Game 7. On May 2, 1985, the Canadiens hosted the Nordiques at the Forum with a ticket to the conference final on the line. Just over three minutes into the game, Quebec's Bruce Bell opened the scoring. After the Nordiques added to their lead early in the second period, the Canadiens scored twice to knot it up at two goals apiece.

When nobody could find the back of the net in the final stanza, the provincial rivals went to sudden death for the third time that series. Early in the extra session, Peter Stastny tapped in a Pat Price rebound to score the biggest goal in Nordiques history, vanquishing the Canadiens to take on the Flyers in the conference final. The Nordiques won the battle, but they ultimately lost the war. It was the farthest the franchise would go in the post-season until the club was relocated to Denver, where they would win the Stanley Cup in their first season as the Avalanche.

MAY 3

HENRI RICHARD PLAYS IN 165TH PLAYOFF GAME, 1973

Henri Richard found the silver lining. Despite losing 7–4 to the Black Hawks in the third game of the Stanley Cup Final on May 3, 1973, the veteran centre still felt the Canadiens could build on their effort for the next game. And if anybody knew how to evaluate a playoff game, it was Richard. Playing in his 16th post-season, the grizzled veteran had played in more playoff games than any other player in NHL history. In fact, the deflating loss to Chicago was actually his 165th career playoff game, a league record. Richard surpassed the benchmark set by Red Kelly, who logged 164 playoff games with Detroit and Toronto.

For Richard, the positive takeaway was that after trailing 5–1 in the third period, his team scored three goals to close the deficit to one before the Black Hawks added two empty-netters to put the game out of reach. Teammate Claude Larose, however, was a little more acerbic in his assessment: "It's about time we told ourselves we have to play three periods in a game instead of one."

MAY 4

HABS ROOKIE BENCH BOSS WINS CUP, 1969

Claude Ruel capped off his first season behind the Canadiens' bench with a Stanley Cup, but as far as GM Sam Pollock was concerned, the skipper was with the club for life. Ruel had impossibly big shoes to fill, taking over for the legendary Toe Blake, who rode off into the sunset the year before after earning his eighth championship as a coach, but the former scout carried on his predecessor's winning ways. But despite supposedly earning a lifetime contract with the team on the heels of his incredible rookie season, Ruel would relinquish his duties far earlier than anyone expected.

The following season, with the Canadiens sputtering and ultimately missing the playoffs, he offered to resign if it would help the team. Ruel stuck it out for the year, but just 23 games into the 1970–71 campaign, he turned in his resignation, citing the pressure of the position and that the players were no longer producing for him. Ruel returned to his former role in player development but was back behind the Montreal bench by the end of the decade.

HENRI RICHARD SCORES
OVERTIME CUP CLINCHER, 1966

After losing the first two games of the Stanley Cup Final to the Red Wings, the Canadiens stormed back, winning four in a row to capture their second straight title on May 5, 1966. With regulation ending in a 2–2 deadlock, they went to sudden death. Just over two minutes into the extra session, Henri Richard clinched the championship, scoring what would be the only overtime goal of his career. But it wasn't exactly a highlight reel goal. According to Richard, Dave Balon shot the puck to him but someone grabbed his stick, and the puck ended up bouncing off Richard and into the net.

The Red Wings, however, had another account. Goaltender Roger Crozier told coach Sid Abel that Richard had actually pushed the puck over the line with his glove. Abel later told reporters he felt it wasn't a clean goal, but he didn't put up much of a challenge on the ice. After Crozier retired to his dressing room, he learned he had been awarded the Conn Smythe, becoming the first player to win the trophy as a member of the losing team.

MAY 6

GILBERT DIONNE WINS IT IN OT, 1993

Gilbert Dionne did something his older brother, Marcel, never accomplished: he scored an overtime goal in the playoffs. On May 6, 1993, just over eight minutes into the extra session, the younger Dionne scored to give the Canadiens a 4–3 victory and take a commanding 3–0 series lead against the Buffalo Sabres. Or did he? Following the game, Sabres coach John Muckler argued that Dionne hadn't actually scored at all. Instead, the Buffalo bench boss insisted that the puck went in off Pat LaFontaine after Patrice Brisebois fired off a weak shot toward the net from the blue line.

Why Muckler was quibbling about how the goal went in was a curious tactic, but it didn't matter; the result remained the same. The Canadiens had won their fourth straight game in overtime, and with the way they were rolling in OT, every Hab was potentially lethal in sudden death. And despite the suggestion the credit should have gone to someone else, Dionne, who hadn't played much that game, skated off the ice with bragging rights over his Hall of Fame brother.

HABS AVOID LIGHTNING SWEEP, 2015

t was a mythic battle: David Desharnais vs. Goliath. On May 7, 2015, the diminutive five-foot-seven forward scored his first goal of the playoffs against Lightning netminder Ben Bishop, who towered above the net with his six-foot-seven frame. It was the third goal the gigantic goalie allowed on 14 shots. Desharnais's tally proved to be the dagger that chased the leviathan from the crease in favour of Andrei Vasilevskiy. The Russian backup, however, didn't fare much better. He allowed two goals on the first three shots he faced as the Canadiens mounted a 5–0 lead.

At the other end of the ice, Carey Price stopped everything that came his way until Nikita Kucherov finally got the Bolts on the board just past the halfway mark in the second period. The Lightning potted another on the man advantage early in the final frame, but that was as far as they would get. Montreal's Brandon Prust added the final goal minutes later as the Canadiens went on to win 6–2 to avoid the sweep and stave off elimination.

MAY 8

HABS AND HAWKS COMBINE FOR 15 GOALS, 1973

When Ken Dryden was asked if he had ever let in eight goals in the NHL, he said he didn't think so, but added that if he did it wasn't on home ice. As studious as Dryden was, he had misremembered a little bit. He had previously allowed eight goals at the Forum twice, but where he was right is that he had never allowed that many goals in Montreal during the playoffs. In fact, up to that point, the Canadiens had never given up eight in a playoff game at the Forum. It simply didn't happen. Until May 8, 1973.

In the fifth contest of the championship series, the Black Hawks got eight by the Habs. But it wasn't a complete whitewashing. The Canadiens found the back of the net seven times as the two teams combined for the biggest offensive spectacle in the history of the Stanley Cup Final. To put things in perspective, when the two teams met in the Cup Final two years earlier, Montreal limited Chicago to just seven goals in three games at the Forum.

MAY 9

KEN DRYDEN'S 10TH SHUTOUT, 1978

Darryl Sittler had a simple message for Yvan Cournoyer: "Keep the Cup in Canada." On May 9, 1978, after the Canadiens swept the Leafs out of the playoffs, the two captains embraced at centre ice, where the Toronto skipper reportedly urged the Habs on. Montreal would be taking on either the Bruins or Flyers in the Final. His team had just been vanquished by the two-time defending Stanley Cup champions, but even Sittler didn't want to see the silver chalice head south of the border, especially to Boston, an archrival of both Canadian clubs.

And that's all Montreal was focused on. Following the victory, which was goaltender Ken Dryden's 10th career playoff shutout, there was no jubilant celebration in the dressing room. There was no hooting and hollering. There was no popping of champagne bottles. They would save the bubbly for the final game of the season. The Flyers or Bruins would be no easy opponents, but neither would the Habs. Dating back to the 1976 Stanley Cup Playoffs, the Canadiens had lost only four playoff games and appeared poised to win a third straight title.

MAY 10

HABS BENEFIT FROM TOO MANY MEN, 1979

The Bruins were a few minutes away from a berth to the Stanley Cup Final. But they quickly went from protecting their lead to killing off a penalty. With less than three minutes remaining in Game 7 against the Canadiens, on May 10, 1979, Boston was whistled for too many men on the ice. They fought off half the infraction, with just over a minute remaining, but Guy Lafleur fired off a shot to tie it up 4–4. When the red light went off, the Forum erupted into bedlam.

Although the Bruins were still alive, it very much felt like the momentum had shifted in Montreal's favour. The Canadiens stormed out in overtime, and just before the halfway mark, Yvon Lambert deflected a pass from Mario Tremblay into the back of the net to send the Canadiens to the Final for the fourth straight year. Following the game, Boston bench boss Don Cherry faced the music: "Any time you get too many men on the ice, it's the coach's fault." He was fired two weeks later.

TOE BLAKE CALLS IT A CAREER, 1968

Within minutes of winning his eighth Stanley Cup as head coach of the Canadiens, Toe Blake made up his mind. It was time to hang up his fedora. On May 11, 1968, the Habs defeated the rookie St. Louis Blues 3–2 to complete the sweep and clinch Lord Stanley's mug at the Forum for the 10th time in franchise history. Following the victory, Blake spoke to reporters in the dressing room. As much as he loved being a bench boss, he said the job was just getting to him. "This has been the longest season of my career and the tension is getting too hard to take," he said.

Blake also added he was turning 56 in a few months and it was time for the players to have a new voice. Although he retired from the game, he was never too far from the Forum. He spent a lot of time behind the bar at his Toe Blake's Tavern at the corner of Guy and Saint-Catherine, just a stone's throw away from the rink.

MAY 12

HABS ADVANCE TO EASTERN CONFERENCE FINAL, 2010

The Canadiens were back to the conference final for the first time in nearly two decades. On May 12, 2010, Montreal's wild post-season ride continued when they defeated the defending-champion Penguins 5–2 in the seventh game of the eastern semifinal. The Habs got off to a hot start, scoring four unanswered goals to chase Marc-André Fleury from his crease just over five minutes into the second period, but Jaroslav Halák was once again a key part of the reason the club was moving on. Halák made 37 saves, including 18 in the final frame, as the Penguins attempted to mount a comeback while trailing by a pair of goals.

Pittsburgh had hoped to get a few more games in Mellon Arena before moving to its new rink, Consol Energy Center, for the next campaign, but it was rather fitting their last game in the building was against the Canadiens. Forty-three years earlier, they hosted the Habs for their first regular-season game at Mellon, but even back then Montreal spoiled the party, defeating the expansion Penguins 2–1.

MAY 13

HABS WIN 10TH STRAIGHT
CUP FINAL GAME, 1978

The Canadiens remained flawless in the Final. On May 13, 1978, Montreal defeated Boston 4–1 in the opening game of the championship series to win their ninth consecutive Stanley Cup Final matchup since 1976. That year the Canadiens defeated the two-time defending Flyers in four straight, halting the formation of a dynasty. The following season, Montreal swept the Bruins to earn back-to-back titles. Taking on Boston again for the second year in a row, the Habs handed their archrivals their fifth straight loss in the Final. But if you go back to 1973, it was actually Montreal's 10th straight Cup Final victory, an NHL record for both the Habs and their netminder, Ken Dryden, who wasn't too busy, making just 15 saves.

Boston's Brad Park opened the scoring just over two minutes into the contest, but the Canadiens scored a pair of goals on power plays. Yvon Lambert potted the eventual game-winner just before the halfway mark of the first period. Montreal added two more in the final frames to move within three victories of a third consecutive crown.

HABS DEFEAT BRUINS IN GAME 7, 2014

t didn't take long for the Canadiens to quiet the Boston faithful at TD Garden on May 14, 2014. Just over two minutes into the seventh and deciding game of the eastern semifinal series, Dale Weise, who had been getting under the skin of the Bruins all series long, especially forward Milan Lucic, opened the scoring. Not long after the halfway mark of the second session, Max Pacioretty added to Montreal's lead, notching what would hold up as the game-winner.

Jarome Iginla finally got the Bruins on the board with two minutes remaining in the stanza, but it would be as close as they would get. Late in the final frame, with Johnny Boychuk in the penalty box for interference, Danny Briere put the game out of reach. When the teams met at centre ice to conclude the chippy affair that had gone the distance, Lucic wasn't ready to let things go. When it was his turn to shake hands with Weise, he held his grip and left him with some choice words that I can't repeat in this book.

MAY 15

SAM POLLOCK BECOMES GM, 1964

After nearly two decades, the Canadiens would have a new general manager at the helm. On May 15, 1964, the club announced that Frank J. Selke, who presided over six championships, would be moving into an advisory role and Sam Pollock, who had been serving as the team's personnel director, would become the new GM. Pollock had long been identified as Selke's successor, and he quickly proved it was indeed a shrewd decision.

In one of his first moves as GM, just over a month later, Pollock — who would come to earn his nickname, "Trader Sam," honestly — sent Guy Allen and Paul Reid to Boston for Alex Campbell and the rights to teenage goaltender Ken Dryden. The transaction was insignificant at the time, but it would pay dividends, with Dryden backstopping the dynastic Habs to five Stanley Cups. Pollock's master class, however, would be the set of manoeuvres he made to ensure the Canadiens landed the first overall pick in 1971 in order to take Guy Lafleur. Pollock would serve as GM for 14 years, winning nine titles along the way.

MAY 16

CANADIENS WIN FIRST OF
FOUR STRAIGHT CUPS, 1976

As the champagne bottles popped in the visitors dressing room of the Spectrum in Philadelphia, the Canadiens, in between sips, reportedly belted out "God Bless America." The song had become synonymous with the Flyers ever since the team's vice-president, Lou Scheinfeld, had Kate Smith perform it before games during the 1969–70 campaign. Although some fans were initially cool to the move, instead wanting to hear "The Star-Spangled Banner," they couldn't argue with the results. More often than not, the Flyers won following a Smith rendition.

But on May 16, 1976, her performance couldn't turn the tide. Montreal defeated Philadelphia 5–3, completing the sweep and thwarting the Flyers' aspiration of three straight Stanley Cups. Some might have accused the Habs of mocking the team by singing their own version of "God Bless America," but it was their tribute to a worthy opponent that was so close to establishing a dynasty. Meanwhile, the Canadiens, a franchise with no shortage of championship epochs, built off that victory against Philadelphia to string together four consecutive titles.

MAY 17

KEN DRYDEN EARNS
POINT IN FINAL, 1979

With time winding down, and the Canadiens holding a 3–1 lead against the Rangers on May 17, 1979, Montreal goaltender Ken Dryden cleared the puck up to Steve Shutt. Barging into the Rangers' zone, Shutt passed it over to Jacques Lemaire, who wired it past New York netminder John Davidson. The goal helped seal the victory and give the Canadiens a 2–1 lead in the championship series, but it also marked an NHL milestone. Picking up an assist on the play, Dryden became the first goaltender in league history to earn a point in a Stanley Cup Final game.

It would prove to be Dryden's last post-season point. Less than a week later, he capped off his career with a sixth Stanley Cup before hanging up his pads. Dryden had actually wanted to retire sooner, but he agreed to stay on for another year with the club. Although the goaltender, who already had a law degree under his belt, could have certainly continued playing, there were other things he wanted to accomplish away from the rink.

MAY 18

BRIAN SKRUDLAND SCORES
FASTEST OVERTIME GOAL, 1986

f you were still in line at the concession stand waiting
for popcorn or visiting the washroom, you would have
missed it. That's how quick Brian Skrudland was. After
recovering from a 2–0 deficit to force overtime on May 18,
1986, the Canadiens won the faceoff. Racing down the ice
with Mike McPhee on a two-on-one, Skrudland caught
a pass from his linemate and fired the puck past Calgary
goaltender Mike Vernon just nine seconds into the extra
session. Nine seconds. That's all it took to win the game
3–2 and even the Stanley Cup Final at one game apiece.
Skrudland's nine-second tally set the record for the fastest
overtime goal in NHL playoff history.

It couldn't have come at a better time for Skrudland.
Through 16 games of the post-season, he had yet to find
the back of the net, and his quick goal gave him another
distinction of being the first player since Chicago's Cy
Wentworth, more than five decades earlier, to score his first
playoff goal in overtime in the Final.

MAY 19

CANADIENS SCORE TWICE IN OT, 1979

The Canadiens thought for sure they had won the game. Just over six minutes into overtime against the Rangers on May 19, 1979, defenceman Larry Robinson ripped a shot from 60 feet out. The puck had apparently gone in over the right shoulder of New York goaltender John Davidson and hit the back of the net with such force that it bounced right out. The Habs believed the game was over, but the goal judge didn't flick the switch for the red light. After the players protested to referee Andy Van Hellemond, he went over and conferred with the judge, but the official upheld the initial ruling. No goal.

Although the Canadiens might have been robbed, things have a way of working themselves out on the ice. Just over a minute later, Serge Savard backhanded a Guy Lafleur rebound past Davidson to win the game for real. While Robinson remained adamant that the puck had gone in earlier in the extra session, it didn't matter who scored the winner. All that mattered was that Montreal was one victory away from a fourth straight Stanley Cup.

HABS SCORE THREE QUICK GOALS, 1986

"We took the wind out of their sails when we got those goals," said Mats Näslund, and that was putting it lightly. On May 20, 1986, after Calgary took a 2–1 lead late in the first period in the third game of the Stanley Cup Final, the Canadiens responded 26 seconds later by scoring three straight goals in just over a minute. Including the Flames' goal, the two teams put four on the board in just 94 seconds, the fastest four goals by two teams in a Final game. After Näslund opened the scoring for Montreal earlier in the frame, he was part of the offensive outburst that chased goaltender Mike Vernon from his net.

Lanny McDonald cut Calgary's deficit just before the halfway mark of the second stanza, but Kjell Dahlin, who was in contention for the Calder that season, potted his second of the post-season to put the game out of reach. Neither team found the back of the net in the third, and the Habs finished with a 5–3 victory to take a 2–1 series lead.

JACQUES LEMAIRE SCORES CUP-CLINCHER, 1979

Jacques Lemaire knew a thing or two about scoring championship-clinching goals. In 1977, he scored the overtime winner against the Bruins to give the Canadiens a second straight title. Exactly two years and a week later, on May 21, 1979, Lemaire found the back of the net just over a minute into the second period of Game 5 in the Final against the Rangers to give the Habs a 2–1 advantage. Later in the frame, after Bob Gainey extended Montreal's lead, Lemaire added another.

In the final stanza, the Canadiens, on the verge of a fourth consecutive championship, limited the Rangers to just four shots to be crowned kings of the hockey world once again. Lemaire's first goal held up as the game-winner, giving him the distinction of being among just a handful of players in NHL history to score two Cup-clinching goals. But just a few weeks after winning his eighth title with the Habs, the 33-year-old signed on to serve as player, coach, and GM of a team in France, ending an incredible career in Montreal.

HABS TRADE FOR WHAT-WOULD-BE GUY LAFLEUR PICK, 1970

S am Pollock had a busy day of trading. On May 22, 1970, the Canadiens made a series of moves. Montreal sent Larry Mickey, Lucien Grenier, and goaltender Jack Norris to Los Angeles for Léon Rochefort, Gregg Boddy, and Wayne Thomas. The Habs also sent Christian Bordeleau to St. Louis for future considerations. But the biggest deal that day was when GM Pollock sent Ernie Hicke and the 1970 10th overall pick to the Oakland Seals for François Lacombe and a first-round pick in 1971. It may have seemed insignificant, but Pollock had his eye on the future.

Ever the shrewd executive, he knew Guy Lafleur would be the top pick that draft and wanted to give Montreal the best odds of landing him. Anticipating Oakland would be cellar dwellers, Pollock even made another move during the season with the Kings, sending Ralph Backstrom to shore up L.A.'s offence, to ensure the Kings stayed above them in the standings. The Seals finished dead last in the 1970–71 campaign, surrendering the first overall pick to Montreal and forever changing the franchise.

MAY 23

JACQUES LAPERRIÈRE
WINS NORRIS, 1966

There was no replacing Doug Harvey, who won six Norris trophies while patrolling the blue line for the Canadiens, but the club had high hopes for Jacques Laperrière. In his first full season with Montreal, the young defenceman was assigned Harvey's No. 2 jersey. While Laperrière wouldn't have the same offensive prowess as his predecessor, he had a poise and calmness to his game that would serve him well in nearly 700 games with the Canadiens. At the end of his debut season in 1963–64, he was awarded the Calder Trophy as the league's top rookie.

Two years later, Laperrière added to his collection. On May 23, 1966, he earned the Norris as the NHL's top defenceman, becoming the first Montreal blueliner since Harvey to take home the award. Standing at six-foot-two, the lanky "Lappy" used his incredible reach to break up plays and get the puck out of the zone. He would be a fixture on the Canadiens' back end for more than a decade until he sustained a career-ending knee injury halfway through the 1973–74 campaign.

MAY 24

PATRICK ROY NAMED PLAYOFF MVP, 1986

t was an incredible way to cap off his first NHL season. On May 24, 1986, after the Canadiens defeated the Flames 4–3 to win the Stanley Cup, goaltender Patrick Roy was given the Conn Smythe Trophy. The 20-year-old became the youngest recipient of the playoff MVP award in league history and just the third first-year winner, joining Bobby Orr and Canadiens legend Ken Dryden. Following the game, Roy was at a loss for words. "I can't believe this has happened to me," he told reporters. It was, in fact, an unbelievable journey.

Roy made his big-league debut the previous season in a cameo to relieve Doug Soetaert, but he made his mark in the 1985–86 campaign when he was called to the crease to replace injured netminders Steve Penney and Soetaert. Despite his age and playoff inexperience, Roy tended the twine like a much older goaltender and backstopped the Canadiens to their 23rd title. Following his first championship run, Roy would remain between Montreal's pipes for another decade, earning another Conn Smythe and Stanley Cup along the way.

MAY 25

LARRY ROBINSON WINS
CONN SMYTHE, 1978

arry Robinson was a force. During Montreal's 1978 playoff run, there was no player as dominant as he was. The six-foot-three blueliner kept the puck out of the Canadiens' end, but he also joined the rush to contribute offensively. He finished the post-season with four goals and 17 assists, tied with teammate Guy Lafleur for the most points. So when Montreal defeated Boston on May 25, 1978, to win their third straight Stanley Cup, with Robinson picking up two assists in that victory, he was an easy choice for playoff MVP, becoming the first defenceman to win the Conn Smythe since Bobby Orr in 1972.

Even his opponents, who played with Orr, were in awe of his performance. Bruins forward Bobby Schmautz said Orr was the best puck-carrying defenceman, "but Orr wasn't as awesome" as Robinson. When he got moving up the ice with his big frame and long reach, few could get the puck off his stick or hope to slow him down. Robinson would remain a fixture on Montreal's blue line for more than another decade.

HABS NAME ALAIN VIGNEAULT HEAD COACH, 1997

When the 1996–97 hockey season ended, Alain Vigneault was a junior coach, but just a few weeks later, he was called up to the big leagues. On May 26, 1997, he was named head coach of the Canadiens. Vigneault had served as an NHL assistant coach to Rick Bowness in Ottawa, but he had spent most of his coaching career in the Quebec Major Junior Hockey League. In his first year with the Hull Olympiques, he led the club to the 1988 league championship. After five more seasons in Hull, Vigneault joined the Senators.

But after spending the better part of four years in Ottawa, Vigneault went back to the Q to helm the Beauport Harfangs. He had actually been planning to return to the NHL in 1997–98 to reunite with Bowness on Long Island — the two had a verbal agreement — but when the Canadiens came calling, the Quebec native had to answer. In his first season behind the Montreal bench, Vigneault guided the Habs to their first playoff series victory since the championship run in 1993.

HABS STAY ALIVE AGAINST TORONTO, 2021

ess than a minute into overtime, on May 27, 2021, Toronto's Alex Galchenyuk, who was originally drafted third overall by Montreal nearly a decade earlier, made the most ill-advised cross-ice pass in his hockey career. He may have been targeting defenceman Jake Muzzin, who scored two goals in the third period to force overtime, but the puck was intercepted by rookie Cole Caufield, who then raced up the middle of the ice with Nick Suzuki to his left. As the duo entered the Leafs' zone, there was nothing that stood between them and goaltender Jack Campbell.

With Muzzin unable to catch up to the Habs youngsters, they passed the puck back and forth, with the tic-tac-toe culminating in Suzuki wiring it over the blocker side of an all but helpless Campbell. As Galchenyuk stared up in disbelief, the Canadiens spilled over the bench to celebrate. Not only had they survived blowing a two-goal lead in the third period, but they had lived to see another game to try to keep their playoff hopes alive.

ST. PATRICK CALLS IT A CAREER, 2003

t was the end of an era. On May 28, 2003, Patrick Roy announced his retirement. Although Roy, who at the time was the winningest goaltender in NHL history, could have certainly continued to play, he felt it was time to hang up the pads. At a press conference at the Pepsi Center in Denver, Colorado, he divulged that he had actually made the decision to retire before the 2002–03 campaign unfolded.

Before Roy was traded to the Avalanche in 1996, there were reports he was contemplating retirement after he won his second championship and Conn Smythe with the Canadiens in 1993, but of course, he would go on to play another decade, picking up another Stanley Cup and a third playoff MVP award, a league record. Habs fans would have certainly preferred to see Roy retire in a Montreal sweater, but it was rather fitting that he made the announcement beside Avalanche GM Pierre Lacroix, who was his original agent before he was even drafted by the Canadiens nearly two decades earlier.

HABS ELIMINATED, 2014

There would be no need for sunglasses at night. Montreal-born singer Corey Hart, who was best known for his hit about a guy in shades, originally had a concert scheduled at the Bell Centre on May 31, 2014, but he moved the performance to May 29 in case the Canadiens were able to return home for a decisive seventh game. The show went on for Hart, but that wouldn't be the case for the Habs.

On the road in New York, Montreal needed a win to keep their playoff hopes alive. But after Canadien-turned-Ranger Dominic Moore opened the scoring late in the second period, Montreal could not mount a response. While Habs goaltender Dustin Tokarski, who valiantly occupied the crease after Chris Kreider violently bowled over Carey Price in the first game of their Eastern Conference Final series, made 31 saves on the verge of elimination, his teammates were able to muster only 18 shots on Henrik Lundqvist. Tokarski gave his team a fighting chance in Price's absence, but Habs fans will always wonder what could have been.

MAY 30

JACKIE LECLAIR'S BIRTHDAY, 1929

We've nearly exhausted our championship content, a tall order for a franchise like the Canadiens, so we've got to dip into some birthdays. I steered clear of birthdays in the original Hockey 365 series, but I've come to embrace them because they give me the opportunity to highlight players who might not have come up otherwise. Take Jean Louis LeClair, who was known as "Jackie." LeClair was born in Quebec City on May 30, 1929, and played three seasons with Montreal, earning two Stanley Cups.

But early into his tenure with the Habs, a pair of incidents nearly ended his career and, quite possibly, his life. During a game against the Bruins, LeClair caught Milt Schmidt's stick in the face and nearly lost his left eye. Just a few weeks later, in a matchup against the Leafs, his throat was slashed when he fell on Larry Cahan's skate. LeClair was rushed to the hospital, where they were able to stop the bleeding to a pair of gashed arteries. He was out for a month but made a full recovery.

HABS DEFEAT LEAFS IN GAME 7, 2021

For just the second time in their long histories, the Canadiens and Leafs squared off in a Game 7. The last time it happened was in 1964. I had never even seen the Habs and Leafs battle each other in the playoffs in my lifetime. Before the 2021 post-season, it had been more than three decades since they'd duked it out. And while I was excited to see the long-standing rivalry renewed in the playoffs, this is where I must divulge I was cheering for the team in blue and white.

I'll be the first to admit that when Toronto had a 3–1 series lead, I thought they had it in the bag. But when those pesky Habs stormed back to force a decisive seventh game, to me, at least, it seemed preordained. So it was no surprise when, on May 31, 2021, Montreal opened the scoring with three straight goals to win 3–1, overcoming a 3–1 series deficit for just the third time in franchise history. But they were just getting started.

JUNE 1

HABS FALL FLAT IN CUP FINAL OPENER, 1993

The Canadiens hadn't suited up for more than a week, and it showed. On June 1, 1993, playing their first game in eight days, Montreal looked rusty against the Kings in the opening matchup of the Stanley Cup Final. They appeared listless on the power play, and there was even a moment when two Habs players collided in open ice. Sometimes a long layoff in the playoffs can be good for bruised and battered bodies, but it can also sap a team's momentum.

Meanwhile, the Kings, playing for the championship for the first time in franchise history, opened the scoring three minutes into the game. The Canadiens evened the score just before intermission, but they didn't really score. It was actually an uncharacteristic error by the Great One in which he accidentally deflected the puck past his goaltender, Kelly Hrudey. Los Angeles added three more goals to cruise to a 4–1 victory over the flat-footed Canadiens. While the Montreal faithful had jeered Wayne Gretzky during the game, by the time the final buzzer sounded, they were booing their own team.

JUNE 2

BOB GAINEY NAMED GM, 2003

ob Gainey was a four-time Selke winner and a Conn Smythe recipient, and he played an integral role in five championships. While there was no arguing with Gainey's legacy on the ice, playing for a contender in Montreal was quite different from building one. But on June 2, 2003, 14 years after his last game, Gainey took on that challenge when the Canadiens named him general manager and executive vice-president, although he wouldn't officially start for another month.

He was the architect of the Dallas Stars' championship a few years earlier, but it had been a long decade since Montreal's last title. The Habs faithful would be patient with one of its own legends at the helm, but only for so long. In his first season as GM, Gainey made an immediate impact, acquiring Alex Kovalev from New York. Despite finding regular-season success, including a division title, under Gainey's direction, they couldn't quite get over the hump in the playoffs. A few months after he resigned in February 2010, the club made an improbable run to the Eastern Conference Final.

JUNE 3

MARTY MCSORLEY GETS DINGED FOR ILLEGAL STICK, 1993

The Canadiens were looking for every advantage they could get. Trailing 2–1 with less than two minutes remaining in the game, they were in jeopardy of going down 2–0 in the Stanley Cup Final. But head coach Jacques Demers had something up his sleeve. On June 3, 1993, with time winding down in the game, he called for a stick measurement on Kings enforcer Marty McSorley. The officials determined that McSorley's curve exceed the half-inch limit and sent him to the penalty box for two minutes.

The Habs maintained that they nosed out the unlawful twig during the game, but McSorley's side of the story is that Montreal wheeled L.A.'s stick rack into their dressing room at the Forum to get a better look. Either way, McSorley had illegal lumber and paid the price. On the ensuing power play, Canadiens defenceman Éric Desjardins, who scored earlier, lit the lamp to force overtime. In the extra session, Desjardins found the back of the net again, becoming the first defenceman to notch a hat trick in the Stanley Cup Final.

JUNE 4

BOB GAINEY WINS FOURTH STRAIGHT SELKE, 1981

t might as well have been called the Bob Gainey. On June 4, 1981, it was announced that the Canadiens winger had won his fourth straight Selke Trophy, bestowed annually to the forward "who best excels in the defensive aspects of the game," as determined by the Professional Hockey Writers Association. Since the Selke was first awarded in 1978, Gainey had been the only NHL player to win it. He had long been heralded for his dogged two-way play, but the 1980–81 campaign proved to be his best year offensively. He racked up 23 goals and 47 points, both career highs.

Gainey had kept a tight grip on the trophy, but it would prove to be his last victory. The next year, Buffalo's Craig Ramsay, who had twice finished as runner-up, earned the Selke, becoming the first NHL player not named Bob Gainey to take home the award. While Boston's Patrice Bergeron later went on to win the Selke six times, the most in NHL history, Gainey remains the only player to earn the trophy in four straight years.

JUNE 5

FIRST DRAFT HELD IN MONTREAL, 1963

For the first time in league history, a draft was held. On June 5, 1963, at the Queen Elizabeth Hotel in Montreal, the league's six clubs took turns drafting players who were over the age of 16 and not members of an NHL-sponsored team. Prior to this, big-league teams graduated players to their ranks from the junior teams they sponsored by signing them to contracts. Although a lot of the top talent was not available at the inaugural draft — many of the premier prospects were already in farm systems — it marked a significant shift in how clubs cultivated players.

While there were concerns that the move would erode the French-Canadian fabric of the Canadiens, the league allowed Montreal to select two French-Canadian players each year, but the club didn't exercise this option until 1968. Instead, in 1963, the Habs selected Garry Monahan first overall, giving him the distinction of being the first player ever drafted to the NHL. Monahan eventually played 11 games for Montreal but spent most of his big-league career with Toronto and Vancouver.

NHL CHANGES MINOR PENALTY RULES, 1956

F rank Selke had some choice words for his colleagues: "Go get a power play of your own!" He reportedly barked this to his fellow managers at the NHL's annual Board of Governors meeting on June 6, 1956, following a rule change. The league agreed to revise the minor penalty rule so that a player serving the infraction could return to the ice once the opposing club scored. Selke was the lone dissenting voice.

Under the previous system, players were stuck in the sin bin for the duration of their transgression regardless of how many times the team on the man advantage filled the net. Selke felt the change was aimed squarely at the Canadiens' voracious power-play unit, which boasted five future Hall of Famers: Jean Béliveau, Maurice Richard, Bert Olmstead, and defencemen Doug Harvey and Tom Johnson. They had feasted on penalized teams for years, but for the league's five other managers, the last straw came earlier in the season when Béliveau scored a hat trick in only 44 seconds on a power play.

JUNE 7

PATRICK ROY'S WINK, 1993

atrick Roy stood up in the Canadiens' dressing room and delivered a message to his teammates. "They're not going to get another goal on me, so don't worry," he reportedly said. "All you guys have to do is get one." Following the second intermission on June 7, 1993, the game was tied at two goals apiece, and if the Habs followed their goalie's advice, they'd be heading back to Montreal with a 3–1 series lead and a chance to hoist Lord Stanley's mug on home ice.

Roy later divulged it was the first time he had said anything like that in the dressing room, but he meant every word. He made some spectacular saves in the final frame, including stopping a sure goal from Kings winger Tomas Sandstrom. After denying Sandstrom, Roy winked at him — an exchange that has been immortalized as one of the most iconic moments in Stanley Cup Final history. While Roy kept his promise, his teammates delivered too. With just over five minutes remaining, John LeClair scored the tiebreaker to seal a 3–2 victory.

JUNE 8

HABS DRAFT ALFIE TURCOTTE, 1983

With their first pick in the draft on June 8, 1983, the Canadiens took Alfie Turcotte 17th overall. Serge Savard, Montreal's managing director, felt the club got a steal. Turcotte was ranked 11th by NHL Central Scouting, but the Canadiens had him ninth on their board. Savard even went as far as saying Turcotte had as much talent as Pat LaFontaine, who went third overall to the Islanders. Few would ever match LaFontaine's skills, but Turcotte had a pro career that lasted nearly two decades.

Thirty-six years after the Habs called Turcotte's name, his son Alex was drafted fifth overall by the Kings. But just before Alex's big moment, Ryan Whitney, former NHLer and co-host of *Spittin' Chiclets*, thought he caught Alfie picking his nose on the televised broadcast. He tweeted out a photo and it quickly went viral. Turcotte, however, later set the record straight in an interview with me. "I'm itching my nose from the outside," he said. Much like Jerry Seinfeld, Turcotte had been falsely accused of a pick, when it was simply a scratch.

HABS WIN CUP, 1993

J.J. Daigneault dreamed of hoisting the Stanley Cup. Growing up as a kid in Montreal, during the Canadiens' dynasty era, he had plenty of opportunities to let his imagination run wild. The first time he got up close and personal with the trophy was during the celebrations after one of the club's four straight championships in the late 1970s. Daigneault later told the *Montreal Gazette*'s Michael Farber that he had skipped school one afternoon to witness the parade. It was a great day for the youngster Daigneault, but there was a better day in store.

Over a decade later, on June 9, 1993, Daigneault, then a blueliner for the Canadiens, finally got to live his dream. Following the victory over the Kings, he told Farber, "It feels better to touch it rather than look at it." Daigneault had come close six years earlier with the Flyers, scoring the game-winning goal to force the decisive seventh game for the Cup against the Oilers, but winning a title with your hometown team was worth the wait.

HABS TAKE GUY LAFLEUR
FIRST OVERALL, 1971

I n an alternate universe, Guy Lafleur saves the California Golden Seals. Had the team been able to draft the talented winger first overall on June 10, 1971, it's possible his superstar skills would have brought much-needed fanfare and stability to the struggling franchise and the club wouldn't have ended up relocating to Cleveland five years later. But that's not how it played out. After trading their pick to the Canadiens a year earlier — when the club was known as the Oakland Seals — the Golden Seals made a different announcement that day at the NHL's annual amateur draft in Montreal.

A representative of the team said something along the lines of: "California regretfully defers its No. 1 choice to the Stanley Cup champion Montreal Canadiens, Mr. Campbell." Habs GM Sam Pollock, feigning surprise, jokingly called for a time out to a chorus of laughter, as if the move and decision had not already been in the works for over a year. The Canadiens then, of course, selected Lafleur first overall. The rest, as they say, is history.

BLACK HAWKS CLAIM TONY O, 1969

Following the NHL's annual interleague draft on June 11, 1969, newspaper coverage was charitable to the Habs. One report from the Canadian Press stated: "The Montreal Canadiens emerged virtually unscathed from the operation, even though they lost three fringe players." It doesn't sound so bad until you remember that one of those so-called fringe players was Tony Esposito. Nabbed by the cellar-dwelling Black Hawks, Esposito wasn't getting much playing time in Montreal behind Rogie Vachon and Gump Worsley on the depth chart, but he would find more opportunities between the pipes in the Windy City.

Esposito earned the starting job out of training camp for the 1969–70 campaign, and through his first 10 games with the Hawks, he recorded six straight wins, the first of which came against his former team, the Canadiens, and three shutouts, earning the nickname "Tony O" for his ability to keep the puck out of the net. Esposito took home the Calder and the Vezina, the first of three, by season's end, as he began a Hall of Fame career in Chicago.

JUNE 12

HABS DRAFT RÉJEAN HOULE, 1969

As Réjean Houle stared out at the Golden Gate Bridge, he couldn't help but think how far he had come. Hailing from the small mining town of Rouyn-Noranda, Quebec, Houle had realized his dreams of suiting up for the Canadiens. Selected first overall by Montreal on June 12, 1969, he was one of the last players drafted using the French-Canadian rule that was granted to the Habs when the league first moved to an amateur draft. Houle played nine games for the Canadiens the following season, but it was that moment, on the shores of San Francisco, that really put things into perspective.

Standing next to him was his roommate, Guy Lafleur, who came from the tiny lumbering village of Thurso, Quebec. But here they were, two young kids from La Belle Province, playing for the Montreal Canadiens on a California road trip. Houle would end up winning five championships with the bleu, blanc, et rouge, but that moment was so special that it has stayed with him more than five decades after he was drafted.

HABS TRADE RED BERENSON, 1966

R ed Berenson had long been the subject of trade rumours. Even after completing just his first full season with the Canadiens in 1964, the left winger, who was a star on the University of Michigan team before turning pro, was linked to Detroit. The Wings expressed interest in him, but they couldn't strike a deal. Berenson spent most of the following season in the American Hockey League with the Quebec Aces but was recalled to Montreal for the playoffs and won the Stanley Cup.

After he split another campaign between the minors and the Habs, Berenson's name was once again in the mix. Although reportedly offered to Boston, he was finally dealt on June 13, 1966, when the Canadiens sent him to the Rangers for Ted Taylor and a player to be determined. Berenson's tenure on Broadway was brief, and he eventually made his way to the expansion Blues, where he would become a franchise player. In his second season in St. Louis, on November 7, 1968, Berenson scored six goals in a road game, a league record.

HABS ACQUIRE GLEN SATHER, 1974

Glen Sather was a hard-nosed winger who broke into the NHL with the Big Bad Bruins. But after a few years in Boston, he made his way to Pittsburgh and then New York, before joining the upstart Blues for most of the 1973–74 campaign. That season, Sather scored 15 goals and 44 points, both career highs, but that would prove to be his only stint in St. Louis. On June 14, 1974, he was sent to Montreal to complete an earlier trade the club had made with the Canadiens for Rick Wilson.

The Habs would be Sather's fifth big-league club since making his debut eight years earlier, but they wouldn't be his last. After one year with the Canadiens, he was dealt to the North Stars for cash. Minnesota would be his final NHL stop, but Sather later joined the Edmonton Oilers of the World Hockey Association, where he would serve as a player-coach. After hanging up his skates, Sather remained with Edmonton as bench boss and later GM, guiding the Oilers to five Stanley Cups.

JUNE 15

HABS TRADE MIKHAIL SERGACHEV TO LIGHTNING, 2017

t was no secret that Jonathan Drouin wanted out of Tampa Bay. Drafted third overall by the Lightning in 2013, the Ste-Agathe, Quebec, native had starred in the QMJHL but struggled early in his big-league tenure. During the 2015–16 season, he had formally requested a trade and was suspended by the team for failing to report to a game after he was sent down to the minors. Despite the turmoil that campaign, Drouin returned to Tampa Bay for the playoffs and played a critical role in the club's run to the Eastern Conference Final.

The next year, with Steven Stamkos on the shelf with a knee injury, Drouin played a more prominent role, collecting 21 goals and 53 points, both career highs. But at season's end, with the expansion draft for Vegas looming, the Lightning decided he was not part of the club's future plans. On June 15, 2017, he was dealt to Montreal for defenceman Mikhail Sergachev, who had been drafted ninth overall a year earlier. Just hours after the trade, Drouin signed a six-year contract extension.

JUNE 16

JEFF PETRY'S BLOODSHOT EYES, 2021

Jeff Petry looked like something ripped from the pages of a Stephen King novel. Even the king of horror would have had a difficult time conjuring up a more nightmarish creature. After missing two games with a hand injury, Petry returned to the ice on June 16, 2021, for the second game of Montreal's Stanley Cup Final series against Vegas. But it wasn't his hand that was terrifying — it was his eyeballs. Calling them bloodshot would be putting it mildly. Rather, the whites of both eyes were completely red. Horrifyingly red.

It was reported later in the evening that his condition was caused by a subconjunctival hemorrhage, the result of broken blood vessels in the eye, but it wasn't clear how it happened. It wouldn't be until after the playoffs were over that Petry revealed the cause: when a doctor set his broken pinky finger, after he got it stuck in one of the photographer's holes in the glass along the boards, the defenceman passed out from the pain, rupturing blood vessels in both eyes.

JUNE 17

CANADIENS TRADE WAYNE THOMAS TO TORONTO, 1975

Wayne Thomas hadn't played all season. With the return of Ken Dryden, who missed the entire 1973–74 campaign, when a contract dispute led him to spend the year working in a law firm, Thomas was bumped back down to third string, behind Michel "Bunny" Larocque. With Dryden articling, Thomas shared the crease with Larocque and Michel Plasse. Thomas, however, got the lion's share of the work, making 40 starts. In one of those games, he made 53 saves, a regular-season Canadiens record that has never been beaten but was matched 35 years later by Carey Price.

But when Dryden returned, instead of sending Thomas down to the minors or trading him elsewhere, the Canadiens kept him as a third goalie. He watched every single game, all 80 of them, from the press box. When the season ended, the Habs mercifully traded him to the Maple Leafs on June 17, 1975, for a first-round draft pick. The next year, Thomas got more time between the pipes in Toronto, making 64 appearances and even representing the Buds at the NHL All-Star Game.

JUNE 18

LUKE RICHARDSON TAKES REINS, 2021

t was not exactly how Luke Richardson envisioned getting his first NHL head coaching experience. On June 18, 2021, with Canadiens bench boss Dominique Ducharme ruled out with Covid-19, Richardson, one of his assistants, was tapped as his temporary replacement for Montreal's third game against the Golden Knights of their third-round series. It was certainly one way to make a debut — Richardson later divulged that he figured his first crack at leading an NHL bench would have been during an exhibition game.

After Josh Anderson scored in the final minutes of regulation to force overtime, the hulking winger found the back of the net again in sudden death to give Richardson and the Habs a 3–2 victory. The rookie coach stayed behind the bench for the rest of the series, punching a ticket to the Stanley Cup Final, until Ducharme returned for Montreal's last few games. It wouldn't be long, however, before Richardson officially got a head coaching opportunity. On June 27, 2022, he was named head coach of the Blackhawks, the 40th in franchise history.

NORTH STARS NAME BOB GAINEY HEAD COACH, 1990

Just a year after hanging up his skates, Bob Gainey was back in the NHL, but it wasn't with Montreal. On June 19, 1990, at a press conference at the Met Center in Bloomington, Minnesota, he was introduced as the head coach of the North Stars. Following his retirement from the Canadiens, Gainey served as a player-coach with the Épinal Squirrels in a tier-two league in France. While he had spent his entire distinguished playing career with the Canadiens, he did find a familiar face behind the bench in Minnesota. One of his assistants was Doug Jarvis, his former centre with the Habs.

Gainey didn't have any big-league coaching experience, but it didn't show. In his first campaign, the North Stars advanced to the Stanley Cup Final but came up two victories shy to the powerhouse Pittsburgh Penguins. By the end of the next campaign, Gainey added GM duties to his portfolio, and while he would step away from coaching in the 1995–96 season, he would engineer a championship a few years later.

JOSÉ THÉODORE WINS HART TROPHY, 2002

José Théodore couldn't believe it. On June 20, 2002, he was awarded the Hart Trophy as the NHL's most valuable player. Théodore led all goalies that season with a sterling .931 save percentage and became the first Canadien to take home the trophy since Guy Lafleur in 1978. It was an incredible night for Théodore and the Habs, but it was not without controversy. The runner-up was Jarome Iginla, who scored 52 goals for an anemic Flames squad. Although Calgary didn't make the playoffs, there was a strong argument that no player was more valuable to his team than Iginla.

Both players finished with the same number of balloting points, but Théodore had more first-place votes, so the trophy went to him. Many in the hockey world felt Iginla was robbed, and he kind of was. While there's no question that Théodore was deserving, it was later reported that a Montreal writer placed Iginla fifth on his ballot. If Iginla was any higher on that list, and he absolutely should have been, he would have won instead.

JUNE 21

HABS TAKE ANDREI KOSTITSYN
10TH OVERALL, 2003

As the saying goes, hindsight is always 20-20. The 2003 NHL draft was one of the deepest and most star-studded classes in league history, rivalling only the 1979 group, which boasted seven future Hall of Famers. With their first pick on June 21, the Canadiens selected Belarusian winger Andrei Kostitsyn 10th overall. Prior to the draft, he was rated third among European skaters by NHL Central Scouting. Joining the Habs full-time for the 2007–08 campaign, Kostitsyn racked up 53 points in 78 games playing on a line with Alex Kovalev and Tomáš Plekanec.

Canadiens fans hoped it was a preview of things to come, but it proved to be Kostitsyn's most productive campaign in Montreal. A few years later, he was traded to Nashville for a pair of draft picks. Looking back, it's easy to say the Habs should have selected another player, but let's not forget that nearly every team passed on Patrice Bergeron at least once, including the Bruins. Now that's a player who would have looked sharp in bleu, blanc, et rouge.

JUNE 22

HABS DRAFT JESPERI KOTKANIEMI, 2018

Her face said it all. After the Canadiens called Jesperi Kotkaniemi's name as the third overall pick at the NHL Entry Draft on June 22, 2018, the camera panned to a fan's reaction in the crowd. A spectacled woman wearing a Habs jersey put her hands on both sides of her face and looked skyward. As Kotkaniemi made his way down to the draft floor from the stands, she just stared blankly with her mouth agape. Montreal's selection of the Finn was a bit of a surprise, and her expression was one of the most enduring moments from the draft.

A couple of years later, as part of the team's coverage of the 2020 draft, they invited her on air to explain her reaction. It turned out that Janie Barrios, a Habs-loving fan from Louisiana, wasn't so much disappointed that the team had picked Kotkaniemi, but rather that she hoped they would've selected Filip Zadina instead. Zadina went three spots later to Detroit, but the one who really got away was Brady Tkachuk, snagged by Ottawa immediately after Montreal's pick.

JUNE 23

MONTREAL TAKES RYAN POEHLING, 2017

t was a familiar look for Ryan Poehling. Playing hockey at St. Cloud University, where the institution's logo bore a striking resemblance to the Canadiens', it was an easy transition for the tall centre. On June 23, 2017, Montreal took Poehling with the 25th overall pick at the NHL Entry Draft. After finishing his collegiate career wearing the "St. C," Poehling was called up for Montreal's final game of the 2018–19 campaign. Making his NHL debut against the Leafs, he became the first Canadiens player to record a hat trick in his first game in nearly eight decades.

Poehling would play two more seasons with the Habs until he was dealt to Pittsburgh, but it was another first-rounder from that draft class who would make his mark on the franchise. Nick Suzuki went 13th overall to Vegas, but before he ever put on a Golden Knights sweater he was sent to Montreal as part of the Max Pacioretty trade. A few years later, the 23-year-old Suzuki would be named captain, becoming the youngest player in franchise history to wear the "C."

JUNE 24

HABS CLINCH CAMPBELL BOWL, 2021

The Montreal Canadiens were Western Conference champions. Well, sort of. Because of a quirk in the playoff format in the pandemic-shortened 2020–21 season, the Habs, after defeating the Maple Leafs and Jets, found themselves in the western bracket, taking on the remaining top-seeded team, the Golden Knights. Even before Montreal squared off against Vegas, the team had already put together an improbable run, but it was about to get even more improbable. On June 24, 2021, while the Province of Quebec was celebrating Saint-Jean-Baptiste Day, they had another reason to cheer.

Less than two minutes into overtime, Artturi Lehkonen put the puck past goaltender Robin Lehner to win 3–2 and clinch a berth in the Stanley Cup Final. When the underdog Canadiens were presented with the Clarence S. Campbell Bowl, historically awarded to the league's Western Conference champion, it looked odd. But in a world that was still upside down from Covid-19, it was almost fitting. And while many hockey players are superstitious about touching the conference trophies, there was no way the Habs were putting their hands on such a foreign prize.

JUNE 25

RICHARD TROPHY CREATED, 1998

t was a unanimous decision. On June 25, 1998, the NHL Board of Governors agreed to create the Maurice "Rocket" Richard Trophy, which would be presented annually to the top goal scorer in the league. The Rocket, of course, was a fitting choice. He was a trail-blazing lamp lighter. He was the first player to record 50 goals in a season and the first player to reach the 500-goal mark. If such a trophy existed when the fiery winger was playing, he would have won it five times. Richard, who was battling abdominal cancer when the award was approved, was humbled to receive the honour.

The following year, Anaheim's Teemu Selänne became the first-ever recipient. But in 2000, just over a month after Pavel Bure, who was known as "the Russian Rocket," earned the award, Richard succumbed to his battle. At the time of this writing, no player has collected the trophy more than Alex Ovechkin, who has won it nine times. Meanwhile, the Montreal faithful are still waiting for one of their own to bring the Rocket home.

CANADIENS ACQUIRE DOUG JARVIS, 1975

D oug Jarvis would never miss a day of work for the Canadiens. Although he was drafted 24th by the Maple Leafs, just a few weeks later, on June 26, 1975, he was traded to Montreal for Greg Hubick. Jarvis quickly found a home with the Habs. Under head coach Scotty Bowman, he became one of the league's premier checking pivots. Centring a line with Bob Gainey, who would win four Selkes flanking him, and Doug Risebrough on the wings, few teams could get anything past the grinding shutdown unit. Jarvis played a dogged style of hockey that could take its toll on players, but he proved incredibly durable and consistent.

Before he was traded to Washington in 1982, Jarvis never missed a regular-season game for Montreal, appearing in 560 straight matches, along with 72 in the playoffs. He continued the incredible run with the Capitals and then later with the Whalers. During his time in Hartford, Jarvis surpassed Garry Unger's NHL record for consecutive games played, topping out at 964, a benchmark that stood for 35 years.

CANADIENS NAME GUY CHARRON
ASSISTANT COACH, 2002

More than three decades after the Canadiens traded him away, the team brought Guy Charron back. On June 27, 2002, he was introduced as one of the club's new assistants, replacing Guy Carbonneau on head coach Michel Therrien's bench. Charron originally played 20 games for the Habs over two seasons before he was traded to Detroit, along with Mickey Redmond, on January 13, 1971, in exchange for Frank Mahovlich and Bill Collins. Following his time in the Motor City, he played with distinction on struggling expansion teams: the Kansas City Scouts and the Washington Capitals, where he recorded back-to-back 30-goal campaigns.

After serving as a player-coach in Switzerland, Charron took up coaching full-time, spending five years with the Canadian national team, which included a gold medal at the 1990 World Juniors. He joined the NHL ranks not long after, serving as an assistant in Calgary, New York, and Anaheim, where he took over the bench after Craig Hartsburg was fired during the 2000–01 season. Charron spent two seasons in Montreal before joining the Panthers.

BRENDAN GALLAGHER BLOODIED IN CUP FINAL, 2021

Brendan Gallagher was a warrior. Late in the first game of the Stanley Cup Final, on June 28, 2021, the Canadiens winger got into a skirmish in front of the Tampa Bay net. After the Lightning's Blake Coleman knocked off Gallagher's helmet with a shot to the head, he was taken down by Mikhail Sergachev, hitting his head on the ice. When the officials pried the Tampa Bay defenceman off Gallagher, he emerged bloodied from a gash he sustained to his noggin.

Ever since he made his debut for the Canadiens, almost a decade earlier, Gallagher had been the team's beating heart, but in that moment, with blood streaming down his face, he truly embodied what it meant to be a Hab. Montreal lost the contest 5–1, but Gallagher demonstrated that the team wouldn't go down without a fight. As bench boss Luke Richardson, still filling in for head coach Dominique Ducharme who was out with Covid-19, said, "You're going to cross-check his face right into the ice, but you're still not going to stop him."

P.K. SUBBAN TRADED IN STUNNING BLOCKBUSTER, 2016

History doesn't repeat itself, but it rhymes. Exactly twenty-six years after the Canadiens traded Norris-winning defenceman Chris Chelios to the Blackhawks for Denis Savard, they did it again. On June 29, 2016, in a blockbuster that happened just 17 minutes after Edmonton traded Taylor Hall to New Jersey for Adam Larsson, Montreal sent P.K. Subban to Nashville for Shea Weber.

Originally drafted 43rd overall by the Canadiens in 2007, Subban joined the club full-time for the 2010–11 season. During the lockout-shortened 2012–13 campaign, he racked up 38 points in 42 games and won the Norris as the league's top defenceman, becoming the first Canadien to win the award since Chelios. But just a few years later, he was dealt away. There were rumblings about a rift in the dressing room between Subban and captain Max Pacioretty, but the two had reportedly quashed those rumours. While the trade initially appeared to favour Nashville, which received the younger and more dynamic blueliner, Weber became Montreal's 30th captain and played his heart out until injuries got the better of him.

JUNE 30

HABS TRADE RYAN MCDONAGH, 2009

When the Canadiens acquired Scott Gomez as part of a six-player deal with the Rangers on June 30, 2009, some of the New York coverage focused on how Chris Higgins, a Long Island native and three-time 20-goal scorer, was the key piece coming to Broadway. This trade would be a lot easier to look back on if only that proved to be true. Higgins didn't even finish the year in New York before he was traded to the Flames, but the Rangers also acquired Ryan McDonagh.

McDonagh, drafted 12th overall by the Canadiens in 2007, was still playing collegiate hockey at the University of Wisconsin, but he would become one of the league's premier blueliners. After turning pro in the AHL, he was called up to the Blueshirts on January 7, 2011, and never looked back. He went on to captain the Rangers and was later an integral part of Tampa Bay's back-to-back Stanley Cups. Meanwhile, in Montreal, a few years after a respectable 59-point campaign, the Canadiens bought out Gomez following a prolonged goal-scoring drought.

HABS SIGN SEBASTIAN AHO
TO OFFER SHEET, 2019

Montreal wanted Sebastian Aho in a Canadiens sweater. On July 1, 2019, the club tendered a five-year, $42.27 million offer sheet to the restricted free agent. Aho, who was coming off a 30-goal campaign with Carolina, signed the deal. The Hurricanes had previously stated they would match any offer sheet for Aho, but they had seven days to officially match the contract. If they chose not to, they would receive draft picks as compensation.

Later that same day, taking to Twitter, the Hurricanes' official account sent out a poll asking if they would match the offer sheet. The two options were "yes" and "*oui*," a direct message to Montreal. And while it seemed there was no way Carolina would let Aho walk, the Canadiens structured the deal with an $11.3 million signing bonus that they thought might give team owner Tom Dundon pause. But Aho was a talent the Hurricanes couldn't afford to lose, and they officially matched the contract on July 7. It was the right move. Aho has hit the 30-goal mark four more times since inking the deal.

CAREY PRICE SIGNS LONG-TERM EXTENSION, 2017

There was nowhere else Carey Price wanted to play than in Montreal. And for the Canadiens, the feeling was mutual. On July 2, 2017, they signed their former Hart- and Vezina-winning goaltender to an eight-year contract that would keep him in a Habs sweater until 2026. With one year left on his current deal, Price would start the 2018–19 campaign under a new contract that would make him the highest-paid goaltender in the NHL. But he was worth every penny.

Although Price struggled with injuries over the next few seasons, he was one of the best goalies in the world. Despite posting a .901 save percentage in 25 games in the 2020–21 campaign, he returned to form in the playoffs, playing otherworldly and leading the Canadiens to the Stanley Cup Final. But following knee surgery after the improbable run, Price voluntarily entered the NHL/NHLPA player assistance program before the start of the next season. He returned later that year, playing in five games and deservedly winning the Masterton Trophy for his perseverance and dedication to hockey.

JULY 3

HABS SIGN GEORGES LARAQUE, 2008

Georges Laraque had a change of heart. Earlier in his career, the Montreal native said he didn't want to play for his hometown team. The hulking winger felt the additional pressure from the media and family would distract him. But a decade into the NHL, Laraque, now a grizzled veteran, was ready to embrace the opportunity. On July 3, 2008, he signed a three-year, $3.5 million contract with the Habs, who were looking to get tougher and not get pushed around in the playoffs.

And there were few players in the league tougher than Laraque. A heavyweight scrapper tipping the scales at 243 pounds, the six-foot-three Laraque had nearly 120 fights under his belt. While he continued brawling in Montreal, he also scored a special goal. On January 14, 2010, just a few days after a devastating earthquake rocked his home country of Haiti, where he still had family, Laraque notched his first tally in almost two years. He exuberantly threw himself into the glass, performing his trademark "Laraque leap" for the first and only time in a Habs sweater.

CANADIENS INK KID FACE-OFF, 2001

Yanic Perreault was one of the league's premier faceoff performers. During the 1999–00 season, the Sherbrooke, Quebec, native took 987 draws for the Maple Leafs and won nearly 62 precent of them. He wasn't taking as many as Adam Oates, who was deployed for nearly twice as many with Washington, but few could match Perreault's proficiency on the dot, leading *Montreal Gazette* columnist Jack Todd to call him "Kid Face-Off." Perreault was also coming off a 52-point campaign with Toronto, a career best, making him a coveted free agent who could play both sides of the puck. When he wasn't re-signed by the Leafs, the Canadiens made their move.

On July 4, 2001, Montreal inked Perreault to a three-year, $8.4 million contract, the team's first signing of the off-season. In his first year with the Canadiens, Perreault racked up 27 goals and 56 points, leading the team in both categories, and won 61.28 percent of his draws. He turned 31 at the end of the season, and while he was no longer a kid, he still lived up to his moniker.

JULY 5

DAVID REINBACHER SIGNS ENTRY-LEVEL CONTRACT, 2023

After Carey Price forgot his last name when the Canadiens selected him fifth overall at the 2023 NHL Entry Draft, things only got worse for David Reinbacher. Despite becoming the highest-drafted Austrian-born defenceman in NHL history, the young blueliner was subjected to online abuse from some who felt as though the team should have used the pick on dynamic Russian winger Matvei Michkov. And while it wasn't exactly how he pictured starting his big-league career, Reinbacher was soon reminded why the Habs have some of the best fans in the hockey world.

When Patricia Néron learned of the vitriol Reinbacher was receiving, she put out a call on Twitter for her fellow supporters to instead spread messages of positivity for the prospect. She collected all the kind words and assembled a scrapbook, which she then delivered to him personally at the team's development camp in Brossard, Quebec. Reinbacher was overwhelmed by the gesture of support. A few days after the touching moment, on July 5, 2023, Reinbacher signed a three-year entry-level contract with the Habs.

JULY 6

ALEX KOVALEV SIGNS WITH THE SENS, 2009

As a contingent of diehard fans gathered outside the Bell Centre, a chant rose up from the crowd. "We want Kovy!" they shouted. They were protesting that the Canadiens had not tendered a contract extension to mercurial winger Alex Kovalev, who was now a free agent. The Russian had spent the past four seasons in Montreal, after he was acquired at the end of the 2003–04 campaign from the Rangers.

Kovalev could dominate a game when he wanted to, but he was enigmatic and seemingly disengaged throughout his tenure with the club. During the 2006–07 season, he occasionally pulled fourth-line duty and there were reports he wanted out, but the following year he recorded 35 goals and 84 points, his most productive campaign since his time with the Penguins seven years earlier. The Habs' Kovalev era officially came to an end on July 6, 2009, when he signed a two-year, $10 million contract with the Senators. In his first game back in Montreal, Kovalev scored a goal and added an assist in a 3–1 victory.

JULY 7

HABS DRAFT JURAJ SLAFKOVSKÝ FIRST OVERALL, 2022

There was an audible gasp in the Bell Centre. With the first pick at the NHL Entry Draft, on July 7, 2022, the Canadiens selected Juraj Slafkovský. While the Slovakian winger's draft stock was on the rise after guiding the national team to its first-ever Olympic medal and being named tournament MVP a few months earlier, Shane Wright had been the consensus number one pick for most of the season. I wasn't among the crowd, but I was in the arena at one of the bars, and my fellow patrons, many of whom were Habs fans, couldn't believe it either.

As we watched Wright get passed over, eventually getting scooped up by the Kraken at fourth overall, before seemingly giving a death stare to Montreal's draft table, the Canadiens weren't done making some surprise moves that evening. Not long after drafting Slafkovský, they traded defenceman Alexander Romanov to the Islanders for the 13th overall pick, which they then sent to Chicago, along with the 66th overall selection, for Kirby Dach, who went third overall in 2019.

JULY 8

SAKU KOIVU SIGNS WITH ANAHEIM, 2009

Teemu Selänne finally got his wish. For years, he had been trying to pry Saku Koivu out of Montreal. The two were linemates for Finland at the 2006 Winter Olympics, but they had to wait a few more years before they would play together again. On July 8, 2009, Koivu signed a one-year deal with the Ducks. Although he had received other offers, including one to join his younger brother, Mikko, in Minnesota, he decided on Anaheim. While it reunited him with the Finnish Flash in southern California, it was the end of an era in Montreal.

Drafted 21st overall by the Canadiens in 1993, Koivu played 13 seasons with the Habs, nine of those as captain. Montreal would always have a special place in his heart, especially when the fans welcomed him back following a courageous battle with cancer, but he felt it was time to move on. There would be no topping that salute, but when Koivu returned to Montreal for a game on January 22, 2011, he received a prolonged standing ovation that came close.

JULY 9

KEN DRYDEN RETIRES, 1979

Ken Dryden was hanging up his pads. On July 9, 1979, the towering netminder, who was often seen resting his arms and chin on his goalie stick during lulls in play, announced his retirement. Dryden had hoped to retire earlier but agreed to stick around for another season. It proved to be the right move, since he capped off his sterling career with a sixth Stanley Cup. While Dryden could have kept playing — he was only turning 32 the next month — he was ready for the next challenge.

Although he did ponder the idea of playing in the Soviet Union, which was quickly shut down by the Soviet Ice Hockey Federation, that would have been more about the cultural experience for the scholarly Dryden than getting between the pipes. Dryden had a law degree from Cornell University, but he'd soon make a name for himself as an author. In 1983, the same year he was inducted into the Hockey Hall of Fame, his first book, *The Game*, was released, which, for me and countless others, remains the gold standard for hockey writing.

CHEERS TO RON ANDRUFF, 1953

R on Andruff was ahead of his time. Born in Port Alberni, British Columbia, on July 10, 1953, Andruff was taken 32nd overall by Montreal in 1973. He only managed to suit up for six games on a stacked Canadiens roster, but he was a standout in the American Hockey League. In the 1975–76 campaign, he racked up 42 goals and 88 points with the Nova Scotia Voyageurs, Montreal's AHL affiliate, and won the Les Cunningham Award as the league's most valuable player. He picked up another 13 points in the playoffs, guiding the Voyageurs to a Calder Cup.

After finishing his professional hockey career in Germany, where he'd win another league championship, Andruff got into sports marketing. He founded the company Dynadx Technologies, and by the early 1990s, he brought dynamic board advertising to the North American big leagues. While the NHL agreed to adopt his system, which allowed multiple advertisers to be featured on rotation, it took the league another three decades to truly realize Andruff's pioneering vision when it adopted digitally enhanced dasher boards to mixed reviews.

JULY 11

HABS RE-SIGN ARTTURI LEHKONEN, 2019

After coming off a 31-point campaign, a career high, Artturi Lehkonen needed a new contract. Drafted 55th overall by the Canadiens in 2013, the Finnish winger made his big-league debut in 2016 and quickly demonstrated his reliability on both sides of the puck. While Lehkonen was a proven double-digit goal scorer, it was his two-way play, particularly on the penalty kill, that really made him a fan favourite. Ensuring he'd keep plying his trade in Montreal, the Habs signed him to a two-year, $4.8 million contract extension on July 11, 2019.

Lehkonen would see his production dip, but in the pandemic-shortened campaign two years later he came up big in the playoffs. During the club's improbable run, he scored the goal that sent the Canadiens to the Stanley Cup Final, arguably the franchise's biggest goal in nearly three decades. Although he and the Habs came up short that year, the next season, Lehkonen, who was sent to Colorado before the trade deadline, once again scored the series-winner in the conference final and then potted the championship-winning goal for the Avalanche.

HABS ACQUIRE MIKE JOHNSON, 2006

The trade caught Mike Johnson by surprise. On July 12, 2006, the Canadiens acquired the right winger from the Coyotes for a fourth-round draft pick. Johnson, who had started his NHL career with the Leafs a decade earlier after going undrafted, had spent the past four years in the desert, where he had played some of his best hockey. In the 2002–03 campaign, he racked up 63 points, a career high, to lead the team in scoring. After missing most of the following season with a shoulder injury, Johnson returned to form after the 2004–05 lockout, collecting 54 points and finishing as one of the Coyotes' top contributors once again.

And although he had only a year remaining on his contract, Johnson was not expecting to be dealt. "I did not see this coming," he told reporters after the news was announced. Johnson would play just one season with the Canadiens, recording 31 points in 80 games. Not long after hanging up his skates in 2009, he became an analyst for TSN and remains one of the shrewdest minds in hockey.

HABS INK ALEXANDER ROMANOV, 2020

Alexander Romanov wouldn't be able to play in the post-season, but he would get to be around his new teammates. On July 13, 2020, the Canadiens officially inked the Russian blueliner to a three-year entry-level contract. Drafted 38th overall by Montreal in 2018, Romanov and the team agreed to terms a couple of months earlier, but with the hockey world still on hiatus because of the Covid-19 pandemic, the start of the deal had not been determined.

But just a couple of weeks before the NHL was set to resume operations, Romanov would start the next chapter of his career. He had spent the past two seasons playing for CSKA Moscow in the Kontinental Hockey League, where he was part of a Gagarin Cup championship in 2019. While Romanov would be able to practise with the Canadiens in the bubble following his seven-day quarantine, he would need to wait to play. The next year, he made his mark in the post-season, scoring a goal in the Stanley Cup Final, becoming the youngest defenceman in Habs history to accomplish the feat.

JULY 14

GUY LAFLEUR SIGNS WITH QUEBEC, 1989

t was the wrong sweater, but at least the Flower was back in Quebec. On July 14, 1989, it was announced that Guy Lafleur had signed a contract with the Nordiques. The deal was reportedly for one year but included the stipulation that Lafleur could keep playing for as long as he wanted, along with a guarantee of employment in the club's front office whenever he decided he was done with hockey. Habs fans would have liked to have seen Lafleur in Montreal, but it was rather fitting for him to be back in Quebec City, where his junior career began two decades earlier with the Remparts.

Following his incredible tenure in junior, the Canadiens, of course, took Lafleur first overall. He went on to win five Stanley Cups in Montreal, before initially retiring in 1984. After taking more than three years off, he was lured out of retirement by the Rangers in 1988. Lafleur would play two seasons with the Nordiques before officially hanging up his skates as one of the game's greatest wingers.

PHILLIP DANAULT SIGNS THREE-YEAR DEAL, 2018

P hillip Danault and the Canadiens had reached a deal. The two-way centre had filed for salary arbitration, but on July 15, 2018, before the case was even heard, he and the club agreed on a three-year, $9.25 million contract. It was significantly more money than his last pact, which had paid him $1.8 million annually, but Danault had proved he had earned the raise. He was limited to just 52 games that season after sustaining a concussion from a Zdeno Chara slapshot, but he could play both sides of the puck, killing penalties and providing offence.

Originally drafted 26th overall by the Blackhawks in 2011, Danault was acquired from Chicago in 2016 for Tomáš Fleischmann and Dale Weise, in what was one of GM Marc Bergevin's masterstrokes during his tenure in Montreal. In his first full season under the new deal, Danault lived up to his billing. He picked up 53 points, a career high, and finished seventh in Selke Trophy voting. But when his contract expired two years later, he opted for free agency, inking a six-year agreement with the Kings.

HABS BRING MIKE MATHESON HOME, 2022

t was a homecoming for Mike Matheson. Born and raised in Montreal, Matheson grew up on the West Island, where he learned to play hockey. After being drafted 23rd by the Panthers in 2012, he went to Boston College before making his NHL debut. Following four seasons in Florida, however, Matheson was dealt to the Penguins. He played two seasons in Pittsburgh and then was traded to his hometown team on July 16, 2022. The trade not only brought the smooth-skating defenceman back to his roots but also reunited him with his former agent, Kent Hughes. Now the GM of the Canadiens, Hughes had negotiated Matheson's eight-year agreement with the Panthers.

There wasn't much to cheer about in the 2022–23 season, but Matheson proved to be one of the club's bright spots, bringing leadership and stability to the blue line. The deal looks even better now. In the 2023–24 campaign, Matheson racked up 62 points, a career high, and the most by a Habs defenceman in more than a decade.

JULY 17

HABS SIGN ANDY MOOG, 1997

For many Canadiens fans, it was difficult news to reconcile. On July 17, 1997, the Canadiens announced they had signed goaltender Andy Moog to a two-year contract. A veteran netminder, Moog was well known to Habs Nation for his history of terrorizing their team between the pipes. Four times he helped eliminate Montreal from the playoffs, once with the Oilers as a rookie and then three times with the Bruins in the early 1990s.

But with the Habs still searching for their first playoff series victory since their Stanley Cup championship in 1993, they hoped Moog could help get them over the hump. Although he was now 37 years old, there were still a number of teams vying for his services, but he chose Montreal because they offered him more opportunities to play than he'd gotten with Dallas. While he and Jocelyn Thibault shared the crease in the regular season, Moog was given the reins for the playoffs. In the first round, he vanquished the Penguins, giving the Habs their first post-season series victory in five years.

TED HARRIS'S BIRTHDAY, 1936

T ed Harris was tough as nails. And for good reason. Not only did he have a rugged upbringing on the Canadian Prairies, but his mentor, Eddie Shore, was one of the toughest players to ever lace them up. Born in Winnipeg, Manitoba, on July 18, 1936, Harris played defence for the Winnipeg Monarchs, where he caught the eye of Shore. During his time on the Bruins' back end, Shore was said to have broken his nose more than a dozen times. Harris would follow down the same path.

After turning professional with the Springfield Indians of the AHL, where he would win two Calder Cups, Harris joined the Canadiens full-time for the 1964–65 season and finished the year as a Stanley Cup champion. He would add three more titles during his stay with Montreal, and another with Philadelphia to cap off his career. By the time he hung up his skates, Harris was said to have broken his nose more times than he could remember, an estimate Shore would have been proud of.

JULY 19

DAVID AEBISCHER SIGNS
WITH COYOTES, 2007

I t was David Aebischer's last chance to be an NHL starter. On July 19, 2007, the 29-year-old Swiss netminder signed a one-year deal with the Coyotes. After spending the past season serving as Cristobal Huet's backup, he was looking to reclaim his place in the crease. Following Patrick Roy's retirement in 2003, Aebischer became the number one netminder in Colorado. He picked up 32 wins in his first season as the Avalanche's starter, but after his play dropped off following the 2004–05 lockout, he was traded to the Canadiens on March 8, 2006, for José Théodore.

In his first and only full campaign with the Habs, Aebischer went 13-12-3. But in Phoenix, unable to wrestle the starting gig from Mikael Tellqvist or even the backup role from Alex Auld, Aebischer played just one game before he was sent down to the minors. When the Coyotes needed to make room for Auld in the American Hockey League after acquiring Ilya Bryzgalov, Aebischer was loaned to HC Lugano in Switzerland, where he played for four seasons before returning to the AHL for 31 games.

JULY 20

NORDIQUES SIGN J.C. TREMBLAY, 1972

J.C. Superstar was going to the World Hockey Association. After failing to reach a new deal with the Canadiens, Tremblay, who earned his moniker for his superb stickhandling and offensive skills from the blue line, signed a lucrative five-year, $1 million contract with the Quebec Nordiques on July 20, 1972. Tremblay had quarterbacked Montreal's power play for more than a decade, setting club records for most points by a defenceman and winning five Stanley Cups along the way. And while he could dazzle fans with his puck-handling abilities, he also drew the ire of the fans and coaches for some of his defensive lapses.

But in the WHA, he got to do what he did best. In his first campaign, he averaged 40 minutes per game, finishing with 89 points, and was awarded the Dennis A. Murphy Trophy as the league's best defenceman. Tremblay played six more seasons with the Nordiques, leading the club to a WHA championship in 1977, before hanging up his skates a couple of years later at the age of 40.

JULY 21

GARRY BAUMAN IS BORN, 1940

Garry Bauman hadn't planned on becoming a netminder. He was actually a winger as a kid, but when his team's goaltender went down with an injury, Bauman put on the pads. The story goes that he picked up a shutout in his first appearance and then never left the crease. After tending the twine for Michigan Tech in college, Bauman, who was born in Innisfail, Alberta, on July 21, 1940, turned professional and eventually joined the Canadiens' organization. On January 15, 1967, he made his NHL debut, making 32 saves in a 3–1 victory against the Bruins.

Just a few days later, Bauman found himself in the All-Star Game. Back then the event pitted the defending Stanley Cup champions against a squad of stars from the rest of the league. With Gump Worsley on the shelf, coach Toe Blake threw Bauman into the game with Charlie Hodge. The two split the goaltending duties and blanked their opponents 3–0, recording the first and, as of this writing, only shutout in the history of the exhibition.

JULY 22

HABS SIGN BOBBY FARNHAM, 2016

During his senior year at Brown University, Bobby Farnham made the decision to change his game. Not known for his scoring prowess, Farnham, who went undrafted to the NHL, knew that if he had any shot of cracking the big leagues, he'd need to add some nastiness to his play. It was then that the Ivy Leaguer decided to embrace the rougher side of the game. The decision paid off. A few years after graduating, Farnham was playing in the NHL for the Penguins. But the road to get there was hell. In three seasons with Pittsburgh's AHL affiliate, he racked up 666 penalty minutes.

Other teams liked the edge that Farnham played with, and when the Penguins waived him early in the 2015–16 season, he was claimed by the Devils. Following 50 games with New Jersey, a career best, he signed a one-year two-way contract with the Canadiens on July 22, 2016. Farnham spent most of the season in St. John's, Newfoundland, but was called up for three contests with the Habs, his final NHL games.

HABS DRAFT LOGAN MAILLOUX, 2021

Many in the hockey world were outraged at the Habs. Even Canadian prime minister Justin Trudeau took part in the criticism. On July 23, 2021, the Canadiens selected Logan Mailloux 31st overall at the NHL Entry Draft. It was a controversial pick. Earlier that season while playing in Sweden on loan from his junior team, Mailloux had taken pictures while engaged in a sexual act with a woman, without her consent, and then shared the explicit images with his teammates. He was charged under Swedish law with defamation and offensive photography and ordered to pay a fine.

Mailloux later released a statement, acknowledging the severity of his actions, and renounced his intentions to be drafted. He rightly noted that being drafted to the NHL is a privilege, and he felt that, based on his behaviour, he had not yet earned that honour. Nevertheless, most pundits still anticipated he would be selected, but the Canadiens shocked the hockey world when they took him with the penultimate pick in the first round, sending a troubling message to their fans, especially their female supporters.

CANADIENS RE-SIGN LARS ELLER, 2014

T he day before Lars Eller was scheduled for his salary arbitration hearing, he struck a deal with the Canadiens. On July 24, 2014, the Danish forward agreed to a four-year contract extension. Originally drafted 13th overall by St. Louis in 2007, he was acquired by Montreal, along with Ian Schultz, a few years later for Jaroslav Halák. Eller quickly provided versatility and dependability to the Habs lineup, killing penalties and providing strong two-way play as either a winger or a centre.

Eller got off to a hot start to the 2013–14 season. Centring Brendan Gallagher and Alex Galchenyuk in what became known as "the Kid Line," Eller racked up nine points in his first 13 games. Although he couldn't maintain the torrid pace, he was a key part of the club's run to the Eastern Conference Final that year, recording 13 points in 17 games. Eller would remain in Montreal for just one season under his new deal before he was traded again. In 2016, the Dane was sent to Washington, where, two years later, he would score the Stanley Cup–clinching goal.

JULY 25

HABS INK MARK STREIT, 2017

t could have been a fitting way to bring his career full circle, but it wasn't meant to be. Just over a month after winning a championship with the Penguins, on July 25, 2017, Mark Streit signed a one-year, $750,000 deal with the Canadiens. Streit was originally drafted 262nd overall by Montreal in 2004 and spent three seasons with the club before joining the Islanders as a free agent in 2008. He patrolled the blue line on Long Island for four years before making his way to Philadelphia and then joining Pittsburgh before the trade deadline, as part of their mission to defend their Stanley Cup.

But just two games into his return with the Habs, Streit was waived. He cleared waivers but refused to report to the club's AHL affiliate in Laval. A few days later, the Canadiens placed the 39-year-old defenceman on unconditional waivers. The saga came to an end the next day when team management announced they had agreed to mutually terminate his contract. Two weeks later, Streit retired from the NHL after 12 seasons.

LARRY ROBINSON LEAVES FOR L.A., 1989

Before Bruce McNall headed out onto the set of *The Pat Sajak Show*, he handed Larry Robinson a small coin for safekeeping. A little while later, Robinson was called out to join him onstage. McNall, an avid coin collector and owner of the Kings, asked the former Conn Smythe Trophy winner if he still had the item he had given him. Robinson fished the coin out of his pocket and handed it over to the executive. That's when the defenceman's jaw dropped. "It turns out that frigging dime was worth a quarter of a million dollars," Robinson recalled more than three decades later.

And that was Robinson's first taste of the L.A. lifestyle. After McNall wined and dined him and his wife, they hammered out a three-year contract agreement. Robinson wanted to stay in Montreal, but when the Habs were unwilling to match the offer, he became a King, officially inking the deal on July 26, 1989. Robinson manned the L.A. blue line for three seasons before hanging up his skates. He returned to the Kings in 1995 as head coach.

JACK LAVIOLETTE IS BORN, 1879

There aren't many people who were more important to the start of the Canadiens franchise than Jack Laviolette. Born in Belleville, Ontario, on July 27, 1879, as Jean-Baptiste, Laviolette grew up in Valleyfield, Quebec, where he earned a reputation as a speedy defenceman. After playing for the Montreal Shamrocks of the Eastern Canadian Hockey Association, he was approached by J. Ambrose O'Brien to assemble a French-speaking squad for the newly formed National Hockey Association in 1909, becoming their first player, coach, and manager.

The club, of course, would be called the Montreal Canadiens, but led by Laviolette's swift skating on the back end, it soon became known as "the Flying Frenchmen." Among the players Laviolette recruited were future Hall of Famers Newsy Lalonde, Didier Pitre, and Georges Vézina. The team struggled in its first campaign, but by 1916 the Canadiens were Stanley Cup champions. When the Habs joined the NHL in 1917, Laviolette played one season, but at the end of the campaign, he lost his right foot in a car accident, ending his playing career.

DAVID SAVARD SIGNS WITH THE HABS, 2021

Just a couple of weeks after vanquishing his hometown team to win the Stanley Cup, David Savard joined them. On July 28, 2021, the Saint-Hyacinthe, Quebec, native signed a four-year deal with the Canadiens. Originally drafted 94th overall by the Blue Jackets in 2009, Savard played with distinction in the QMJHL. At the end of the 2009–10 season, he needed to reinforce his trophy case after earning the Kevin Lowe Trophy as the Q's best defensive defenceman, the Emile Bouchard Trophy as the top defenceman, and the Canadian Hockey League's Defenceman of the Year award.

Savard then spent a decade patrolling the Columbus blue line before he was acquired by the Lightning to defend their title. Following the loss to Tampa Bay, times were tough in Montreal, but the veteran blueliner proved to be a bright spot, valiantly blocking shots with aplomb and earning the adoration of the fans. At the end of the 2022–23 campaign, he received the Jacques Beauchamp-Molson Trophy, awarded annually to the Hab who played a dominant role during the regular season without earning any particular honour.

JULY 29

HABS SIGN MATHIEU PERREAULT, 2021

Mathieu Perreault once almost netted a fan a million dollars. During his tenure with the Jets, Perreault scored four goals in an 8–2 rout of the Panthers on January 13, 2015. But if he had notched another goal, a random fan, identified early in the game as Gail McDonald, would have won the grand prize as part of a contest offered by the grocer Safeway. Not known for scoring in bunches, it was Perreault's first four-goal performance. The versatile forward wouldn't record another hat trick for six years.

After signing a one-year deal with the Canadiens on July 29, 2021, Perreault, who grew up in Drummondville, Quebec, lit the lamp three times in his fifth game for the Habs, becoming the first Quebec native to score a hat trick for the Canadiens in Montreal since Vincent Damphousse more than two decades earlier. Perreault had always dreamed of playing for the Canadiens, but he later said that, even in his wildest dreams, he didn't think he'd ever score a hat trick in a Habs sweater at home.

CANADIENS DRAFT CAREY
PRICE FIFTH OVERALL, 2005

When the Canadiens drafted goaltender Carey Price fifth overall on July 30, 2005, there were some raised eyebrows. The team already had José Théodore between the pipes, and he was just a few seasons removed from his Vezina- and Hart trophy-winning campaign. But GM Bob Gainey told reporters this wasn't a move for the present. He was thinking long-term and talked about Price as the club's goaltender of the future. While general managers often talk in those platitudes, Gainey's words proved to be prophetic.

After dominating the Western Hockey League that year, Price played two more seasons in junior before joining the Canadiens for the 2007–08 campaign. Within a few years, he had established himself as a franchise goalie, racking up 38 victories, the most by a Habs netminder in more than three decades. By 2014, Price had not only become what Gainey had hoped for, he was arguably the best goalie in the world. That year he backstopped Canada to Olympic gold, and the following season, he earned the Vezina and Hart trophies.

JULY 31

HABS SIGN ALEXANDRE PICARD, 2010

When free agency opened, Alexandre Picard had a few offers on the table. But they weren't exactly what he was looking for. He hoped to sign a one-way contract in order to stay in the NHL. Drafted 85th overall by the Flyers in 2003, the defenceman had bounced around the league, unable to find a consistent spot on the blue line. He initially didn't want to sign a two-way deal, only to wind up in the minors, but changed his tune when he got a call from the Canadiens.

Picard had been born and raised in Gatineau, so the offer was a no-brainer. "It's a dream for every guy who's born in Quebec," he later told reporters. So on July 31, 2010, Picard inked a one-year, two-way agreement with the Habs. He wasn't guaranteed a spot on the roster, but with Andrei Markov still on the shelf with a knee injury to start the season, he got the chance to play alongside P.K. Subban for stretches throughout the campaign. Picard appeared in 43 games for the Canadiens.

AUGUST 1

HABS START BUBBLE HOCKEY, 2020

When the 2019–20 season was ground to a halt by the Covid-19 pandemic, the Canadiens were sitting outside of a playoff spot. But when the NHL resumed operations a few months later, they suddenly found themselves in the post-season after the league expanded the playoffs to 24 teams. The top four teams from each conference received a bye to the first round of the playoffs, while the remaining 16 teams battled it out in a best-of-five series. The other twist was that there would be only two venues for the games, one in the east and one in the west, in a controlled setting that quickly became known as "bubble hockey."

And while the league was adamant this qualifying round was not the playoffs, it certainly felt like Montreal playoff hockey. The only thing standing between the team and the actual playoffs was the higher-seeded Penguins. On August 1, 2020, the Canadiens took the first game with a 3–2 victory in sudden death. Carey Price made 39 saves, while Jeff Petry was the unlikely overtime hero.

GEORGES LARAQUE CALLS
IT A CAREER, 2010

Georges Laraque already had his next gig lined up before he had even retired. On August 2, 2010, the NHL tough guy officially hung up his skates. The announcement was not a surprise — he played his last game with the Canadiens six months earlier before he was bought out of his contract. What may have been a surprise was that a few days before confirming his retirement, Laraque was named the new deputy leader of the Green Party of Canada. The political appointment may have been a curious choice for the pugilist, but it was the perfect fit for him.

When he wasn't chucking his knuckles on the ice, he stood up for environmental and humanitarian causes. Laraque caught the Green Party's eye after he started advocating and making presentations about becoming a vegan. A few years after being named deputy leader, Laraque threw his name into the ring to run for the federal seat in Montreal's Bourassa riding, but a few months later, he was forced to step down when he faced allegations of fraud from a former business partner.

AUGUST 3

PATRICE BRISEBOIS RETURNS TO HABS, 2007

P atrice Brisebois was right back where he wanted to be. After spending the past two seasons with the Avalanche, he returned to where he started his career, signing a one-year deal with the Habs on August 3, 2007. Drafted 30th overall by the Canadiens in 1989, the defenceman was a fixture on the Montreal blue line for parts of 14 seasons, winning a Stanley Cup in 1993. And while he had played an important role quarterbacking the power play, by the end of his tenure, he was often booed by fans who felt he was not living up to his contract. GM Bob Gainey stuck up for his blueliner, sometimes calling the fans names we can't print, but Brisebois left for free agency in 2005.

While Brisebois was no longer a top-four defenceman in 2007, he was healthy again after undergoing back surgery the previous campaign. Following his first season back, the Canadiens signed him to another one-year contract. In what would be his final NHL campaign, Brisebois capped off his career with a milestone, appearing in his 1,000th game on March 14, 2009.

AUGUST 4

THE ROCKET IS BORN, 1921

Maurice Richard was not always known as "the Rocket." Born as Joseph Henri Maurice Richard on August 4, 1921, he grew up in the Bordeaux neighbourhood of Montreal. As he got older and became more skilled at hockey, he used aliases so he could play on more than one team. By the time he was attending the Montreal Technical School to become a machinist, Richard had caught the eye of the Canadiens and signed on with Montreal's affiliate in the Quebec Senior Hockey League. He eventually made his NHL debut for the 1942–43 season but appeared in just 16 games after breaking his ankle in December.

The next season, however, Richard, now sporting No. 9 as a nod to his daughter Huguette, who was born weighing nine pounds, racked up 32 goals in 46 games and was dubbed "the Comet" by the media for his blazing speed and shot. By the time he scored 50 goals the next year, a new nickname had caught on, and Richard would be forever known as "the Rocket."

AUGUST 5

TOMÁŠ TATAR SIGNS WITH NEW JERSEY, 2021

wanted Tomáš Tatar to stay in Montreal forever because, if nothing else, it meant he would always be known as Tomáš Tataaaaaaaaaarrrr. Acquired from Vegas as part of the Max Pacioretty trade in 2018, Tatar quickly became a fan favourite, especially with one supporter. When the Canadiens hosted the Golden Knights on November 10, 2018, a fan named Daniel Toulouse went viral when he put a little extra emphasis on the Slovakian winger's last name while strolling the Bell Centre concourse with a Molson in his hand.

And if Toulouse's beer-laced pronunciation wasn't already epic enough, Tatar scored the game-winning goal that night against his former team. Over the next two seasons, playing with Phillip Danault and Brendan Gallagher on one of the league's most potent even-strength lines, Tatar set career milestones in points. But in his final campaign with the Habs, he struggled and watched most of the team's 2021 deep playoff run from the press box. And then, on August 5, 2021, the Tataaaaaaaaaarrrr era was officially over when he signed with New Jersey as a free agent.

AUGUST 6

HABS ACQUIRE JEFF PETRY (AGAIN), 2023

Jeff Petry was a Hab again, but for how long? After spending six seasons in Montreal, he was dealt to Pittsburgh in the 2022 off-season. During the 2021–22 campaign, Petry's wife, Julie, who was pregnant with their fourth son, had grown increasingly frustrated by the lingering protective measures against Covid-19 in Quebec; she returned to the family's home in Michigan with their three young boys, while Petry stayed behind. He played out the season but requested a trade.

But after spending a year with the Penguins, Petry was sent back to the Canadiens on August 6, 2023, as part of a three-way deal that allowed Pittsburgh to net reigning Norris Trophy winner Erik Karlsson. Although a lot had changed in the world in the past year, it seemed unlikely Petry would stay in Montreal. Sure enough, just over a week later, the Habs sent him to the Red Wings for Gustav Lindstrom and a conditional fourth-round draft pick. It was a fitting destination for Petry. His father, Dan, had won a World Series with the Detroit Tigers in 1984.

AUGUST 7

HABS OUST PENGUINS, 2020

Artturi Lehkonen spoiled Sid the Kid's party. On August 7, 2020, Sidney Crosby's 33rd birthday, the Canadiens and Penguins squared off for the fourth game of their playoff qualifying series. It was a pivotal matchup; Pittsburgh needed a victory to stay alive. Although Penguins netminder Tristan Jarry was making his first post-season start, he was poised and made timely saves against Paul Byron and Brendan Gallagher in the second period. At the other end of the ice, Carey Price, who was spectacular all series, stymied the birthday boy just before the halfway mark of the middle frame.

Byron was denied in the second session, but with just over four minutes remaining in the game, mobbed by Penguins as he proceeded toward the net, he drew a delayed penalty. The power play wasn't needed. Byron got the puck out front to Lehkonen, who broke the scoreless deadlock. Pittsburgh desperately looked to force overtime, but Montreal captain Shea Weber added an empty-net goal with just 22 seconds left on the clock to complete the upset of the fifth-seeded Penguins.

KEN DRYDEN'S BIRTHDAY, 1947

When Ken Dryden was born in Hamilton, Ontario, on August 8, 1947, he had the whole world in front of him. But even his parents, Murray and Margaret, might have balked at the idea that he would not only grow up to be a six-time Stanley Cup champion but also a Hockey Hall of Famer. And he accomplished even more off the ice. During his Habs tenure, Dryden earned a law degree from McGill University. And a few years after that he became a bestselling author with the release of his book *The Game*, which remains one of the greatest hockey books ever written.

He wrote more books, including a novel, and even developed a six-part documentary series. And that was before he got into politics. Dryden served as member of Parliament and cabinet minister in the Paul Martin government. So today is not just about celebrating a Canadiens goaltending legend. It is also about recognizing how much Dryden contributed to the game and to society after he put away his blocker and trapper.

AUGUST 9

HABS ACQUIRE JOCELYN LEMIEUX, 1988

Jocelyn Lemieux would have been a Canadien earlier if he hadn't broken his leg. During the 1987–88 campaign, Montreal had a trade drawn up that would have netted it Lemieux, younger brother of Claude, from the Blues, but when he went crashing into the boards in a game against the Flyers on January 7, 1988, he fractured his fibula and tore tendons in his left leg. He needed surgery and missed the rest of the campaign, so the deal was scrapped. But in the off-season, the Habs revisited the trade.

On August 9, 1988, they finally acquired Lemieux, along with Darrell May and a second-round draft pick, from the Blues for Sergio Momesso and Vincent Riendeau. Head coach Pat Burns welcomed Lemieux's hard-nosed style of play, but he spent most of the year in the minors. The next season, however, he made the team out of camp and opened the 1989–90 campaign playing on a line with his older brother. The younger Lemieux played 34 games for Montreal that year before he was traded to Chicago.

MIGHTY DUCKS COMPLETE FIRST-EVER TRADE WITH THE HABS, 1993

t was a historic trade. On August 10, 1993, the Mighty Ducks of Anaheim, set to begin their inaugural NHL season at home on October 8, made their first-ever deal when they acquired Patrik Carnbäck and Todd Ewen from the reigning Stanley Cup champion Canadiens for a third-round draft pick in 1994. In Montreal, Ewen was no stranger to the penalty box, but he would become even more familiar with the sin bin out west. Serving as a bodyguard for Anaheim's stars, Paul Kariya and Teemu Selänne, the pugnacious Ewen racked up 272 penalty minutes in his first campaign as a Duck. A couple of seasons later, he would collect 285, a team record that, as of this writing, still stands.

But the right winger's hard-hitting brand of hockey came at a heavy cost. Nearly two decades after hanging up his skates, Ewen, who had been suffering from depression for years, died by suicide. An examination of his brain later revealed the presence of chronic traumatic encephalopathy, a degenerative brain disease caused by repeated head trauma.

FLOYD CURRY'S BIRTHDAY, 1925

Floyd Curry's teammates knew him as "Busher" because of his tireless work ethic. Born in Chapleau, Ontario, on August 11, 1925, but raised in the gold mining town of Kirkland Lake, Curry had a dogged determination on both sides of the puck. After winning a Memorial Cup with the Oshawa Generals in 1944, he caught the eye of the Canadiens. He spent a handful of seasons in the minors before joining the Habs full-time for the 1950–51 campaign.

Curry was known more for his defensive play, but he once gave an offensive effort that was fit for a queen. On October 29, 1951, with Princess Elizabeth and the Duke of Edinburgh taking in a game at the Forum during a royal tour of Canada, he recorded his first and only NHL hat trick in a 6–1 victory against the Rangers. Following that performance, you could understand if the royals might have assumed Curry was the league's best player. He won four Stanley Cups in Montreal as a player and then spent more than four decades working in the club's front office.

SERGE SAVARD ANNOUNCES RETIREMENT, 1981

John Ferguson had other plans for his former teammate. When Serge Savard announced his retirement on August 12, 1981, Ferguson, who was then the general manager of the Winnipeg Jets, had something up his sleeve. A few months later, when the Canadiens had mistakenly failed to put Savard on the voluntary retirement list, Ferguson plucked him in the league's annual re-entry draft. The Winnipeg GM figured that if anyone could talk Savard into lacing up his skates again it was him. But the big defenceman initially rebuked Ferguson's proposal.

During his tenure in Montreal, Savard had already made a fortune on real estate and held one of the province's first lottery licences — he seemed destined to skate off the ice and into the business world. Ferguson, however, would not take no for an answer. After a few months, Savard relented and made his Jets debut on December 20, 1981. He spent two seasons in Winnipeg before returning to the Canadiens as GM. Under Savard's direction, the Habs won championships in 1986 and 1993.

AUGUST 13

RANDY EXELBY'S BIRTHDAY, 1965

Randy Exelby really put the relief in relief goaltender. During a game against the Sabres on January 27, 1989, one of the linesmen skated over to the Canadiens' bench to inform coach Pat Burns that Patrick Roy needed to go to the washroom. Burns looked down at Exelby, who was the backup goaltender that night, and told him he was going in. While Roy relieved himself, Exelby made his NHL debut.

Born in Toronto, Ontario, on August 13, 1965, Exelby had been picked up by the Canadiens in the league's first supplemental draft in 1986. He spent parts of two seasons in the minors until he was recalled in January 1989 to serve as a backup for Brian Hayward while Roy was battling a case of tonsillitis. When Roy was healthy enough to return, Hayward went down with an illness of his own and Exelby got to stick around a little while longer. He stopped one shot in just under three minutes of action before Roy returned to the crease. It proved to be Exelby's only appearance with the Canadiens.

HABS BLANK FLYERS, 2020

This one was for the skipper. Following the first game of the Canadiens' quarterfinal series against the Flyers, head coach Claude Julien was complaining of chest pain. He was taken to hospital and had a stent placed in a coronary artery. Julien was expected to make a full recovery, but he was out of the series. In his absence, associate coach Kirk Muller took over behind the bench.

When the Habs played their next game, on August 14, 2020, they had Julien on their mind but were focused on the job they had to do. Just over a minute into the contest, Tomáš Tatar bulged the twine to give the Canadiens the early lead. They racked up three more unanswered goals to chase goaltender Carter Hart from his crease. The Habs added another halfway through the final frame to seal a 5–0 victory and even the series at one game apiece. Following the game, Muller had a heartfelt message for his boss: "To Claude, I'm sure he's listening, this one was for you."

AUGUST 15

HABS INK JEFF WOYWITKA, 2011

Jeff Woywitka thought he was going to be a Hab. But just over a month after signing a one-year deal with Montreal on August 15, 2011, he was waived on the eve of the regular season. Woywitka, however, would not be reassigned to the minors. Instead, the defenceman was claimed by the Rangers. And New York needed all the help it could get on the blue line. When the campaign commenced, the Rangers' top defenceman, Marc Staal, was still on the shelf with an injury.

Woywitka started in the press box, but he got into the lineup when Michael Sauer went down with a shoulder injury, forming the third pair with Steve Eminger, who was his defence partner at the World Juniors for Team Canada nearly a decade earlier. While Woywitka was sometimes the odd man out on the back end, he played 26 games on Broadway until Staal returned in January. After he was recalled from the minors a month later, Woywitka suited up for what would be his final NHL game on March 2, 2012.

HABS ACQUIRE THE RIGHTS
TO KARRI RÄMÖ, 2010

t was not likely that Karri Rämö would be a Montreal Canadien anytime soon. Although the Habs acquired his rights from the Lightning in exchange for minor-leaguer Cédrick Desjardins on August 16, 2010, the Finnish goaltender was still under contract with Avangard Omsk of the KHL for another year. Originally drafted 191st overall by Tampa Bay in 2004, Rämö spent parts of three seasons with the Bolts before heading to Russia for the 2009–10 campaign.

Rämö would never suit up for the Canadiens, but he was part of a notable moment in franchise history a couple of years later. Remember when Mike Cammalleri was traded to Calgary in the middle of a game? Well, Rämö was also included as part of that deal. He was still playing for Omsk at the time, but he signed a two-year contract with the Flames that off-season and made his return to the NHL. He earned the starting job in Calgary for the 2013–14 season, and ended up playing for three years in Alberta before returning to Europe to finish out his career.

AUGUST 17

MIKE MCPHEE TRADED TO NORTH STARS, 1992

Mike McPhee was Bob Gainey's type of player. He was strong on both sides of the puck. While McPhee started his tenure with the Canadiens just as Gainey's playing career was coming to a close, the two were eventually reunited in Minnesota. The Habs decided to protect McPhee in the 1992 expansion draft, a change of heart from their original plan, but a few months later, on August 17, 1992, he was traded to the North Stars, where Gainey was the coach and GM, for a fifth-round draft pick in 1993.

In his final season with the Habs, McPhee saw his ice time curtailed, but under Gainey's direction, his game flourished again. In his first campaign with the North Stars, the 33-year-old McPhee collected 18 goals and 40 points. The following year, with the team now in Dallas, he hit the 20-goal mark for the fourth time in his career. After sitting out the 1994–95 campaign while he recovered from knee surgery, McPhee was forced to hang up his skates in September 1995.

JIMMY ROBERTS TRADED BACK TO BLUES, 1977

Jimmy Roberts had a well-earned reputation for shutting down the league's top players. As an original member of the St. Louis Blues, he had done such an impressive job shadowing the Bruins' superstar defenceman Bobby Orr during the Stanley Cup Final that at least one Boston reporter started referring to him as "Lamont Cranston," the alter ego of the fictional pulp and radio hero *The Shadow*. While that particular moniker didn't stick, Roberts's notoriety for being able to shadow his opponents did.

After breaking into the NHL with the Canadiens in 1963, Roberts won two Stanley Cups in Montreal before he was eventually plucked in the 1967 expansion draft by St. Louis. He played there for five seasons before being traded back to the Habs, where he added three more championships to his collection. But after his fifth title with the Canadiens, on August 18, 1977, the hard-working Roberts was dealt back to St. Louis, where he continued to reside in the off-season, for future considerations. He played one final season for the Blues and then retired.

AUGUST 19

HABS LIVE TO FIGHT ANOTHER DAY, 2020

The Canadiens stayed alive. On August 19, 2020, Montreal defeated Philadelphia 5–3 to stave off elimination in its quarterfinal playoff series. Flyers goaltender Carter Hart had been flawless in the past two games, turning aside every shot he faced, but early in the contest, the Habs finally found a way to beat him again. Less than three minutes after puck drop, with the Flyers on the man advantage, Joel Armia caught a rebound from an Xavier Ouellet blast from centre ice and put it over Hart's left pad.

Philadelphia scored two straight goals early in the second period on a five-minute major to pull ahead, but a few minutes later, Armia notched his second of the night to tie the game. Just over a minute after that, Brendan Gallagher, who hadn't scored since March 3, potted his first of the playoffs to extend the lead. The Flyers knotted it up midway through the final frame, but the Habs remained relentless. Twenty-two seconds later, Nick Suzuki recorded the go-ahead goal, with Phillip Danault adding an empty-netter to seal the victory.

HABS TRADE SYLVAIN
LEFEBVRE TO LEAFS, 1992

After the Maple Leafs lost defenceman Ric Nattress to the Flyers, they went looking to fill the hole on their blue line. Their search led them to the Canadiens. On August 20, 1992, Toronto acquired Sylvain Lefebvre from Montreal for a third-round draft pick in 1994. A reliable stay-at-home defenceman, Lefebvre joined the Habs organization as an undrafted free agent. He made his NHL debut in 1989, but by the end of his third season with the Canadiens, he was often in the doghouse of head coach Pat Burns, finding himself frequently stapled to the bench or watching the team from the press box.

Although Burns would once again be his bench boss, Lefebvre reached career highs for games played with the Leafs until he was part of the trade to Quebec that landed Toronto Mats Sundin. A couple of years later, Lefebvre won a Stanley Cup with the Avalanche, and when it was his turn to spend the day with the trophy, he had his daughter baptized in the silver chalice.

AUGUST 21

HABS ELIMINATED, 2020

A ll good things must come to an end. The Canadiens got further in the bubble than most expected, upsetting the higher-seeded Penguins in the qualifying round, but they ran out of runway against the Flyers. On August 21, 2020, Montreal lost 3–2 to Philadelphia and was eliminated from the playoffs. With a little more puck luck, it's possible the Habs could have pushed the series further and even taken it.

When the final buzzer sounded for the series, the Canadiens had actually outscored the Flyers 13–11, but what really did them in was that they just didn't get the bounces. Six of Philadelphia's goals went in off a Montreal player, including four in the final two games. And although Carey Price admirably turned aside 138 of the 149 shots he faced, it's tough to win games when the other team is seemingly skating around with lucky horseshoes on the ice. Philly got plenty of breaks, but Carter Hart proved to be the difference-maker, turning in back-to-back shutouts and making 31 saves in the final game.

HABS INK DOUGLAS MURRAY, 2013

have a confession to make. For the longest time, I had no idea Douglas Murray was Swedish. With a Scottish name like that, you could understand my mistake, but there was a lot more I didn't know about Murray. Before he broke into the NHL, the hulking defenceman, who was known as "Crankshaft," which is a pretty badass nickname, earned a degree in hotel administration from Cornell University. During his time there, he and his friends patented the UberTap, a hands-free, multi-spout dispenser for beer kegs, the kind of device that could only be invented by someone with an Ivy League education who answers to "Crankshaft."

After graduating from Cornell, Murray turned pro and spent a decade with the Sharks organization before he was traded to the Penguins. Following a brief stint in Pittsburgh, he signed a one-year deal with the Canadiens on August 22, 2013. At six-foot-three and 240 pounds, Murray brought size to the Montreal blue line. He suited up in 53 regular-season games and a few more in the playoffs for the Habs, his final NHL appearances.

AUGUST 23

HABS SIGN GEORGE HAINSWORTH, 1926

I t was rather fitting that George Hainsworth was the first-ever winner of the Vezina. Signed by the Canadiens on August 23, 1926, he was brought in to fill Georges Vézina's crease after the goaltender, who had tended the twine for the Habs since 1910, passed away five months earlier following a battle with tuberculosis. No one could ever possibly replace the Chicoutimi Cucumber, but Hainsworth was a worthy candidate to carry on his legacy between the pipes.

At the end of his first season in the NHL, Hainsworth had finished with 28 victories and 14 shutouts, the most in the league, and was named the inaugural winner of the Vezina Memorial Trophy, which the Canadiens had donated to honour the memory of their late goalie. Two years later, he won it for the third straight time following an incredible campaign that included 22 shutouts, an NHL record that will likely stand the test of time. Hainsworth would backstop the Habs to a Stanley Cup in 1930, their first title without Vézina, and another the next year.

LE GROS BILL AND BOOM BOOM INDUCTED, 1972

When Ted Lindsay was inducted into the Hockey Hall of Fame in 1966, he declined the invitation to the ceremony because women and children were not allowed to attend. The archaic rule was finally done away with six years later. On August 24, 1972, when the Hall welcomed its new members, families could be there, and two of Montreal's greatest were among the esteemed group: Jean Béliveau and Bernie Geoffrion.

Béliveau, who had hung up his skates a year earlier and was serving as vice-president of the Canadiens, had the standard three-year waiting period waived, but his formal induction was pushed to the following year because he was in Munich for the Summer Olympics and then heading to Moscow for the Summit Series. While le Gros Bill couldn't be there, Boom Boom, who had been waiting for his call, received his honour. Geoffrion's wife, Marlene, couldn't attend because she was recovering from surgery, but he acknowledged it was a special moment for their family because he was joining his late father-in-law, Howie Morenz, in hockey's pantheon.

HARRY MUMMERY BORN IN CHICAGO, 1889

H arry Mummery was one of the heaviest players of his generation. The NHL officially listed him at 220 pounds, but it's been suggested that he tipped the scales at closer to 250. Growing up on the Manitoba Prairies after being born in Chicago on August 25, 1889, Mummery had the appetite of a good farm boy, but even his western Canadian counterparts couldn't pack it away like him. There was nothing he liked more than frying up a five-pound steak after a match and washing it down with a quart of cream, which he reportedly drank after every meal.

When Mummery turned in his meal expenditures to GM George Kennedy when he reported to the Canadiens in 1920, the Habs executive was flabbergasted. He assumed Mummery must have had help from several cats to lap up all that cream. But Mummery contended the cream gave him strength. It was hard to argue with the results. In the 1920–21 campaign, he scored 15 goals in 24 games, leading famed Montreal sportswriter Elmer Ferguson to call him "a one-man power play."

HOCKEY HALL OF FAME OPENS, 1961

The Hockey Hall of Fame would finally have a home. Established during the Second World War to honour the game's greatest players, the collection was without a permanent installation for nearly two decades. It began as an exhibit at the Canadian National Exhibition in Toronto in 1955, and plans were soon developed to create something more fitting for hockey's pantheon. With funding from the NHL's six teams, the half-million-dollar building, which was shared by Canada's Sports Hall of Fame, opened at the CNE fairgrounds on August 26, 1961.

After Prime Minister John Diefenbaker opened the facility to much fanfare, 17 members were inducted into the Hall of Fame. Among those honoured were Canadiens Maurice Richard, George Hainsworth, and Joe Hall, who was inducted posthumously more than four decades after succumbing to the Spanish flu during Montreal's Stanley Cup Final series against Seattle. But as the Hall of Fame's ranks swelled, it wasn't long before the building ran out of exhibit space. In 1993, the Hall moved to BCE Place (now Brookfield Place) and has been there ever since.

HABS LAND VINCENT DAMPHOUSSE, 1992

Oilers GM Glen Sather once called Vincent Damphousse the second-best French Canadian in the NHL. The other, of course, was Mario Lemieux. So when the Habs had the chance to land Damphousse, a Montreal native, they jumped at the opportunity. And Damphousse was also eager to get out of Edmonton. Following a separation from his wife early in the 1991–92 campaign, he requested a trade. Despite what was happening off the ice, he finished the season with 38 goals and 89 points, leading the team in both categories. In the off-season, on August 27, 1992, Sather traded him to the Canadiens, along with a fourth-round pick, for Shayne Corson, Brent Gilchrist, and prospect Vladimir Vůjtek.

Damphousse flourished in Montreal. In his first season with the club, he racked up 39 goals and 97 points, both career benchmarks. In the playoffs, he added 23 points in 20 games and was critical in the team's Stanley Cup victory that year. Damphousse played five more seasons with the Canadiens before he was dealt to San Jose in 1999.

CANES SIGN JESPERI KOTKANIEMI TO OFFER SHEET, 2021

The Hurricanes did not forget. Two years after the Canadiens signed Sebastian Aho to an offer sheet, on August 28, 2021, Carolina inked Jesperi Kotkaniemi to one of their own. Although the Canes ended up matching the deal that was extended to Aho, they seemed intent on exacting some measure of revenge and relished the opportunity to pry Kotkaniemi out of Montreal. Not only did the contract include a $20 signing bonus (yes, $20!), a nod to the number worn by Aho, but the club also tweeted out the announcement *en français* and changed its bio to French on Twitter.

While the pettiness abounded on social media, the Canadiens had until September 4 to match the offer, otherwise they would receive first- and third-round draft picks from Carolina as compensation. Seven days later, the Habs announced they would not match, and Kotkaniemi officially became a Hurricane, the first NHL player in over a decade acquired with an offer sheet. Just over halfway through his first season with his new club, he signed an eight-year contract extension.

AUGUST 29

AURÈLE JOLIAT IS BORN, 1901

Aurèle Joliat was one of the smaller players of his day, but he played his heart out on the ice. Born in Ottawa, Ontario, on August 29, 1901, he wound up on the Prairies for work but made his way back east when the hockey team that held his rights in Saskatoon traded him to the Canadiens for Newsy Lalonde. In Montreal, Joliat quickly endeared himself to the fans and earned the nickname "the Little Giant." What he lacked in size, he more than made up for in skill and determination.

Joliat played nearly two decades with the Habs, capturing three Stanley Cups and the Hart Trophy in 1934, but one of his most enduring moments happened long after he retired. In 1984, as part of the Canadiens' 75th anniversary celebrations, an 83-year-old Joliat, the oldest living member of the franchise, took to the ice wearing his trademark black cap and even the same skates from his playing days. He took a few tumbles, but the octogenarian delighted the crowd by sneaking the puck past Jacques Plante.

KIRK MULLER GETS THE "C", 1994

Much like the starship *Enterprise*, the Canadiens would have their own Captain Kirk. On August 30, 1994, the club announced that Kirk Muller would become the 21st captain in franchise history. He replaced Guy Carbonneau, who had worn the "C" with distinction for five seasons until he was traded to St. Louis a few months earlier. When Carbonneau was initially appointed captain in 1989, he shared the role with Chris Chelios when the team vote ended in a tie. The two served as co-captains for the 1989–90 campaign until Chelios was dealt to Chicago for Denis Savard at the end of the year.

Looking to avoid a similar outcome and a potential rift within the dressing room, Muller was appointed captain by management. Regardless of where the decision came from, he was an obvious choice, having been a heart-and-soul player for the club for the past three years. But Captain Kirk wouldn't even get a full season. With just over a dozen games remaining on the calendar, he was traded to the Islanders.

AUGUST 31

HABS ACQUIRE BRIAN BELLOWS, 1992

When Brian Bellows was introduced as the newest member of the Canadiens, he came with a guarantee: he would score more than 30 goals. It wasn't necessarily a lofty promise — he had reached the 30-goal mark six times, which included a 55-goal campaign, during his tenure with the North Stars — but it signified his commitment to perform for his new team. Before Bellows was traded to Montreal on August 31, 1992, in exchange for Russ Courtnall, there were reports he would be unhappy about a move to a Canadian club, something he indicated when he was the subject of trade rumours in Minnesota.

But Bellows was quick to dispel that notion, stating that "it's every kid's dream to play for the Canadiens" and that Ken Dryden had been his boyhood hero. While his words courted the Habs faithful, Bellows made good on his pledge. He scored 40 goals and 88 points in the regular season and then added 15 more points in the playoffs to help the club clinch its 24th Stanley Cup championship.

SEPTEMBER 1

HABS REACQUIRE HOWIE MORENZ, 1936

The Stratford Streak was back where he belonged — in Montreal. On September 1, 1936, the Canadiens purchased Howie Morenz from the Rangers for cash. Morenz, the NHL's first superstar, made his debut for the Habs in 1923, and over the next decade he lived up to his billing. He would earn three Hart trophies and led the Canadiens to three Stanley Cup titles. But after 11 seasons with the club, Morenz was traded, along with Lorne Chabot and Marty Burke, to Chicago for Leroy Goldsworthy, Lionel Conacher, and Roger Jenkins.

While Morenz was about to turn 34 years old and could no longer streak up the ice the way he once could, there was still a buzz about his return to Montreal. He got off to a hot start, collecting five points in his first six games, but his season came to a tragic end. Morenz shattered his leg in four places in a game against the Rangers on January 28, 1937, and just over a month later, he died when a blood clot caused a coronary embolism.

SEPTEMBER 2

HABS ACQUIRE JAKE ALLEN, 2020

Jake Allen knew exactly what his job would be. "The role that I'll be playing is obviously behind one of the best goalies in the world," he told reporters after he was acquired from the Blues, along with a seventh-round pick, for third- and seventh-round picks on September 2, 2020. Allen, who was drafted 34th overall by St. Louis in 2008, had spent the last two seasons backing up Jordan Binnington and won a Stanley Cup in 2019. In Montreal, he would help lighten Carey Price's workload, but he would prove to be more than a dependable backup.

When Price missed a stretch of games at the end of the 2020–21 campaign, Allen took over the starting duties and kept the Habs in the playoff picture. Following the club's run to the Stanley Cup Final that year, Price agreed to waive his no-movement clause so that the Canadiens could protect Allen in the 2021 expansion draft. With Price unable to play the next campaign, Allen shared the crease with the up-and-coming Sam Montembeault.

SEPTEMBER 3

BONNE FÊTE, CRISTOBAL HUET, 1975

Cristobal Huet ended up between the pipes the way many young netminders do: his big brother needed a goalie. Born in Saint-Martin-d'Hères, France, on September 3, 1975, Huet dutifully answered the call but probably never imagined where his sibling servitude would lead. After making his World Hockey Championship debut in 1997, he appeared in the tournament 13 more times over the next two decades. In between representing his country with distinction, Huet became the first goalie trained in France to suit up in the NHL.

Drafted 214th overall by the Kings in 2001, Huet was eventually acquired by the Canadiens, where he wrestled the starting job from José Théodore. Following a few seasons in Montreal, which included winning the Molson Cup in the 2006–07 campaign for the most three-star selections, he made his way to Chicago, where he hoisted the Stanley Cup in 2010. Huet's career came full circle when he played his final games on home ice when France hosted the World Championship in 2017. Six years after hanging up his blocker and trapper, he was inducted into the IIHF Hall of Fame.

SEPTEMBER 4

HABS ACQUIRE CHRISTIAN DVORAK, 2021

When the Canadiens decided to walk away from Jesperi Kotkaniemi, they didn't sit around and lick their wounds. The same day he officially became a Hurricane, on September 4, 2021, Montreal acquired Christian Dvorak from Arizona for a first-round pick in 2022 and a second-round pick in 2024. With an extra first-rounder in hand from the compensation owed to them from Carolina, the Canadiens had some extra manoeuvrability. I still remember Dvorak ripping up the Ontario Hockey League in the 2015–16 season, racking up 121 points, the second most that year, playing alongside future NHL stars Mitch Marner and Matthew Tkachuk, but by the time he made his way to the Habs he had adjusted his game for the big leagues.

Although he was still good for double-digit goals and 30-plus points, nothing to scoff at on some pretty anemic Coyotes teams, he was strong on both sides of the puck. Dvorak brought that two-way game to Montreal, adding some defensive upside to the team's bottom six, and became one of head coach Martin St-Louis's most trusted players.

SEPTEMBER 5

JOHN FERGUSON'S BIRTHDAY, 1938

John Ferguson was arguably the NHL's first enforcer. Brought in to protect captain Jean Béliveau, Fergy took his job seriously. Just 12 seconds into his very first game with the Canadiens, he took on the Bruins' "Terrible Ted" Green, whose nickname tells you all you need to know about his reputation on the ice. Ferguson made short work of his opponent, establishing himself as one of the league's toughest players, a title he wouldn't relinquish until retirement.

Ferguson, who was born in Vancouver, British Columbia, on September 5, 1938, was not a player you wanted to tangle with, but there was more to his game than fisticuffs. Playing alongside Béliveau in his debut season, Ferguson recorded 45 points, the most among rookies, but finished runner-up to teammate Jacques Laperrière for the Calder Trophy. In the 1968–69 campaign, he recorded 29 goals and 52 points, both career highs. It's even more impressive when you realize that only two players, Forbes Kennedy and Jim Dorey, spent more time in the penalty box than him that year, and neither of them hit the double-digit mark in goals.

SEPTEMBER 6

MONTREAL ACQUIRES SCOTT THORNTON, 1996

Andrei Kovalenko wasn't with the Canadiens very long, but he is forever linked to the team's history. Acquired from the Avalanche as part of the unceremonious Patrick Roy trade, Kovalenko ended up scoring the final regular-season goal in the Montreal Forum in a 4–1 victory against Dallas on March 11, 1996. He finished the campaign with 17 goals for the Habs, to go along with the 11 he notched in Colorado. It was a career year for the Russian, but he wasn't part of the Canadiens' long-term plans.

A month before the next season began, on September 6, 1996, he was dealt to the Oilers for Scott Thornton. On paper it was certainly a mismatch trade. Thornton, who was drafted third overall by Toronto in 1989, had never scored more than 10 goals in a season, while Kovalenko appeared poised to hit the 30-goal mark. While the Habs had concerns about whether Kovalenko's heart was in it, they knew Thornton, a hard-nosed player known for his two-way play, would run through a wall for his teammates.

SEPTEMBER 7

JEFF HALPERN SIGNS WITH HABS, 2010

Everything was going Jeff Halpern's way. Just over a week after signing a one-year deal with the Canadiens on September 7, 2010, he shot a hole-in-one at the team's golf tournament. It was the first ace for the veteran centre, and you couldn't blame him for thinking it was a sign of things to come that season. Halpern had spent the past two seasons with the Lightning until he was traded to Los Angeles before the deadline. In 16 games down the stretch with the Kings, he couldn't find the back of the net.

With the Habs, he was reunited with Mathieu Darche, whom he had good chemistry with in Tampa Bay, and they once again found *belle chimie* in Montreal. Halpern finished the year with 11 goals and 26 points, his most productive season in four years. Following his campaign with the Canadiens, he signed with Washington, where his NHL career had begun as an undrafted free agent. More than a decade after suiting up for the Habs, Halpern won a Stanley Cup against them as an assistant coach with Tampa Bay.

SEPTEMBER 8

COURNOYER CALLED TO THE HALL, 1982

Yvan Cournoyer wished his call could have come a little later. Although he was elated to be inducted into the Hockey Hall of Fame on September 8, 1982, the Roadrunner had hoped to attempt a comeback after he was forced into retirement by a nagging back. He started the 1978–79 season, his 15th full campaign with the club, but just 15 games into the schedule, Captain Cournoyer had to hang up his skates. Just over a year later, he was able to lace 'em up for a charity old-timers game at Maple Leaf Gardens, but that was as far as he got to returning to big-league ice.

In retirement, Cournoyer took a page out of his former coach Toe Blake's book and opened a bar called Brasserie No. 12, a nod to his number with the Canadiens. He also found himself behind the bench. In 1994, he became the inaugural coach of the Montreal Roadrunners, a team on the Roller Hockey International circuit, which was, of course, named in honour of Cournoyer's blistering speed.

SEPTEMBER 9

HABS TRADE ROD LANGWAY, 1982

The Canadiens blew up their blue line. On September 9, 1982, the team traded defencemen Rod Langway and Brian Engblom, along with Doug Jarvis and Craig Laughlin, to the Capitals for Rick Green and Ryan Walter. They didn't have much choice. Langway, who had grown disgruntled with Quebec's high taxes and, as a U.S. citizen, was tired of filing tax returns in two countries, wanted out. It was arguable that swapping Langway for Green and Jarvis for Walter was fair, but Engblom was one of Montreal's top rearguards, leaving a hole in the defence corps. The deal, however, only looked worse with time.

In Washington, Langway was named captain and became known as "the Secretary of Defense" for his strong play in his own end. He and Engblom helped turn around the porous Caps and led the team to a playoff berth for the first time in franchise history. At the end of his first season in D.C., Langway won the Norris as the league's top defenceman and took home the trophy again the next year.

SEPTEMBER 10

MAX PACIORETTY TRADED, 2018

f you're like me, you probably woke up to this news, but then again, if you're a night owl, you might have caught this trade in real time. In the early morning hours of September 10, 2018, the Canadiens announced they had traded captain Max Pacioretty to the Golden Knights for Tomáš Tatar, Nick Suzuki, and a second-round draft pick in 2019. It was arguably one of the most significant trades in the Marc Bergevin era, and much of the hockey world was sleeping when it happened. The Habs got a proven 20-goal scorer in Tatar, but GM Bergevin noted that Suzuki was, of course, the "key piece" in the deal.

Taken 13th overall by Vegas a year earlier, Suzuki was a promising centre who modelled his game after Boston's Patrice Bergeron. The Canadiens also had their eye on Cody Glass, another Golden Knights blue-chip prospect who was drafted seven spots ahead of Suzuki, but it worked out even better than they could have imagined. Within a few years, Suzuki was putting up 60 points in the NHL and was wearing the "C" for Montreal.

SEPTEMBER 11

BUTCH BOUCHARD IS BORN, 1920

Growing up in the working-class neighbourhood of Le Plateau in Montreal, Butch Bouchard couldn't afford skates. Born as Joseph Émile Alcide Bouchard on September 11, 1920, he and his family struggled during the Great Depression. Bouchard was forced to borrow skates from other kids for five cents an evening, and when he was short on change, he simply tended the twine in boots. When he was 16 years old, his brother loaned him some cash to finally purchase his own set of hockey equipment. The investment paid off.

Bouchard joined his hometown Canadiens for the 1941–42 campaign. At six-foot-two and 205 pounds, he towered over the opponents of his era and became a stalwart on the Montreal blue line. Known for his strong passing and hockey IQ, it was Bouchard's defensive prowess that allowed future defence partners like Doug Harvey to freewheel from end to end. After Toe Blake hung up his skates in 1948, Bouchard assumed the captaincy and wore it with distinction for nearly a decade. He played 15 seasons with the Habs, winning four Stanley Cups.

HABS ACQUIRE ROBERT LANG, 2008

The Canadiens had been pursuing Mats Sundin all summer, but when it became clear the club was not going to land the former Leafs captain, they made other plans. And so, on September 12, 2008, they acquired Robert Lang from Chicago for a second-round pick. Lang was just a few months from turning 38, but the Czech forward could still produce. In the 2007–08 campaign, he recorded 21 goals and 54 points in 76 games.

While Sundin stayed in Sweden until signing with the Canucks in December, Lang proved to be a solid consolation prize for the Habs. By the halfway mark of the season, Lang had 18 goals and was the team's leading scorer. He was on pace for a banner year when his left Achilles tendon was sliced during a game. Lang was optimistic he could return if the team made a deep playoff run, but the Habs just squeaked into the post-season and were then swept in four games by the Bruins. In the off-season, Lang signed with the Coyotes.

SEPTEMBER 13

HABS AND BLACKHAWKS
PLAY AT WEMBLEY, 1992

t was the first time in more than three decades that the NHL had played games in England. On September 13, 1992, the Canadiens and Blackhawks squared off for the final set of a two-game pre-season series at Wembley Stadium in London. With the NHL looking to grow the game globally, it sent two of its premier teams across the pond in what was billed as the Molson Challenge. Montreal took the first game 3–2, but Chicago won two shootouts the next day to take the series.

When the second game ended in a 4–4 tie, the Blackhawks scored two goals in the shootout, while four Habs shooters were stymied by goaltender Jimmy Waite. With the series tied, they went to another shootout. Montreal replaced André Racicot with Patrick Roy for the finale, but it didn't matter. Waite stayed hot, stopping all but one shot he faced, and Chicago took the series with a 2–1 victory in the shootout. The NHL returned to Wembley again the next year, with the Leafs and Rangers duking it out.

HABS HIGHLIGHT FRIENDSHIP TOUR, 1990

Two years before the Canadiens made their way to the United Kingdom, they played their first-ever games outside North America as part of a nine-game tour of Europe that included stops in Sweden, Latvia, and the Soviet Union. Known as the Friendship Tour, it also featured the North Stars, but neither NHL club faced each other; instead they played local clubs on each leg. After the Habs opened the exhibition with two wins in Stockholm and Leningrad (now St. Petersburg), they squared off with Dinamo Riga in the Latvian capital on September 14, 1990.

Led by Montreal's new top line of Denis Savard, Stéphane Richer, and Shayne Corson, who each scored goals, the Habs defeated their Soviet League counterparts 4–2. Head coach Pat Burns said it was the best team they had played so far. More interesting than the outcome on the scoresheet, however, was that the day before the game was held, NHL president John Ziegler announced at a news conference that he had turned down a request to have a Soviet team join the league.

SEPTEMBER 15

THE ROCKET RETIRES, 1960

There was no replacing the Rocket, but when head coach Toe Blake was asked who he would put in Maurice Richard's place next season, he said wryly, "Two men." He then added that they were going to petition the league to let them play seven players. The bench boss was having a chuckle with the media, but that's how much Richard meant to Montreal and French Canadians across the province. Ever since he stepped onto the ice at the Forum nearly two decades earlier, he had captured the imagination of the fans and inspired a generation.

So when Richard announced on September 15, 1960, that he was hanging up his skates, it was not only a sad day for hockey, it was a tough day for Quebec. The fiery winger helped the Habs establish a dynasty, winning five straight Stanley Cups to go along with his three other titles, and was so revered in the province that some believe he helped ignite a social revolution. You could never replace someone who meant so much to so many.

SEPTEMBER 16

CANADIENS HIRE YOUPPI!, 2005

The Canadiens were bringing Youppi! out of retirement. On September 16, 2005, the Habs announced that the former Montreal Expos mascot would be joining the team's payroll. An orange and furry giant, Youppi! was the brainchild of Bonnie Erickson, who brought Miss Piggy to life as a designer for Jim Henson and the Muppets. The popular mascot had been with the Expos in Major League Baseball until the team moved to Washington and became the Nationals.

But Youppi! wasn't out of work for too long. His last official event with the Expos was on September 29, 2004, when the club played its final home game at Olympic Stadium. Youppi! might have found a gig with the Canadiens even sooner if the NHL hadn't locked its doors for the 2004–05 season, but he was there now and ready to go from the diamond to the ice. As you probably already guessed, Youppi! was the first mascot in the history of North American major professional sports leagues to switch leagues. Not as if the orange fuzzball had much of a choice.

SEPTEMBER 17

HABS TRADE ANDREW CASSELS, 1991

Andrew Cassels wanted out of Montreal. After suiting up for 54 games in the 1990–91 campaign, his first full season with the Canadiens, Cassels, who had been drafted 17th overall by the club in 1987, skipped training camp the following year. Dissatisfied with his deployment, he was looking for more playing opportunities. Well, he wouldn't find them with the Habs. On September 17, 1991, the team traded the disgruntled centre to the Whalers for a second-round draft pick in 1992.

In Hartford, Cassels found more ice time and soon became one of the club's top scorers, collecting 85 points a couple of years later. Meanwhile, the Habs used the pick to select Valeri Bure 33rd overall. The younger brother of Pavel "the Russian Rocket" Bure, Valeri was known for his nifty playmaking skills. Some deemed him undersized by NHL standards at the time, but he wasn't actually all that small at five-foot-10. But when he, Saku Koivu, and Oleg Petrov, whom he had a few inches on, played together for part of the 1995–96 season, they were known as "the Smurf Line."

SEPTEMBER 18

NEWSY LALONDE TRADED OUT WEST, 1922

The Canadiens didn't just trade Newsy Lalonde. They sent him to a whole other league. On September 18, 1922, the Habs shipped their premier goal scorer to the Saskatoon Crescents of the Western Canada Hockey League for cash and the rights to Aurèle Joliat. In Saskatchewan, Lalonde served as both a player and manager. And although he doubled his salary, he didn't warm to the idea that Joliat would be replacing him in Montreal.

When the two squared off in an exhibition game, Joliat, who was wearing Lalonde's old No. 4, recalled that his predecessor was waiting for him. "One second I was on the left wing, the next I was on the right wing," Joliat said years later. "He crushed me. Split my lip in two." Lalonde finished his first campaign with the Crescents with 30 goals, the most in the WCHL. He spent three more years out west, before heading back to the NHL for one game with the New York Americans. In retirement, Lalonde returned to the Canadiens, serving as head coach for eight seasons.

SEPTEMBER 19

ANDRÉ BOUDRIAS CELEBRATES A BIRTHDAY, 1943

André Boudrias had his work cut out for him. Sitting behind Jean Béliveau, Henri Richard, and Ralph Backstrom on the Canadiens' depth chart down the middle, it would have been nearly impossible for any player to find a regular spot in that position on that roster. Born in Montreal on September 19, 1943, Boudrias made his NHL debut with his hometown team for the 1963–64 campaign, but he spent most of the next few seasons in the minor leagues, appearing in just seven games for the Habs.

When the league doubled its circuit in 1967, Boudrias was traded to the newly minted North Stars. With more opportunities in Minnesota, he picked up 53 points, just a few off the team lead. After spending some time with Chicago and St. Louis, he was dealt to the Canucks a few months before the club's inaugural season. In Vancouver, Boudrias immediately became a fan favourite and emerged as the team's first star player. After hanging up his skates, he returned to the Canadiens as a scout and, later, assistant GM, winning two championships.

JONATHAN DROUIN OPENS UP ABOUT HIS ANXIETY, 2021

When Jonathan Drouin abruptly left the Canadiens in April 2021 for personal reasons, it wasn't clear what was going on in his world, and quite frankly, it wasn't any of our business. But a few months later, following the team's improbable run to the Stanley Cup Final, Drouin opened up in an interview on September 20 with RDS, the French-language sister channel of TSN. The 26-year-old forward explained that his leave of absence stemmed from insomnia brought on by anxiety.

Drouin noted that he had been dealing with the condition for years, but he reached an impasse toward the end of the 2020–21 campaign. After taking part in a pre-game skate in Calgary, he just hit a wall. He hadn't slept for three nights and realized he needed some time away from the game if he hoped to get better. Drouin wasn't under any obligation to shed light on why he stepped away from the ice, but his courage to deal with a mental health issue and then speak openly about it was brave and inspiring.

FRANCIS BOUILLON RETURNS TO THE PREDS, 2009

Francis Bouillon was going back to the Predators. Undrafted out of college, Bouillon signed with the Canadiens organization and made his NHL debut in the 1999–00 campaign. A few seasons later, however, the Habs waived him and he was claimed off waivers by Nashville. But after playing just four games with the Predators, Bouillon was once again placed on waivers, but this time it was the Canadiens who scooped him back up.

After returning to Montreal, Bouillon patrolled the Habs' blue line for the next six years. As he approached free agency, he suffered an abdominal muscle injury and missed the last two months of the 2008–09 campaign, but he returned to the lineup for one game in the playoffs. After going unsigned for most of the off-season, on September 21, 2009, Bouillon finally inked a deal to return to Nashville that was contingent on him passing a physical. He spent the next three years with the Predators before once again returning to the Canadiens for a pair of seasons to close out his career.

HABS FANS BOO CAREY PRICE
IN PRE-SEASON GAME, 2010

The Canadiens have some of the most loyal fans in hockey, but sometimes that passion can boil over. On September 22, 2010, in a pre-season matchup against the Bruins, Carey Price was making his first start since the club traded Jaroslav Halák to the Blues in the off-season. Halák had played brilliantly during the team's run to the Eastern Conference Final, and there were people who felt the team traded the wrong goalie. And during that exhibition game against Boston, some fans made that sentiment loud and clear.

After Patrice Bergeron scored his second goal of the evening on Price, they let the netminder have it. Boos erupted from the Bell Centre, and when he made easy stops when the puck trickled in from centre ice, they weren't shy about giving him the Bronx cheer either. Fans were quick to jump on Price in a meaningless game, but it didn't take long for their tune to change. Price finished the season with 38 victories, the most by a Canadiens goaltender in more than three decades.

SEPTEMBER 23

SCOTTY BOWMAN INDUCTED INTO THE HOCKEY HALL OF FAME, 1991

E ven if Scotty Bowman had decided he was done with coaching after his illustrious tenure with the Habs, he still would've been destined for the Hockey Hall of Fame. On September 23, 1991, Bowman, the winningest coach in hockey, was inducted into hockey's pantheon as a builder. He earned his big-league bona fides in St. Louis and then took over the bench in Montreal, where he guided the team to five Stanley Cups.

Following his time with the Habs, Bowman went to Buffalo, where he served as GM and coach, before leaving the bench for the television booth for a couple of seasons. In 1990, he joined the Penguins as an assistant coach to "Badger" Bob Johnson and earned his sixth championship later that year. When Johnson was diagnosed with brain cancer ahead of the 1991–92 campaign, many expected the newly minted Hall of Famer to be named his replacement. Just over a week after his induction, Bowman took over the Penguins. He guided Pittsburgh to another title, a tribute to Johnson, who passed away in November.

SEPTEMBER 24

MOLSON CANADIEN, 1957

Molson was getting into the hockey business. On September 24, 1957, the brewery, which had been operating out of Montreal since the late 18th century, purchased the Forum and the Canadiens. In the first season under ownership of the beer barons, the Habs earned their third straight Stanley Cup. The club stretched that run to five consecutive titles and added five more championships before Molson sold the team to the Bronfman family in 1971. But the brewery bought the team back seven years later.

Molson held on to the team for another two decades until, after complaining the Habs were hemorrhaging cash, the family-owned brewery sold majority ownership of the club to communications mogul George N. Gillett in 2001. Eight years later, Gillett sold his 80.1 percent stake in the team back to a Molson family ownership group helmed by brothers Geoff, Justin, and Andrew, the grandsons of Thomas Molson, who first purchased the team with his brother, Senator Hartland, more than a half-century earlier on that crisp autumn day in Montreal.

SEPTEMBER 25

CAROL VADNAIS IS BORN, 1945

Whenever I think of Carol Vadnais, one image immediately comes to mind, and that is of him being held up by André the Giant, who is also holding Bobby Orr on his other massive arm. The two defencemen look diminutive next to the gentle giant, who was seven-foot-four and over 500 pounds. The photograph was taken during Vadnais's time with the Bruins, but he had reportedly forged a connection with the goliath celebrity a few years earlier while he was playing in California with the Seals.

Born in Montreal on September 25, 1945, Vadnais started out as a forward until he was switched to defence in his final season of junior hockey. After graduating from the Jr. Canadiens, he joined the Habs for part of the 1966–67 campaign. Vadnais split his time in the NHL and the minors again the following year, until he was nabbed by Oakland in the 1968 NHL Intra-League Draft. Following a few seasons out west, he was acquired by Boston, where, playing behind superstar Orr, he won a Stanley Cup.

SEPTEMBER 26

CHRIS CAMPOLI SIGNS WITH
THE CANADIENS, 2011

t was a tough way for Chris Campoli to end his season. In overtime in Game 7 against the Canucks, the Blackhawks defenceman turned the puck over in his own zone. Alex Burrows retrieved the disc and absolutely wired it past Corey Crawford, slaying the dragon for Vancouver and ending Chicago's dream of repeating as Stanley Cup champions. During the off-season, as a restricted free agent, Campoli filed for salary arbitration. The blueliner was awarded a one-year, $2.5 million contract, but the Blackhawks chose to walk away from the arbitrator's decision, making Campoli a free agent.

Just over a week before the next season began, on September 26, 2011, he inked a one-year deal worth $1.75 million with the Canadiens. Campoli made 43 appearances for the Habs; they would prove to be his final NHL games. He spent the next four seasons playing in Switzerland. After hanging up his skates in 2016, he came out of retirement a couple of years later to play senior hockey in pursuit of the Allan Cup.

SEPTEMBER 27

AL MACNEIL IS BORN, 1935

Not even the Stanley Cup could save Al MacNeil's job. In the fifth game of the Stanley Cup Final against the Black Hawks, with the Habs trailing 2–0, MacNeil benched Henri Richard. Following the loss, a frustrated Richard told reporters that MacNeil was incompetent and the worst coach he had ever played for. The two embraced a few days later when the Canadiens defeated Chicago in Game 7 to win the championship, but MacNeil stepped down at the end of the season and was replaced by Scotty Bowman.

Following his departure, MacNeil, who was born in Sydney, Nova Scotia, on September 27, 1935, returned to Montreal's AHL affiliate, the Voyageurs, in his home province. Over the next six years, he led the club to three Calder Cup titles. Although there was no love lost between Richard and MacNeil, the future captain might have been too harsh in his assessment. After all, it was MacNeil who made the decision to start rookie Ken Dryden for the playoffs, a move that certainly paid off.

PATRICK TRAVERSE CLAIMED ON WAIVERS, 2006

The French word "*traverse*" means "cross" in English. It proved to be rather fitting for defenceman Patrick Traverse, who wove his way across the NHL in less than a season. After finishing the 1999–00 campaign with Ottawa, Traverse, who had a career year with 23 points in 66 games, was traded to Anaheim. Less than two months into the season, he was dealt to Boston. And then, finally, a few months later, he was shipped to Montreal. Traverse, however, found a home with the Canadiens for parts of the next few seasons.

Following a sojourn in the minor leagues, he signed a one-year two-way contract with the Sharks organization in the 2006 off-season. But after playing in two pre-season games for San Jose, he was claimed off waivers by the Habs on September 28, 2006, as an insurance policy for the club's ailing blue line. Traverse's second stint with Montreal was brief. After playing 26 games in Hamilton for the club's AHL affiliate, he was traded back to San Jose for Mathieu Biron.

BRIAN GIONTA NAMED CAPTAIN, 2010

When Brian Gionta was introduced as the 28th captain of the Canadiens on September 29, 2010, it was hard not to notice that his assistant captains, Hal Gill and Andrei Markov, were towering over him. And while Gionta may have been small in stature, especially next to his imposing defencemen, he played with a big heart. After signing with the Canadiens as a free agent in 2009, the five-foot-seven winger led the team in goal-scoring with 28 tallies, but it was his tenacity and willingness to do the dirty work that endeared him to his teammates and the fans.

A native of Rochester, New York, Gionta was just the second American-born player to wear the "C" for the Canadiens; the first was Chris Chelios, who shared the duties with Guy Carbonneau two decades earlier. Gionta led the Habs with distinction, on and off the ice, for the next four seasons until he signed with his home-state Sabres as a free agent in 2014. In Buffalo, he was once again an easy pick for the captaincy.

SAKU KOIVU NAMED CAPTAIN, 1999

Mike Keane said there was a saying about being captain of the Canadiens: "Around here, the 'c' stands for see ya later." He would know. Keane was named captain following the departure of the club's former leader, Kirk Muller, who was traded to the Islanders. Just a few months after Keane earned the captaincy, he was shipped out to Colorado as part of the Patrick Roy blockbuster. Pierre Turgeon replaced Keane for the rest of the 1995–96 campaign, but not long into the next season, he was dealt to St. Louis.

Vincent Damphousse brought some stability to the role for a couple of years, but in 1999 he, too, was traded. Although Keane's sentiment held true for much of the '90s, that changed when the Habs named Saku Koivu as Damphousse's replacement on September 30, 1999. Koivu, entering his fifth season with the club, narrowly beat out Shayne Corson in a tight player vote to become the 28th captain in franchise history. Koivu served as captain for nine seasons — the longest-tenured captain since the great Jean Béliveau.

OCTOBER 1

TRAVIS MOEN SCORES FIRST
GOAL AS A HAB, 2009

Travis Moen started off his tenure with the Habs with a bang. On October 1, 2009, the hard-nosed winger scored early in the second period against the Maple Leafs to notch his first goal with the Canadiens. Signed as a free agent in the off-season, Moen brought sandpaper, depth scoring, and a championship pedigree to the bottom of the lineup. Two years earlier, he won the Stanley Cup with Anaheim, where he was credited with the title-clinching tally, although it was actually Ottawa defenceman Chris Phillips who, under pressure, put the puck into the back of his own net.

But it was another contribution to the team that really showcased why Montreal inked him. Just before the halfway mark of the opening session, Moen fought Jay Rosehill. Later in the game, after barrelling into Toronto goaltender Vesa Toskala, which, in his defence, could have been avoided if Leafs blueliner Mike Komisarek hadn't shoved him into his own netminder, Moen answered the bell and dropped the gloves with Komisarek for his second tilt of the evening.

OCTOBER 2

A STELLAR ALL-STAR FORMAT, 1954

I don't know about you, but I rarely watch the All-Star Game. Sure, I always tune in for the skills competition, but for me, the tournament is a bit of a snooze-fest. The players certainly aren't always interested in the game, and it has become a bit gimmicky. What I would love to see is a return to the league's earlier format in which the reigning Stanley Cup champions squared off against an all-star squad. It would definitely be more challenging today with so many more teams, but I really like the idea of the champs vs. everybody else.

For example, on October 2, 1954, for the eighth annual event, the Red Wings, who knocked off the Habs to win the Cup a few months earlier, took on players from around the league that included Canadiens Doug Harvey, Bernie Geoffrion, Maurice Richard, Ken Mosdell, and Jean Béliveau, who was making his second All-Star Game appearance. This format continued until 1970, when the league, after doubling in size a few years earlier, switched to conference-based teams.

OCTOBER 3

JESPERI KOTKANIEMI MAKES NHL DEBUT, 2018

J ust a few months after he was taken third overall by the Canadiens, Jesperi Kotkaniemi made his debut. Stepping out onto the ice at Scotiabank Arena in Toronto, on October 3, 2018, he became the first player born in the 2000s to appear in an NHL game. Just writing that makes me feel old. He made more history once the puck was dropped. After assisting on Andrew Shaw's tying goal in the second period, Kotkaniemi, who had just turned 18 in July, became the second-youngest player in Habs history to record a point.

The other assist on that goal came from Max Domi, son of the former Leafs pugilist Tie, who was also making his Montreal debut after he was traded there in the off-season for Alex Galchenyuk. But it was Auston Matthews who stole the show, scoring two goals, including the overtime winner. Kotkaniemi finished the season with 34 points, ninth among rookies, but in the coming years, many felt his development was rushed and that he could have benefited from more time in the minors.

OCTOBER 4

HABS SIGN ARBER XHEKAJ, 2021

Some Habs fans know Arber Xhekaj as "Wifi," but the blueliner always had a better nickname. During his time with the Kitchener Rangers, he was called "the Sheriff" for his ability to dole out frontier justice on the ice. The tag "Wifi," however, came about because some suggested his Albanian last name resembled the typical random combination of characters used for wifi network passwords. Xhekaj embraced this sobriquet when he joined the Canadiens, after signing a three-year entry-level contract on October 4, 2021, but "the Sheriff" is much more fitting.

A hard-hitting defenceman, Xhekaj plays with an edge and isn't afraid to drop the gloves to stick up for his teammates. Although the Habs sent him back to junior after inking his deal, he made the team the following year. He finished the season with 13 points and led the club in penalty minutes, and he was one of the few bright spots in an otherwise dim campaign. And now, for the first time in a long while, it seems Montreal finally has a sheriff in town.

OCTOBER 5

JEFF PETRY SCORES PENALTY SHOT GOAL, 2019

You didn't need to be a proficient lip reader to know what Max Domi said. Late in a game against the Maple Leafs, on October 5, 2019, after Jeff Petry scored on a penalty shot, a broadcast replay showed Domi leaning over the Canadiens' bench, yelling in the direction of Toronto defenceman Kasperi Kapanen. His words were as clear as day: "Atta boy, Kapanen, you [a word that neither the publisher nor my mother would ever let me put in a book] idiot."

Before the taunt, the Habs were on the power play and Petry took a shot from the point, hitting Kapanen's stick and breaking it into two pieces. When the biscuit came back to Petry, Kapanen threw what remained of his broken twig directly at the Montreal blueliner and the puck. Petry was still able to make a play, but Kapanen was whistled for interference and Petry was awarded a penalty shot. Petry buried it to tie the game at four goals apiece, and the Canadiens later won the match 6–5 in a shootout.

OCTOBER 6

HABS CLAIM PAUL "BREAKAWAY" BYRON, 2015

P aul Byron was not known for his breakaway prowess. In fact, during his time with the Flames, one fan put together a compilation video that showcased all the times he didn't convert when he was all alone with the puck. The montage was definitely a jab at Byron, but it actually helped him land his next gig. After Calgary put him on waivers before the 2015–16 season began, Montreal snagged him on October 6, 2015.

The Habs later acknowledged that the video was a key reason they put in a claim for him. The club saw past the failed breakaways and were taken by Byron's speed. Canadiens assistant general manager Larry Carrière said that "speed kills," and he was exactly right. The following season, with time winding down in a 1–1 game against the Predators, Byron switched on his afterburners and beat Nashville defenceman Matt Irwin in a footrace for the puck. With no one between him and goaltender Pekka Rinne, Byron put the puck into the back of the net to take the lead with 8.3 seconds remaining.

OCTOBER 7

FINAL OPENER AT THE FORUM AND JACQUES PLANTE RETIREMENT, 1995

The Habs final home opener at the Forum was a disaster. On October 7, 1995, they hosted the Flyers for what would be their last start of the season at the historic arena; later in the year, the Canadiens moved to the new Molson Centre. Philadelphia got on the board first just over three minutes into the game, and after scoring three more goals in quick succession halfway through the frame, the Flyers went into intermission with a 4–0 lead.

Two minutes into the second period, the Flyers struck again and chased Patrick Roy from his net. Roy's performance was all the more glaring because before the game began, the club honoured the late Jacques Plante, who passed away nearly a decade earlier, by raising his No. 1 to the rafters. Plante, of course, pioneered the goalie mask and was one of the greatest netminders in franchise history, but even with his spirit in the hallowed building, Roy could not stop the puck. His backup, Patrick Labrecque, fared only slightly better, allowing two goals in a 7–1 shellacking.

OCTOBER 8

HABS ACQUIRE JOSH ANDERSON, 2020

J ust a couple of days after acquiring Josh Anderson from the Blue Jackets in exchange for Max Domi, on October 8, 2020, the Canadiens signed the hulking winger to a seven-year, $38.5 million contract extension. Anderson, originally drafted 95th overall by Columbus in 2012, was the type of player every NHL team still covets. At six-foot-three and 224 pounds, he brought a physical presence to the ice and could also reliably contribute 20 goals a year. And while most would indeed refer to Anderson as a power forward, Tomáš Tatar had a better name for his new teammate: "powerhorse," a portmanteau of power forward and workhorse.

While he was limited to just 26 games the previous season with a shoulder injury, Anderson was only a year removed from a 27-goal and 47-point campaign, both career highs. He finished his first season in Montreal with 17 goals in 52 games and 139 hits. In the playoffs, Anderson added five more tallies, including an overtime winner against Tampa Bay to give the Habs its only victory in the Stanley Cup Final.

OCTOBER 9

GUY LAFLEUR MAKES NHL DEBUT, 1971

T he NHL was on notice. When Bruins head coach Eddie Johnston was asked about how tough the competition would be in the league's East Division for the 1971–72 season, he immediately thought of the Habs. "To begin with there's Montreal, the Stanley Cup champions, with a rookie named Guy Lafleur," he said. Lafleur, drafted first overall a few months earlier, was poised to make an impact. On October 9, 1971, the Flower made his debut in a game against the Rangers.

Lafleur later said he was disappointed with his performance, but he still managed to record a point, getting a pass to Yvan Cournoyer, who caught a breakaway — as he often did — and put the puck past Eddie Giacomin. Lafleur felt there would be some adjustment moving from the junior ranks to the big leagues, but he didn't think it would take him long to get dialed in. He finished the season with 29 goals and 64 points, the most by a Canadiens rookie. In just a few years, Lafleur punched his ticket to the vaunted century club.

OCTOBER 10

HABS TROUNCE RANGERS, 1998

T hings went from bad to worse for the Rangers in the third period against the Canadiens on October 10, 1998. Although the Habs were only up 2–1, they quickly blew the doors off their Broadway visitors. Just over two minutes into the final frame, Craig Rivet extended Montreal's lead. Less than two minutes later, the Rangers thought they caught a break when they were awarded a power play, but it was the Canadiens and not the Blueshirts who converted on the man advantage. Benoit Brunet scored a short-handed goal, but it went undetected by the goal judge and referee Lance Roberts.

Since it was not called on the ice, play continued for over a minute until the next stoppage. Following a lengthy review between the video replay judge and NHL officiating ombudsman Jim Gregory, it was ruled a good goal, making the score 4–1. The Canadiens added three more, capping off a five-goal third period and a 7–1 win, their largest margin of victory in a season opener in more than two decades.

OCTOBER 11

BOOM BOOM GETS 100TH VICTORY, 1979

Bernie Geoffrion had always dreamed of coaching the Canadiens, and on October 11, 1979, it became a reality. That day, Geoffrion, who had an illustrious career with the club as a player, took his post behind the bench for the first time. Prior to returning to Montreal, he had stints as an NHL head coach in New York and Atlanta until he was forced to resign from both clubs due to ailing ulcers.

Taking on his former team, the Flames, the Canadiens picked up a 3–1 win, giving Geoffrion his 100th career victory as a head coach and making his first night as the Habs' skipper even sweeter. But two months later, Geoffrion's dream had turned into a nightmare. Just 30 games into the campaign, he resigned. He was in good health this time around, but prior to taking the job, he'd assured his wife, Marlene, daughter of Habs legend Howie Morenz, that if he couldn't handle it, he would walk away. Habs executive vice-president Irving Grundman tried to talk him out of it, but Geoffrion kept his promise to his wife.

NICK SUZUKI SIGNS
EIGHT-YEAR DEAL, 2021

The Habs had locked up Nick Suzuki. On October 12, 2021, the team announced it had signed the young centre to an eight-year, $63 million extension. Acquired from the Golden Knights a few years earlier in the trade for Max Pacioretty, in just two seasons with the Canadiens, Suzuki had already demonstrated he was the franchise centre the club had been looking for. After finishing the 2020–21 campaign with 26 points in 56 games, Suzuki led the team in scoring in the playoffs, racking up 16 points in 22 games during Montreal's Cinderella run to the Stanley Cup Final.

Suzuki's new deal would not kick in until the end of the year, but he proved he was worth the money that season. He collected 21 goals and 66 points, both career highs, and was named the winner of the Molson Cup Player of the Year, awarded annually to the Canadiens player who earned the most three-star selections. A month before hitting the ice under his new contract, Suzuki, who had just turned 23, was named captain, the youngest in team history.

OCTOBER 13

ARTTURI LEHKONEN MAKES NHL DEBUT, 2016

Arturri Lehkonen was honest in his assessment of his first NHL game. After making his debut against the Sabres on October 13, 2016, the Finnish winger acknowledged he had some work to do. "I had some scoring chances, including two on one shift, but I had some bad turnovers in the second period," he told reporters. He didn't manage to get on the scoresheet, but Lehkonen led the Canadiens with five shots on goal in a 4–1 loss to Buffalo. Two nights later, on the road in Ottawa to play the Senators, he notched his first goal with Montreal. He finished the season with 18 goals, the most by a Habs rookie in a decade.

While Lehkonen was quick to own his defensive lapses in his first appearance, he was committed to working on them. In just a couple of years, he became one of the club's most trusted two-way players and was relied upon heavily to kill penalties. Lehkonen remained with the Canadiens until 2022 when he was traded to Colorado, where he scored the Stanley Cup–clinching goal against the Lightning.

BUTCH ELECTED CAPTAIN, 1948

The Canadiens weren't taking any chances. When the time came to elect a new captain in advance of the 1948–49 season, the club reportedly went as far as constructing a voting booth and commissioning a police officer to guard it in the name of upholding the sanctity of the secret ballot. It was probably a tad overkill with such an obvious choice on the docket. On October 14, 1948, after counting up all the ballots, the Habs announced that Émile "Butch" Bouchard would be the team's next captain.

Although the Canadiens had been around for nearly four decades, Bouchard became the first Quebec-born captain of the squad. He wore the "C" for the next eight seasons, setting the gold standard for leadership with the Habs, until he hung up his skates in 1956. When Jean Béliveau became captain in 1961, he later said that Bouchard was his role model for upholding the captaincy in Montreal. Fittingly, Béliveau was the first player in franchise history to have a longer tenure as captain than Bouchard.

OCTOBER 15

TOMÁŠ PLEKANEC HITS 1K, 2018

When Tomáš Plekanec made his NHL debut in 2003, he didn't yet have a goatee, but he was sporting a black turtleneck beneath his jersey. Over the next 14 seasons, both formed part of his signature look. He was forced to shave his facial hair during a brief stint with the Maple Leafs, but by the 2018–19 season, Plekanec was back in a Canadiens sweater, the goatee was growing back, and everything was right in the world. When he returned to the Habs as a free agent, he was just two matches away from hitting the 1,000-game mark. While he nearly reached the milestone in Toronto, it was only fitting he did it in Montreal.

On October 15, 2018, when the Canadiens hosted the Red Wings, Plekanec hit the ice for his 1,000th career contest. To top it off, the Czech native scored a lucky goal on Jimmy Howard in the first period, becoming just the fourth Hab to score in his 1,000th game. Plekanec appeared in one more game for good measure, before he and the club mutually agreed to part ways, bringing his NHL career to a close.

JIŘÍ SEKÁČ'S FIRST NHL GOAL, 2014

No one was more excited about Jiří Sekáč's first NHL goal than his father, Jiří Sr. On October 16, 2014, after the Czech winger banged in a rebound late in the second period against the Bruins, his dad, who was in the stands at the Bell Centre, jumped to his feet and jubilantly raised his arms above his head. Following the game, Jiří Jr. joked with reporters that "he can get excited, but never like that." After seeing the shot of his proud papa in the crowd, he said, "I've seen that quite a few times already. I think it's going to be all over the Internet."

And it was. Before the game had ended, Sekáč Sr.'s reaction had gone viral. Somewhat lost in the moment was that his son's goal sparked a comeback. Just over a minute later, P.A. Parenteau found the back of the net to take the lead. The Canadiens added two more in the final frame to defeat the Bruins 6–4. Sekáč scored six more goals for the Habs before he was traded to Anaheim for Devante Smith-Pelly.

OCTOBER 17

VICTOR METE AND NICK SUZUKI EACH SCORE FIRST GOALS, 2019

After 127 games, the puck finally went Victor Mete's way. On October 17, 2019, the defenceman notched his first career NHL goal. Drafted 100th overall by the Canadiens a few years earlier, the Woodbridge, Ontario, native played two full seasons with the Habs but had yet to bulge the twine. While Mete put in his time to earn his goal, Nick Suzuki did not have to wait as long. Less than five minutes after Mete's tally, Suzuki, who was playing in his seventh NHL game, backhanded a loose puck past Wild goaltender Alex Stalock with 37 seconds left in the first period.

Following a 4–0 victory for the Habs, Suzuki told reporters that when he saw Mete score earlier in the frame, he couldn't contain his excitement. "I hope we can both score some more goals," he explained. Mete collected three more tallies that season, while Suzuki added 12 more to round out his rookie campaign. While more goals were in store for Suzuki in Montreal, those proved to be Mete's last with the Habs.

ALEXANDER RADULOV SCORES FIRST GOAL AS A HAB, 2016

t had been more than four years since Alexander Radulov scored an NHL goal. Originally drafted 14th overall by the Predators in 2004, the Russian winger played a couple of seasons in Nashville before going home to play in the KHL despite still being under contract with the Predators. He returned to the NHL and the Preds for nine games in the 2011–12 campaign before, once again, heading back to Russia. After playing four years in Moscow, Radulov eyed a return to North America, and the Canadiens managed to sign him to a one-year, $5.75 million contract when free agency opened in 2016.

In his third appearance with the Habs, on October 18, 2016, Radulov scored his first NHL goal since March 31, 2012. The Penguins initially challenged the tally for goaltender interference, but it was upheld and Radulov was able to celebrate twice. He finished the season with 18 goals and 54 points, along with seven points in the playoffs. As free agency approached, many teams lined up for his services, and Radulov ended up inking a five-year, $31.25 million deal with the Stars.

OCTOBER 19

TERRY RYAN PLAYS LAST NHL GAME, 1998

erry Ryan went out swinging. When he entered the rink on October 19, 1998, before the Canadiens took on the Blackhawks, he figured he had a long future ahead of him in Montreal. Drafted eighth overall by the Habs in 1995, Ryan was coming off a solid campaign in the AHL when he was called up early in 1998–99. He hoped for more opportunities with the Canadiens, but it was no secret that he and coach Michel Therrien did not see eye to eye.

So when Ryan was stapled to the bench for the first period that evening, he figured he might not get into the game at all. But he got the nod early in the second frame. Not long after hopping over the boards, he dropped the gloves with Chicago's Cam Russell. It wound up being Ryan's last bout of NHL action, but he wouldn't have had it any other way. "That was a great fight with a heavyweight experienced NHL player, so it was one of my favourite memories playing up there," he told me later in an interview.

OCTOBER 20

HABS SNAP HOME LOSING STREAK, 2009

The Bell Centre was aching for a win. The last time the Habs celebrated a victory at home was March 31, 2009. After the team was swept out of the playoffs by the Bruins, they opened the 2009–10 campaign with back-to-back victories before losing five straight, which included their first two matchups in Montreal. When the Habs hosted the Thrashers on October 20, they were in jeopardy of getting off to their worst start in nearly seven decades.

After regulation ended in a 1–1 tie and overtime solved nothing, the game went to a shootout. When Mike Cammalleri and Ilya Kovalchuk were both unsuccessful in their respective attempts, it was up to Scott Gomez, who was playing in his first season with the Habs. Gomez put the puck up and over Ondřej Pavelec's glove to send the fans into a frenzy. After Atlanta's Rich Peverley missed, Brian Gionta had the game on his stick. With the Bell Centre fans on their feet, Gionta pulled off a nice forehand, backhand move to win the game and give the Habs their first win at home in 203 days.

OCTOBER 21

HABS WIN ON BUZZER-BEATER, 1995

Mario Tremblay didn't have much time to develop a game plan. Just three hours before the Habs hosted the Leafs on October 21, 1995, he was named head coach. The Canadiens had cleaned house a few days earlier, firing GM Serge Savard and coach Jacques Demers, after the team got off to a 0-4 start. Tremblay was no stranger to Montreal — he had played there for more than a decade, winning five Stanley Cups — but had no coaching experience. And with the club still searching for its first victory of the campaign, the task fell to the newly minted bench boss.

The Canadiens opened the scoring with a goal from Pierre Turgeon, but they allowed two straight goals from Toronto and trailed until early into the final frame. After Brian Savage gave the Habs the lead, the Leafs tied it up with less than five minutes remaining. Overtime seemed inevitable, but with less than a second remaining in regulation, Turgeon scored his second of the night, a buzzer-beating backbreaker, to give Tremblay and the Habs their first win of the season.

OCTOBER 22

HABS EXTEND REGULATION WINNING STREAK, 2016

Through the first four games of the 2016–17 campaign, the Habs had not lost in regulation. After winning their season opener on the road against Buffalo and then losing in a shootout to Ottawa a couple of days later, Montreal recorded two straight wins at home. Taking on the Bruins in Boston on October 22, 2016, the Canadiens were looking to add to the streak. Following a scoreless first period, the Habs struck first just over halfway through the second session. Brendan Gallagher netted his third of the season, and before the frame came to a close, Phillip Danault extended the lead.

The Bruins got on the board early in the final stanza, and the two teams traded special-teams goals before Torrey Mitchell found the back of the net to clinch a 4–2 victory, giving the Habs a run of five games without a regulation loss. Montreal strung together five more consecutive wins to remain the league's only undefeated regulation team before the run ended in a spectacular fashion ... but we'll get to that.

OCTOBER 23

ANDREI MARKOV GETS FIVE EN ROUTE TO 500, 2015

Heading into a game against the Sabres on October 23, 2015, Andrei Markov was sitting at 495 career points. The Russian defenceman was coming off a 50-point campaign and had once racked up 64 points in a season, but nobody, including Markov himself, thought he would make history that night in Buffalo. Going into the third period, the Habs were up 4–2 and Markov had a goal and an assist to his name. But in the final frame, he collected three more helpers to cap off a five-point game (a career high) and reach the 500-point milestone, becoming just the third Canadiens defenceman to accomplish the feat, joining Larry Robinson and Guy Lapointe.

Markov added 72 points over his final two seasons with the Habs to finish with 572, tying him with Lapointe for the second most in franchise history for defencemen. Robinson, however, remained untouchable. Before wrapping up his career with L.A., he left the Canadiens with 883 points, a record that will likely stand the test of time among blueliners in Montreal.

OCTOBER 24

HABS PUSH WINNING
STREAK TO NINE, 2015

The Habs were one win shy of matching league history. On October 24, 2015, the team picked up its ninth straight victory from the start of the season with a 5–3 triumph over the Leafs. Montreal had long since shattered its franchise record for the most wins from the start of a season, which was a paltry four, first established in 1955 and then equalled only twice by the dynastic squads in the 1970s. Another victory and they would match the 1993–94 Leafs and 2006–07 Sabres as the only teams in NHL history to rack up 10 consecutive wins to start a campaign.

But the game against Toronto didn't exactly inspire confidence. The Habs managed only 27 shots on Jonathan Bernier and got lucky in that he allowed five of them, including a goal by Michael Grabner that was awarded to David Desharnais. Meanwhile, Carey Price faced 52 shots, stopping all but three. A few nights later against the Vancouver Canucks, the wheels finally fell off. Montreal allowed three straight goals in the first period and lost 5–1, halting the streak at nine.

OCTOBER 25

TONY O GETS FIRST WINDY CITY WIN, 1969

t was only fitting that Tony Esposito's first victory as a member of the Black Hawks was against his former team, the Canadiens. On October 25, 1969, Esposito turned aside every one of the 30 shots he faced to record his first shutout and win with Chicago. Plucked from the Habs a few months earlier in the NHL's annual intra-league draft, Esposito found more opportunities between the pipes in the Windy City than when he was serving as Rogie Vachon's understudy in Montreal, where he played just 13 games.

Esposito's first win was the start of an incredible record-setting season with the Black Hawks. By the end of the campaign, he had 38 wins, a franchise record, and an astonishing 15 shutouts, another Chicago benchmark, and the most by an NHL goaltender in more than four decades. His performance earned him the nickname "Tony O" for his uncanny ability to blank opponents. Esposito was an easy choice for the Vezina and Calder trophies, while finishing runner-up to superstar Bobby Orr for the Hart.

BRIAN SAVAGE RECORDS FINAL NHL HAT TRICK, 2001

During the prime of his teenage development, Brian Savage took two years off from playing hockey so he could focus on other sports. So much so that he actually gave his skates away to one of his buddies. But after his sabbatical away from the ice, he returned to play high school hockey. He took home MVP honours that year and then went on to play a season of Junior B before heading to Miami University in Ohio, where he was drafted 171st overall by Montreal after his first year of collegiate hockey.

Despite his detour and unconventional path, Savage made the Canadiens a few years later and established himself as a consistent 20-goal scorer. He was actually the first Hab to score a hat trick at the Molson Centre (now the Bell Centre). Five years later, on October 26, 2001, he scored his seventh career three-goal performance in a game against the Sabres. It proved to be his last hat trick with the Canadiens, and in the NHL. A few months later, Savage was traded to the Coyotes.

OCTOBER 27

UNBEATEN HABS BEAT
UNBEATEN FLYERS, 1981

Only one team would remain unbeaten. When the Habs and Flyers squared off in Montreal on October 27, 1981, neither team had been defeated. The Canadiens started off the season with five victories and three ties, while the Broad Street Bullies opened the campaign with a draw and then rattled off seven straight wins. Less than a minute into the game, the Habs struck first and scored six unanswered goals, including two from Keith Acton, to head into intermission with a commanding 6–1 lead.

The Canadiens added three more in the second session, with Acton completing his first career hat trick, and two more in a fight-filled final frame to trounce the Flyers 11–2. Although Philly head coach Pat Quinn said he was devastated by the loss, it was tough to feel too bad for him. Two years earlier, the Flyers went unbeaten for 35 straight games, a North American major professional sports record that will likely stand the test of time. The Habs pushed their mark to 10 games but finally lost on Halloween.

THE FIRST BATTLE OF QUEBEC
AT THE COLISÉE, 1979

G illes Lupien was one of the first casualties in the Battle of Quebec. When the Nordiques joined the NHL as part of the merger with the WHA, many in the hockey world didn't give them much credit. When they squared off in their inaugural game, Montreal won it 3–1. So before the Habs travelled to Quebec City for a rematch on October 28, 1979, Lupien, the six-foot-six defenceman, might have been feeling a little cocky. He said the Habs would take the game by 10 goals. When Lupien hit the ice that night, the fans at the Colisée let him have it.

Every time the towering blueliner touched the puck, he was booed mercilessly. Heading into the final frame, they were tied at three goals apiece, but Quebec pulled away to take it 5–4. But that wasn't Lupien's last humiliation by the Nordiques. By season's end, Lupien wanted out of Montreal, and when it was rumoured the Canadiens offered him to Quebec, the Nordiques flatly denied the report and stated they were not interested in his services.

OCTOBER 29

PIERRE TURGEON TRADED, 1996

Pierre Turgeon got his wish. On October 29, 1996, the Canadiens dealt their captain, along with Craig Conroy and Rory Fitzpatrick, to the Blues for Shayne Corson, Murray Baron, and a fifth-round draft pick in 1997. Turgeon was coming off of a 96-point campaign, but he had been relegated to the third line with the emergence of Saku Koivu down the middle and, after growing frustrated with his usage, had requested a trade. In St. Louis, Brett Hull welcomed the move. Following the departure of Adam Oates, he had been looking for a play-making centre.

Dishing the puck to Hull, Turgeon racked up 49 assists in his first season with the Blues. Meanwhile, in Montreal, Vincent Damphousse assumed the captaincy and Corson was back for a second tour of duty. Originally drafted eighth overall by the Habs in 1984, Corson spent six seasons with the Canadiens before he was traded to Edmonton for Damphousse. The next year, in his second season back with the Habs, he collected 55 points, his most productive campaign in Montreal since he recorded 75 points in 1989–90.

OCTOBER 30

BILL DURNAN PLAYS FIRST GAME, 1943

think Canadiens GM Tom Gorman described goaltender Bill Durnan best when he said he was "as big as a horse, but nimble as a cat." Durnan, who tended the twine at six feet tall, was one of the bigger netminders of his day, but that was only one of the reasons he stuck out. After making his NHL debut on October 30, 1943, Durnan played seven seasons in Montreal, winning the Vezina in all but one of those campaigns.

But one of the most remarkable things about Durnan's playing style was that he was ambidextrous and quite adept at wielding his goalie stick in either hand. He was also the last NHL goaltender permitted to serve as captain on the ice. Officials claimed his frequent trips from the crease to argue calls slowed down the game, and it wasn't long before the league forbade it. The only time Durnan didn't earn the Vezina was the 1947–48 season when he wore the "C," so maybe the rule change was for the best.

OCTOBER 31

MAURICE RICHARD MAKES DEBUT, 1942

anadiens fans were in for a treat on Halloween 1942. That evening, in a game against the Bruins, a young Maurice Richard played his very first game for Montreal. Sporting No. 15 on the back of his jersey for his debut, Richard reportedly "played spectacular hockey" according to the newspaper coverage. Less than a minute into the contest, he helped set up Tony Demers for the opening tally. The other assist on the goal belonged to Elmer Lach, whom Richard would play with the following season, along with Toe Blake, forming the formidable Punch Line.

Just over a week later, Richard potted his first NHL goal against the Rangers. But only 16 games into his rookie campaign, he broke his leg in a game against Boston. Having unfairly developed a reputation as injury-prone as an amateur, some questioned if Richard could stay healthy enough to hack it in the big leagues. But he returned the next season and scored 32 goals, and the following year, he became the first player in league history to reach the 50-goal mark.

NOVEMBER 1

JACQUES PLANTE STARTS A REVOLUTION, 1959

Jacques Plante changed the game forever. After taking a puck to the face from Rangers forward Andy Bathgate during a game on November 1, 1959, the Canadiens goaltender retired to the dressing room to get medical repairs. After he was stitched and bandaged up, he returned to his crease with a different look: he was wearing a fibreglass mask. He had sported a protective face covering from time to time during practices, but it was the first time he wore a mask during an NHL game.

While Plante wasn't the first goalie to wear a mask in the big leagues — that distinction belonged to Clint Benedict of the Montreal Maroons — following that fateful evening, he became the first goaltender to wear facial protection on a regular basis. Plante's decision was met with derision from his coach, Toe Blake, but when his masked netminder continued to rack up victories, the bench boss gradually came around. Plante's courageous move revolutionized the game for goaltenders, and now it's almost impossible to imagine how anyone tended the twine without face protection.

HOWIE MORENZ MEMORIAL
ALL-STAR GAME, 1937

The hockey world came together for the Morenz family. On November 2, 1937, players from the Canadiens and the Montreal Maroons, including coach King Clancy, who came out of retirement that evening to play defence, teamed up to take on a squad of NHL all-stars. The game was to pay tribute to Howie Morenz, who passed away tragically in March after succumbing to complications brought on by a broken leg he sustained during a game against the Black Hawks, and to raise money for his family.

Prior to the exhibition, the Canadiens retired Morenz's No. 7, marking the first time in franchise history that a jersey was raised to the rafters. While his sweater hung proudly high above the ice at the Forum, his son Howie Jr. skated out onto the ice for warm-ups, much to the delight of the crowd. During the game, souvenirs and memorabilia were auctioned off in support of the family, and in a touching moment, Joe Cattarinich, former part-owner of the Canadiens, bought Morenz's uniform and equipment and dutifully presented them back to Howie Jr.

NOVEMBER 3

DICK IRVIN'S FIRST GAME, 1940

Long before Dick Irvin coached his first game for the Canadiens, on November 3, 1940, he had already earned a reputation as a formidable taskmaster. Following a professional hockey career that included winning the Allan Cup with the Winnipeg Monarchs in 1915, along with three seasons in the NHL, Irvin got into coaching. After spending nearly a decade in Toronto, where he guided the Leafs to a Stanley Cup, Irvin was appointed bench boss of the Canadiens prior to the 1940–41 season.

When he held his first Canadiens training camp, he immediately demanded excellence from his players. The story goes that when Toe Blake reported to camp, he had packed on a few extra pounds. Irvin reportedly told him that he could play this year, but if he was going to show up like that again next year, he might as well not even bother making the trip. While he and Blake got off on the wrong foot, they won two Stanley Cups together. Fittingly, it was Blake who succeeded Irvin behind Montreal's bench.

NOVEMBER 4

BLUE JACKETS TROUNCE HABS 10–0, 2016

You may just want to turn the page. I won't mind. I get it. This story is one that most Habs fans would like to forget. On November 4, 2016, the replica Civil War cannon that's fired after every Blue Jackets goal at the Columbus Blue Jackets' Nationwide Arena was put through its paces in a 10–0 rout of the Canadiens. The last time Montreal gave up that many goals in a game was more than two decades before, when Patrick Roy was hung out to dry for nine goals in an 11–1 thumping against the Red Wings that proved to be his last game between the pipes for the Canadiens — but we don't need to revisit that just yet.

After Cam Atkinson opened the scoring just over the halfway mark of the first period, poor Al Montoya let in nine more goals. The only Blue Jackets who didn't register at least a point were Ryan Murray, Lukáš Sedlák, and goaltender Sergei Bobrovsky, who made 30 saves in the lopsided shutout victory.

CANADIENS SIGN DAVID DESHARNAIS, 2008

Despite racking up back-to-back 100-point campaigns in the QMJHL, David Desharnais was passed over in two separate NHL draft classes. Many teams felt he was too small to make it in the big leagues, but the diminutive winger made up for his lack of size with plenty of talent and a fierce work ethic. After he was invited to the Canadiens' camp in 2007, Desharnais earned an assignment to the Cincinnati Cyclones, Montreal's affiliate in the ECHL, two rungs down.

He finished the regular season with 106 points in 68 contests, the most in the league, earning both the rookie of the year and MVP awards. Desharnais continued his torrid pace in the post-season, leading all playoff scorers with 33 points in 22 games and helping the Cyclones capture the Kelly Cup. Following his breakout year, he signed a two-year contract with the Habs on November 5, 2008. After spending most of the next few years in the AHL, Desharnais joined the Canadiens full-time in 2011 and became a fan favourite for five seasons.

NOVEMBER 6

BOOM BOOM HITS 100, 1954

Bernie Geoffrion loved taking slapshots. "When I slapped it, I thought it was the greatest thing ever," he once said. Geoffrion, of course, was one of the pioneers of the cannonading shot, so much so that his nickname "Boom Boom" came from the sound of his stick connecting with the puck and the subsequent sonic boom when the disc smashed into the boards. Geoffrion first started tinkering with the slapshot when he was just a youngster playing on a rink behind his neighbourhood church. By the time he made it to the NHL ranks, he had perfected the thundering shot.

After a few seasons with the Canadiens, intimidating goaltenders around the league, Geoffrion established himself as a fearsome goal scorer. On November 6, 1954, he scored two goals in a game against the Red Wings to record his 100th career marker with the Canadiens. Over nine more campaigns with the Habs, Geoffrion slapped, smacked, or wired 371 more goals into the net, finishing his tenure in Montreal with the second-most goals in franchise history, behind only his boyhood idol, Maurice Richard.

NOVEMBER 7

HABS DEBUT PARTITIONED PENALTY BOX, 1963

The penalty box had a new look at the Forum. Following a dust-up in the sin bin between Montreal's Terry Harper and Toronto's Bob Pulford a week earlier, the Canadiens became the first team in the league to debut a partitioned penalty box, a move that probably should have happened years before. Harper and Pulford certainly weren't the first players to slug it out in the confined space.

After battling each other on the ice with their sticks and fists, it wasn't surprising at all that tensions between bruised and bloodied opposing players sometimes boiled over. The NHL had even gone as far as stationing police officers near the penalty box, but it didn't always prevent a flare-up. So on November 7, 1963, when the Canadiens hosted the Black Hawks, the penalty box had been renovated to include separate entrances and a divider made from steel piping. Before the game began, as a gag, the sign over the Canadiens side said "good guys," while the visitors side, of course, designated the "bad guys."

MIKE HOFFMAN SCORES TWICE, 2022

Mike Hoffman scored only one goal through the first 10 games of the season, but he knew he just had to keep grinding it out and eventually he would get rewarded. Just over five minutes into a game against the Red Wings on November 8, 2022, he opened the scoring. And then with 15 seconds remaining in the first period, he fired a Brendan Gallagher rebound into a wide-open net for his second of the night. Following the game, Hoffman told reporters it was "just simple hockey" and that being in the right place at the right time finally paid off for him. It was his first and what would prove to be his only multi-goal effort for the Canadiens.

After finishing the campaign with 14 goals and 34 points, Hoffman was traded to the Penguins, along with Rem Pitlick, for Jeff Petry, Casey DeSmith, Nathan Légaré, and a second-round pick. But Hoffman wasn't in Pittsburgh for very long. That same day, he was sent to San Jose as part of a blockbuster trade for reigning Norris Trophy winner Erik Karlsson.

NOVEMBER 9

CLAUDE PROVOST SCORES IN FOUR SECONDS FLAT, 1957

Claude Provost wasted no time at all. Just four seconds after the puck was dropped for the second period in a game against the Bruins on November 9, 1957, the Canadiens winger had put it into the back of the net, establishing a new NHL record for the fastest goal from the start of any period. Provost eclipsed Merlyn Phillips's benchmark with the Montreal Maroons from 1926 when he scored five seconds into a matchup against the Black Hawks. Provost also added an assist just before the halfway mark of the final frame as the Habs cruised to a 4–2 victory.

In the decades that followed, a couple of players matched the speedy feat but none surpassed it. Nearly three decades after Provost's record, Denis Savard, who later played a few seasons for the Canadiens, equalled the mark to start the third period for Chicago against Hartford. Most recently, in 2014, James van Riemsdyk lit the lamp for Toronto four seconds into the middle period in a game against his former team, the Flyers.

ARMAND MONDOU TAKES FIRST NHL PENALTY SHOT, 1934

All that stood between Armand Mondou and NHL history was George Hainsworth. On November 10, 1934, in the third period of a game against Toronto, Montreal's Georges Mantha was tripped on a scoring chance. A minor penalty — but under a new rule it was a penalty shot. The league introduced the free shot, billed as a "sniper's delight," to add more excitement to the game. When a penalty shot was awarded, the puck was placed in a designated area, 38 feet away from the goal. A player could either shoot from a stationary position or skate up to the circle in full stride and try to hammer the puck into the net.

After Mantha was hauled down, head coach Newsy Lalonde decided to have Mondou take the freebie. A curious choice since he was coming off a five-goal campaign. But Mondou gave it his best shot. He didn't beat Hainsworth, but he still made hockey history by taking the first big-league penalty shot. A few days later, Ralph "Scotty" Bowman, scored the NHL's first penalty shot goal against the Montreal Maroons.

P.K. SUBBAN SCORES FIRST REGULAR-SEASON GOAL, 2010

t was his first regular-season goal, but it wasn't his first NHL tally. A few months earlier, in the opening game of a playoff series against the defending-champion Penguins, P.K. Subban notched his first big-league goal against Marc-André Fleury. But on November 11, 2010, playing in his first full campaign for the Canadiens, Subban blasted a cross-ice pass from Tomáš Plekanec into the back of Boston's net to record his first regular-season goal.

The puck was deflected by a stick and was bobbling significantly when he received it, but Subban made no mistake and absolutely wired a one-timer from just above the faceoff circle, a play that became one of his signature moves in Montreal. Following the game, when asked about his milestone goal, Subban joked that "I scored in the playoffs, but I guess that doesn't count." But what did count was that this one was against one of Montreal's oldest rivals. Subban finished his inaugural season with 14 goals, the most by a rookie Habs defenceman since Guy Lapointe racked up 15 four decades earlier.

NOVEMBER 12

NO. 12s RETIRED, 2005

Yvan Cournoyer joined the Canadiens just as Dickie Moore left, but their careers did overlap in one notable way: they were the two greatest players ever to wear the No. 12 for Montreal. Cournoyer, one of the most decorated Habs, had a Conn Smythe as playoff MVP to go along with his 10 championships. Moore, a star in his own day, won two Art Ross trophies, along with six Stanley Cups during his tenure with the Habs.

Few players could ever match their list of accomplishments. Fittingly, on the 12th day of November 2005, the Canadiens raised both their jerseys to the rafters in separate ceremonies. Before the game, the Habs players all skated out wearing No. 12 with either Moore's or Cournoyer's name on the back, a lineup that would have terrified opposing teams because there was no catching Cournoyer and you certainly weren't out-battling Moore. For Cournoyer, it was the ultimate honour. Growing up in Quebec, he dreamed of playing for the Canadiens but never imagined his sweater would be immortalized high above the ice.

NOVEMBER 13

MICHAEL PEZZETTA GETS
FIRST NHL POINT, 2021

Michael Pezzetta took the long road to the NHL. Drafted 160th overall by the Canadiens in 2016, he played another two seasons of junior before signing an entry-level contract with Montreal. He spent the next four seasons in the minors, and it seemed as though he might be destined to stay there. But fans who recalled Pezzetta's time with the Sudbury Wolves knew he would never give up. Early into the 2021–22 campaign, his hard work finally paid off when he was recalled by the Canadiens.

A few games after his big-league debut, on November 13, Pezzetta collected his first NHL point, an assist, on the road in Detroit. He finished the season with 11 points, his most productive campaign at any level since his final stint in junior. The next year, he played his first full NHL season, racking up 239 hits and 77 penalty minutes. That season was one most Habs fans would like to forget, but Pezzetta's hard-hitting style and effort on every single shift gave them something to cheer about.

NOVEMBER 14

HABS CLAIM ANTTI NIEMI, 2017

The Canadiens needed help between the pipes. After Carey Price went down with a lower-body injury, Al Montoya took over until he, too, was sidelined. With third-string netminder Charlie Lindgren on the front lines, the Habs recalled Zach Fucale from Laval on an emergency basis. Lindgren performed admirably in his starts, but Montreal needed some stability in the crease while Price and Montoya recovered. And so on November 14, 2017, the Canadiens claimed goaltender Antti Niemi on waivers from Florida. Although the former Stanley Cup champion was winless to start the season with the Panthers, the Habs hoped he could find his game again and become the steady backup they desperately needed.

He did just that. In 17 starts, Niemi picked up seven wins and recorded a sterling .929 save percentage. He performed so well that once Price returned, he kept the backup job and Montoya was traded to Edmonton for a conditional draft pick. Following his resurgence, Niemi was Montreal's nominee for the Bill Masterton Trophy, awarded annually in recognition of sportsmanship, perseverance, and dedication to hockey.

NOVEMBER 15

SERGEI GONCHAR HITS 800, 2014

Sergei Gonchar was in his 20th season in the NHL, but he still felt like he had some game left in him. He had been used sparingly in Dallas to start the year, so Gonchar, the all-time leading scorer among Russian-born NHL defencemen, waived his no-trade clause to come to Montreal for checking winger Travis Moen. Gonchar was nearly a decade removed from a potent 67-point campaign with the Penguins, but he could still quarterback the man advantage, and the Habs were desperate for help to turn around their anemic power play.

Gonchar was held off the scoresheet in his first game with the Canadiens, but in his second contest on November 15, 2014, he collected two assists to reach the 800-point mark. A few weeks later, in a game against Chicago, Gonchar, who would turn 41 in April, found the back of the net to become the oldest player in franchise history to score a goal. Following 45 games with the Canadiens, the Russian hung up his skates and returned to Pittsburgh as a defensive development coach.

THE BIONIC BLUEBERRY
SCORES FIRST GOAL, 1974

As far as hockey nicknames go, this one might be one of my absolute favourites: "le Bleuet Bionique," which translates from French to "the Bionic Blueberry." Before he was drafted 12th overall by the Habs in 1974, Mario Tremblay had grown up in Alma, Quebec, an area renowned for its lush, sweeping blueberry fields. I often lament how today's hockey monikers, at least those shared with the media, seem to lack the ingenuity of what we used to see in the past.

Serge Savard was known as "le Sénateur" because of his stately presence in the dressing room, and Tremblay was known as "le Bleuet Bionique" because, well, he grew up in a blueberry patch. It was a bit of a stretch, but it had a nice ring. After the 18-year-old Tremblay notched his first goal for the Habs on November 16, 1974, setting a franchise record as the youngest player to light the lamp, the Bionic Blueberry went on to score 258 career goals for the Canadiens, winning five Stanley Cups along the way.

NOVEMBER 17

TOO MUCH RED, 1932

The fans were seeing red. When the Red Wings showed up to take on the Canadiens for a game at the Forum on November 17, 1932, both teams, of course, were wearing red sweaters. Realizing it would be difficult to follow the action on the ice from the stands with both teams sporting the same colours, it was decided that Detroit would don white pinnies. The only problem with the solution was that, while it made it clear who played for which team, the pinnies obscured the numbers on the back of the jerseys, making it challenging to identify the Wings' players.

When they squared off at the Olympia in Detroit less than a week later, the Canadiens wore the white pullovers. The pinnies worked in a pinch, but the following season, the Habs solved the problem by introducing a white uniform. Fittingly, they debuted this new look in a game against Detroit on November 27, 1933. It wasn't long before other NHL teams added to their wardrobes to distinguish themselves at home and on the road.

SAKU KOIVU BAGS FIRST HAT TRICK, 2002

There would be no topping Saku Koivu's triumphant return to Montreal following his battle against cancer, but this was pretty close. Playing in his first full season since entering remission, emotions were still running high whenever he was on the ice. After opening the scoring just over a minute into a game against the Penguins on November 18, 2002, the Bell Centre faithful started chanting "Saku! Saku! Saku!" in honour of their captain.

Less than a minute into the second period, Koivu struck again, recording a short-handed goal to give the Habs a 2–1 lead. Ten minutes later, he scored his third of the night, his first three-goal performance in the NHL. After 365 games, the Finnish centre had finally bagged a big-league hat trick. Following the game, Koivu acknowledged how special it was to accomplish the feat not long after his return, but he hoped it wouldn't take him seven years to do it again. But it actually took longer. Koivu netted his next hat trick, and his last, on January 10, 2012, as a member of the Ducks.

NOVEMBER 19

COLE CAUFIELD SCORES BUZZER-BEATER, 2022

The Canadiens were running out of time. Trailing by a goal to the Flyers in a game on November 19, 2022, the Habs were giving Philadelphia goalie Carter Hart everything they had to try to tie it up in the dying seconds. After some nifty passing between Mike Matheson, Cole Caufield, and Nick Suzuki led to a shot and scramble in front of the net, Montreal regained the puck. Matheson fired it, but Hart turned it aside.

Keeping the pressure on, the Habs got the puck back again and got it over to Caufield with just over six seconds remaining. The undersized winger uncorked a shot, but it went wide. In a last-ditch effort, Suzuki passed it over to Caufield on the other side of the ice. With just 1.9 seconds remaining, "the Short King" fired a buzzer-beater to force overtime. The extra session solved nothing, but Suzuki, who did everything in his power to knot it up, notched the deciding, and only, goal in the shootout to give the Habs a 5–4 victory.

NOVEMBER 20

HALLWAY BRAWL, 1986

As Chris Nilan was heading off the ice at the Boston Garden on November 20, 1986, he was just trying to keep his head down. The hard-nosed Canadiens winger had just been tossed from the game, and even though he was playing in his hometown, the fans let him have it. They hurled cups of beer and pizza at him as he made his way to the dressing room. But as he passed by the Bruins' bench, he saw Ken Linseman stand up suddenly.

Nilan had been in enough altercations to know better. In his own words, "If you trust Ken Linseman, you're an idiot, so I just threw a shot at him." That's when all hell broke loose. A brawl ensued in the hallway, and more skirmishes erupted on the ice. Things got so heated that referee Andy Van Hellemond sent both teams to their dressing rooms with five minutes remaining in the second period just to cool off. By the time they cleared the ice, Van Hellemond had issued 11 game misconduct penalties.

BUDDY O'CONNOR PICKS UP 10 POINTS IN TWO GAMES, 1943

B uddy O'Connor's stick was white-hot. After racking up five points on the road against the Leafs, the very next night, November 21, 1943, he picked up a hat trick and added two assists in a 13–4 shellacking of the Bruins to record back-to-back five-point performances. O'Connor's third goal late in the second period that night made it 10–2, but they added three more in the final frame, falling just a few goals shy of matching the NHL record for the most goals in a game.

That benchmark, of course, belonged to the 1919–20 Canadiens, who trounced the Quebec Bulldogs 16–3 that season. While the Habs came up short in 1943, O'Connor became the first player in franchise history to collect five points in consecutive games. Although his twig cooled off in the next two games — he was held scoreless — he then rattled off 18 points in the next eight. O'Connor finished the season with 54 points in 44 games. A few years later, on December 28, 1946, he notched his final five-point performance with the Habs.

HERITAGE CLASSIC, 2003

When goaltender José Théodore was asked how he stayed warm, his response was simple. "I didn't," he said. "I stayed cold." On November 22, 2003, Théodore and the Canadiens, along with 57,167 fans, braved frigid temperatures to take on the Oilers at Commonwealth Stadium in Edmonton. Billed as the Heritage Classic, it was the first time the NHL had taken to the great outdoors for a regular-season contest. Prior to that, the league had held exhibition games outside at venues that ranged from a Michigan prison to Caesars Palace in Las Vegas, but there was never anything on the line.

The outcome had an impact on the standings, but it was also about hearkening back to hockey's roots. One of the most enduring images from the game is of Théodore with a wool Canadiens toque stretched over the top of his mask, with his breath floating in the freezing air, reminiscent of chilly nights on backyard rinks. Despite sipping hot chocolate between periods, Théodore couldn't shake the cold, but Montreal's 4–3 victory undoubtedly warmed his spirits.

HABS SWAP LATENDRESSE
FOR POULIOT, 2009

H eading into his draft year, Benoît Pouliot drew comparisons to Vincent Lecavalier. When Pouliot was selected fourth overall by the Wild in 2005, Lecavalier was a Stanley Cup champion and a two-time 30-goal scorer, and he would soon reach the 50-goal mark. While they were both big francophone players, few could live up to those lofty expectations.

After spending the early part of his career in the minors, where he put up underwhelming numbers, Pouliot was traded to the Canadiens on November 23, 2009, for another player who had not yet lived up to his billing: Guillaume Latendresse, taken 45th overall by the Habs in the same draft class. Montreal had grown tired of the hulking winger not utilizing his size, especially in front of the net. The swap initially paid off for both players. In his first season with the Canadiens, Pouliot recorded 24 points in 39 games, while Latendresse scored 25 goals down the stretch with Minnesota. Pouliot's production, however, soon trickled off, and a year later the Habs opted not to qualify him, making him a free agent.

DICKIE MOORE HITS 20 IN 21 GAMES, 1960

D ickie Moore seemed poised to hit the 50-goal mark. The two-time Art Ross winner was on a torrid pace when the Canadiens squared off against the Red Wings on November 24, 1960. Early in the third period, Moore found the back of the net to record his 20th goal in just the 21st game of the campaign. The only other player to reach the benchmark in so few games was Maurice Richard in 1944. Of course, that was the same year the Rocket became the first player in NHL history to notch 50 goals.

While they both reached the 20-goal mark in 21 games, Richard also collected four others that night to give him 24 tallies in 21 contests. Nevertheless, with Moore nearly matching Richard's pace, many expected he would be the next player to punch his ticket to the 50-goal club. But after collecting another 15 goals, he fractured a bone in his foot and missed the last 13 games of the season. Moore still managed to finish third in NHL goal-scoring that year. Although Moore missed the mark, teammate Bernie Geoffrion made it to 50 that year with a couple of games to spare.

NOVEMBER 25

CAREY PRICE LEAVES GAME WITH AN INJURY, 2015

Habs fans held their collective breath. After playing two periods of a game against the Rangers on November 25, 2015, goaltender Carey Price left the ice with an apparent injury. The reigning Hart and Vezina winner was off to a hot start, picking up 10 victories through his first 12 games, including the win that night in New York. Five days later, it was announced that Price would miss a minimum of six weeks with a lower-body injury.

If there was any good news, it was that he would not require surgery. And while Price would not be able to tend the twine for the Habs in the Winter Classic against their archrival Bruins, there was some solace that he would be back in the New Year. But he never played another game that year. Eventually, at the end of the campaign, the team disclosed that Price had strained the medial collateral ligament in his right knee, and the treatment did not go according to plan. The following season, he returned to form and was named a finalist for the Vezina.

NOVEMBER 26

THE FLOWER RETIRES, 1984

t was a sad day in the hockey world: the Flower was hanging up his skates. On November 26, 1984, Guy Lafleur announced his retirement. Lafleur had seriously contemplated calling it a career at the end of the previous season but decided to come back for another tour of duty. While he no longer had the dazzling speed that sent his blond mane flying back with the wind, earning him another moniker, "le Demon Blond," he figured he could still help the team. But after collecting just two goals and three assists in 19 games, he decided it was time to move on.

Lafleur cited his sluggish start as one of the reasons, but his strained relationship with former teammate and head coach Jacques Lemaire certainly played a part in his decision. A few years later, after he was inducted into the Hockey Hall of Fame, Lafleur was lured out of retirement by the Rangers. He played on Broadway for a year before retiring for good after a pair of seasons with the Nordiques.

NOVEMBER 27

ANOTHER TRIPLE LOW-FIVE, 2010

t had become a common sight after a Habs victory. At the end of a win, rookie defenceman P.K. Subban and goaltender Carey Price celebrated with a triple low-five, a move that is exactly as it sounds: three low high-fives. Neither player could say who exactly initiated it, but it quickly became their signature celebration. On November 27, 2010, after Price made 34 saves and was just over a minute away from recording his fourth shutout in his past nine starts, in a 3–1 triumph over the Sabres, the two, of course, did the triple low-five.

The pair continued the move for a couple of seasons, until head coach Michel Therrien banned it — much to the chagrin of fun-loving hockey fans around the league — insisting that end-of-game celebrations should be team focused. Subban and Price, however, had the last laugh. When the Canadiens honoured Subban on January 12, 2023, just a few months after he retired, Price made a cameo and the two re-enacted the triple low-five, drawing a chorus of cheers from the Bell Centre faithful.

NOVEMBER 28

GEORGES VÉZINA'S FINAL NHL APPEARANCE, 1925

You would be hard-pressed to find a Hab more dedicated to his craft than Georges Vézina. After making his debut for the Canadiens in 1910, the goaltender went on to start 328 consecutive regular-season games for the club and added another 39 straight in the playoffs. And even when he was feeling under the weather, the Chicoutimi Cucumber still reported for duty. When the Habs opened the 1925–26 campaign against the Pittsburgh Pirates on November 28, Vézina was between the pipes, but he had been battling an illness. He thought he could play through it, but he was forced to leave the game early in the second period. Vézina was later given the grim diagnosis that he was suffering from tuberculosis.

The stoic, unflappable netminder returned to his hometown to live out his final days. A few months later, in the early morning hours of March 27, 1926, Vézina passed away at the age of 39. The next year, Montreal's ownership group honoured the late goaltender by donating the Vezina Memorial Trophy to the NHL. It is awarded annually to the league's best goalie.

FIRST NHL GAME PLAYED
IN THE FORUM, 1924

When the Montreal Forum opened in 1924, it wasn't actually meant for the Canadiens — it was for the club's crosstown rivals, the Maroons, who were the key tenants in the building. But when the Habs opened the 1924–25 campaign, the ice-making plant at their Mount Royal Arena was malfunctioning, so the game was moved to the Forum. On November 29, the Canadiens "hosted" the Toronto St. Patricks and christened the ice. Nine thousand patrons, the largest reported crowd to watch a hockey game in Canada at that time, filled the stands at the newly minted arena.

Finished just 159 days after the shovels hit the ground, an incredible feat of construction, the Forum became one of hockey's most cherished cathedrals. Montreal's Billy Boucher scored the first goal in the new building, and the Canadiens added six more to trounce the St. Patricks 7–1. The Habs, however, wouldn't call the Forum home permanently until the 1926–27 season, when they shared the ice with the Maroons. They would go on to win 12 of their 24 Stanley Cups at the corners of Sainte-Catherine and Atwater.

HAL GILL BLOCKS SHOTS LIKE A GOALIE, 2011

H al Gill was a shot-blocking machine. The six-foot-seven defenceman was never afraid to put his big body in front of the puck. "You try to do whatever you can to get in front of a shot to take the pressure off," Gill once said. The previous season, during a matchup against the Capitals on February 10, 2010, Gill blocked 11 shots in a 6–5 overtime victory, just one off Sean Hill's mark for the most in a single NHL game at the time.

Gill continued to risk life and limb in the playoffs, blocking 68 shots, the second most in the league that post-season, and was a critical part of Montreal's run to the Eastern Conference Final. The Canadiens boasted other key shot-blockers, such as Josh Gorges and Jaroslav Špaček during Gill's tenure in Montreal, but no one did it like Gill. In one of his final shot-blocking masterpieces for the Habs, on November 30, 2011, he blocked another 11 shots. As of this writing, other than goaltenders, no Canadien has blocked more shots in one game than Hal Gill.

DECEMBER 1

HABS HIT 5K, 1997

When the NHL was formed in 1917, there were only four teams. Eighty years later, only two of those original clubs remain: the Maple Leafs, who originally started out as the Toronto Arenas, and the Canadiens. So it's no surprise that when you've played for eight decades, you can rack up a lot of games. On December 1, 1997, the Habs became the first team in league history to reach the 5,000-game mark, although the Leafs weren't that far behind — they reached the milestone just a week later.

Heading into that landmark contest against the Penguins, Montreal had 2,625 victories, 1,602 losses, and 772 ties in the regular season. Of course, if you counted the playoffs, the Habs had reached the 5K mark a long time before that, playing 631 post-season games and winning 24 Stanley Cups along the way. But unfortunately, the Penguins spoiled the party. Early in the third period, after Patrice Brisebois misplayed the puck, Jaromír Jágr went on to score the lone goal of the evening, handing the Canadiens their third straight loss.

PATRICK ROY PLAYS FINAL
GAME FOR THE HABS, 1995

T hat was it. Patrick Roy was done. There was no going back. After being left in net for nine goals in a game against the Red Wings on December 2, 1995, Roy was finally, mercifully, relieved midway through the second period. The veteran goaltender, who had twice been playoff MVP for the Canadiens, backstopping them to a pair of Stanley Cups, rightfully felt he had been hung out to dry. After leaving the crease and arriving at the Habs' bench, he brusquely passed by head coach Mario Tremblay to take a seat.

But before finding a spot on the pine, Roy turned around and made his way back to where team president Ronald Corey was sitting. The story goes that Roy told Corey he had played his last game in Montreal. The club tried to calm the waters the next day, but Roy's words proved to be prophetic; he had, in fact, played his last game as a Canadien. A few days later, the team traded him to Colorado, where he'd win another championship and Conn Smythe.

DECEMBER 3

HABS DOMINATE BUT LOSE TO CAPS, 2015

Anyone who has followed hockey long enough knows that the team that wins a game doesn't always deserve it. The website MoneyPuck even went as far as creating a "Deserve to Win O'Meter." As the name suggests, it projects which team deserves to win based on simulations of all the expected goals in a game; when a team is in command of the matchup, the metre skews in its favour. If the metre existed in 2015 when the Habs hosted the Capitals on December 3, the needle would have been off the charts for Montreal.

The Canadiens lost 3–2, but it was arguably one of their best games of the season and one they probably should have won. While limiting Washington to just 19 shots, the Habs fired 35 of their own on net, including nine from captain Max Pacioretty alone, along with 26 that were blocked, and another dozen that went off target. Brian Flynn even had a nifty short-handed breakaway goal early in the third period, but goaltender Braden Holtby ultimately played spoiler.

DECEMBER 4

THE HABS ARE FOUNDED, 1909

The Canadiens were born out of turmoil. After a few clubs in the Eastern Canadian Hockey Association voted to disband the league and form a new circuit without the Montreal Wanderers in late 1909, one of the club's angry representatives, Jimmy Gardner, approached Ambrose O'Brien, who had a stake in his hometown team, the Renfrew Creamery Kings, and squads in Cobalt and Haileybury, about forming their own loop. Gardner's kicker was that they would also include an all-French-Canadian team to draw support from Montreal.

They met in early December and founded the National Hockey Association. Two nights later, on December 4, 1909, they convened again and ironed out the plans for a French-Canadian team that would be called "le Canadien." There wasn't much coverage about the nouveau club, but O'Brien went to work to build his team of flying Frenchmen. He hired Jack Laviolette, one of the game's fastest skaters, to play and assemble the squad. Although their first season was disastrous, the Canadiens would be Stanley Cup champions by 1916 — and the rest, of course, is history.

DECEMBER 5

TONY O MAKES FIRST START, 1968

The scheduling couldn't have worked out any better for the Esposito family. A little over a week after the Canadiens had recalled goaltender Tony Esposito from the minors, on December 5, 1968, he made his first NHL start against the Bruins. Of course, this wasn't just any other opposing team. Besides the long-standing rivalry between the two clubs, Boston also boasted Tony's older brother, Phil, who was on the path to stardom in his second full campaign with the Bruins. And like many older siblings, Phil spoiled the fun.

After opening the scoring against his little brother, the elder Esposito scored again just before the halfway mark of the final frame to tie the game and, ultimately, deny Tony his first victory; the game ended in a 2–2 draw. But Tony didn't have to wait too long for his first win. Two nights later, Esposito stopped every shot he faced to earn a shutout against Chicago, where Phil began his career and where, in a quirk of fate, Tony would become a Hall of Famer.

DECEMBER 6

A DARK DAY IN MONTREAL, 1989

Just a few hours before the Canadiens were scheduled to take on the North Stars in Minnesota, something unthinkable happened in Montreal. A gunman stormed an engineering classroom at École Polytechnique de Montréal and began firing on women in a violent act of misogyny. By the time his rampage came to an end, 14 people had been murdered simply because they were women. While the Habs played that night, Quebec and the rest of Canada came to grips with what had transpired. The outcome on the ice was the farthest thing on the nation's mind as it grieved the unspeakable tragedy.

To honour the lives of the young women who died and to pledge your commitment to battling the hatred that led to the horror that day in Montreal — and that unfortunately still exists today — read their names and keep their memory alive: Geneviève Bergeron, Hélène Colgan, Nathalie Croteau, Barbara Daigneault, Anne-Marie Edward, Maud Haviernick, Barbara Klucznik-Widajewicz, Maryse Laganière, Maryse Leclair, Anne-Marie Lemay, Sonia Pelletier, Michèle Richard, Annie St-Arneault, and Annie Turcotte.

DECEMBER 7

JOHN FERGUSON GETS TRIPLE MINOR, 1967

I don't know about you, but one of the last people I'd want to get into a stick-swinging duel with is John Ferguson in his prime. From the minute he broke into the league, fighting Boston tough guy Ted Green just 12 seconds into his first shift, Ferguson established himself as one of the most fearsome pugilists around. When he fractured his hand early in the 1967–68 campaign and was out of commission, players around the league breathed a sigh of relief knowing that Fergy wasn't patrolling the ice, if only for a little while.

In his first game back, on December 7, the Canadiens were hosting the Red Wings. Just over the halfway mark of the opening frame, Ferguson collided with Detroit defenceman Gary Bergman. When they got up, they both started wildly swinging their sticks at each other like they were in a jousting match. Luckily, neither player was hurt, but Ferguson got dinged with a rare triple minor penalty — two minutes for charging, two minutes for slashing, and two minutes for, of course, high-sticking.

CAREY PRICE POUNDS KYLE PALMIERI WITH HIS BLOCKER, 2016

Carey Price had had enough. After the goaltender was bowled over on New Jersey's first goal against the Canadiens on December 8, 2016, Price was steaming. The Habs netminder had missed most of the previous year's campaign with a knee injury, so he was on high alert. Late in the first period, it happened again. This time Kyle Palmieri knocked him over as he skated through the crease. Price, rightfully, took exception. As Palmieri lay on the ice, Price began pummelling him in the back with his blocker. He continued to tenderize Palmieri's kidneys as a scrum broke out in front of the net.

When the dust settled, Price was lucky to have skated away with only a double minor for roughing. The NHL rule book allows referees to impose a match penalty on a goalie if he hits a player with his blocker with the intent to injure. But Price wasn't trying to hurt Palmieri — he was simply showing him that he didn't care for the unnecessary contact and wasn't going to take it anymore.

DECEMBER 9

HABS ACQUIRE TOMÁŠ KABERLE, 2011

Tomáš Kaberle made an immediate impact with the Habs. Acquired from the Hurricanes in exchange for Jaroslav Špaček on December 9, 2011, Kaberle was brought in to help ignite Montreal's moribund power play. The Czech defenceman, who started his NHL career with the Maple Leafs in 1998, had been quarterbacking power-play units around the league for more than a decade. The day after the trade, he made his Canadiens debut in a matinee game against the Devils.

Just over a minute into the second period, Kaberle helped set up Max Pacioretty's power-play goal, the club's first tally on the man advantage in three games. He also assisted on another goal early in the final frame to clinch a 2–1 victory. The Habs still finished with one of the worst power plays in the league, but Kaberle had done his best. Of the 22 points he picked up that season, more than half were on the man advantage. He played 10 more games for Montreal in the 2012–13 lockout-shortened campaign before his contract was bought out.

DECEMBER 10

HABS WIN 10–1, 2016

n a sport like hockey, you can't get too worked up over a single game. Whether you win or lose is not necessarily a true reflection of the state of the team. Sometimes you get the bounces, and sometimes you don't. Even when you lose in spectacular fashion, like when the Habs were trounced 10–0 by the Blue Jackets, you can't read too much into it. A poignant reminder of this came less than a month after that humiliating loss, when the Canadiens were on the other side of the coin.

On December 10, 2016, the Habs scored six unanswered goals in the opening period against the Avalanche to go into the first intermission with a 6–1 lead. It was the club's first six-goal period in more than a decade. Montreal added four more in the final two frames to win 10–1. Captain Max Pacioretty, who highlighted the high-scoring affair with a career-best four-goal performance, was still in diapers the last time the Canadiens found the back of the net that many times.

DECEMBER 11

GUY LAFLEUR NETS FIRST HAT TRICK, 1971

n his final season of junior, Guy Lafleur scored 130 goals
with a stacked Quebec Remparts team that went on to win
the Memorial Cup. When he arrived on the NHL scene the
next season as the first overall pick with the Canadiens, one of
the key differences he noticed in adjusting to the big leagues
was how much more difficult it was to score and how much
each goal mattered. Through his first 25 games, Lafleur had
found the back of the net just six times.

But on December 11, 1971, in a game against the North
Stars, the rookie had a breakthrough performance, bagging
a hat trick, including the game-winning goal. After a 4–3
victory, he told reporters that "with each goal I get, I'm
building confidence. You wait, I'm only getting started." The
Flower was a man of his word. Six days later, he recorded
another three-goal effort against the Canucks. Despite his slow
start, Lafleur's confidence grew, and he finished the season
with 29 goals, the most by a Habs rookie in two decades.

DECEMBER 12

DOUG GILMOUR'S FIRST GOAL, 2001

We're almost near the end of the book, so I think I can safely divulge again that I am a Leafs fan. I made no secrets about that in the introduction, but I have tried to check my blue-and-white baggage at the door. But this is a tough one. For me, Doug Gilmour will always be a Leaf. Sure, I know he started out with St. Louis and Calgary, where he won a Stanley Cup, but he truly became a star in Toronto. And while he spent time with the New Jersey Devils, Chicago Blackhawks, and Buffalo Sabres after his time with the Buds, it's always difficult for me to picture him in a Canadiens sweater, but I'll do my best.

After signing with Montreal in the 2001 off-season, Gilmour, who was known as "Killer" for his fierce determination, struggled to find the back of the net. Finally, on December 12, he notched his first goal with the Habs. Gilmour added nine more to finish the season in double digits for the 18th time in his career.

DECEMBER 13

PATRICE BRISEBOIS NETS GOALS
IN BACK-TO-BACK GAMES, 2008

Patrice Brisebois was once booed so badly by Habs fans that GM Bob Gainey felt the need to intervene. And that's putting it mildly. Gainey actually referred to the hecklers as "gutless bastards" and asked them to stay away from the games if that's how they were going to act. Brisebois endured the taunts throughout the 2003–04 season and ended up signing with the Avalanche following the 2004–05 lockout.

But after a pair of seasons in Colorado, Brisebois was ready to return to Montreal. Although his departure was filled with jeers, Brisebois gave the fans plenty to cheer about in his second stint. With defencemen like Andrei Markov and Roman Hamrlik in starring roles, Brisebois was able to provide depth on the blue line and still contribute. During his second season back, on December 13, 2008, he lit the lamp for the second game in a row, marking the first time he scored goals in back-to-back games since 2002. Brisebois finished the year with 18 points, before hanging up his skates after 16 NHL seasons.

PIT LÉPINE RECORDS FIVE POINTS IN A PERIOD, 1929

P it Lépine played in the shadow of Howie Morenz in Montreal, but on December 14, 1929, he stole the show from his star teammate. Lépine got the Canadiens on the board late in the first period against Ottawa. However, he saved his best performance for the second frame. After scoring just before the halfway mark, Lépine added three more goals and an assist to finish the middle stanza with five points, establishing a club record for the most points in a single period, a mark that has since been equalled but never surpassed.

His six-point feat that game was just one point shy of matching the franchise benchmark shared by Joe Malone and Newsy Lalonde. Lépine completed the season with 24 goals and 33 points in 44 games, finishing runner-up to Morenz in team scoring. Canadiens manager Frank Selke Sr. later said that on any other team Lépine would have been a "blazing meteor" but was outshone by Morenz. Sure enough, in the first campaign after Morenz was traded to Chicago, Lépine led the Habs in scoring.

DECEMBER 15

TUXEDO NIGHT, 1979

Winnipeg dressed up for the Canadiens. On December 15, 1979, the Jets hosted the Habs for "Tuxedo Night," but they weren't wearing their finest just for Montreal: the new NHL club wanted to show the rest of the league they were one of the classiest operations. A reported 1,000 fans showed up to the game wearing tuxedos, and even the staff — from the ushers to the Zamboni driver — were dressed to the nines as the *Hockey Night in Canada* cameras descended on the Winnipeg Arena for the first time to broadcast the matchup between the fledgling Jets and the reigning Stanley Cup champions.

The Habs had clobbered the Jets 7–0 in their first meeting that season, but head coach Tom McVie, who was also sporting a tux, made good on his pledge that the team would avenge the loss and eventually beat the Canadiens. While Montreal opened the scoring just 44 seconds into the game, the Jets rattled off six unanswered goals, including a hat trick from Willy Lindström, to trounce the Habs 6–2.

ALEX GALCHENYUK NETS FIRST CAREER HATTY, 2014

After Alex Galchenyuk scored his first goal of the night, his linemates celebrated with him. After he scored his second, they celebrated with him once more. But when Galchenyuk potted his third in a game against the Hurricanes on December 16, 2014, to complete his first career hat trick, he was all alone. Evidently, his new linemates, Max Pacioretty and Brendan Gallagher, decided to have a little fun with the young centre, who was recently promoted to Montreal's top line. The two wingers apparently made a pact that if Galchenyuk reached the three-goal mark, neither player was going to celebrate with him.

After Pacioretty, who had assisted on both of Galchenyuk's goals, made a slick pass in front of the Carolina net to set Galchenyuk up for his third, Gallagher, who was trailing the play, immediately turned around and skated back up the ice when he saw the puck was in the back of the net. So when Galchenyuk realized there was no one around to celebrate the milestone, all he could do was laugh.

DECEMBER 17

BOB PERREAULT RECORDS FIRST SHUTOUT, 1955

When you're as colourful a character as Bob Perreault was, getting a shutout in your NHL debut probably isn't even in your top five stories. Before the Canadiens called him up in 1955 to replace an injured Jacques Plante, Perreault had already made a name for himself in the Quebec Hockey League with the Shawinigan Cataracts. One game, he went out onto the ice to take his usual spot between the pipes, but he was sporting some extra accessories and had a companion in tow. Perreault was chomping on a cigar under a straw hat, while pulling a monkey on a chain.

He had apparently bought the primate on a trip to Florida and named it Chief. Although the crowd might have delighted in the goaltender's antics, after he placed his pet on top of the net, the referee told him to ditch it or he'd be out of the game. But when Perreault made his Habs debut on December 17, 1955, there was no monkey business. He stopped all 18 shots he faced to record his first career shutout.

DECEMBER 18

JEAN BÉLIVEAU RECORDS
FIRST HAT TRICK, 1952

Jean Béliveau was in no hurry to turn pro. He had carved out a great living and name for himself in the Quebec Senior Hockey League, and since he had signed a "B form" with the Canadiens, which only contractually committed him to play for the club when he was ready, the ball — or better yet, the puck — was in his court. After he played a couple of games for Montreal in the 1951–52 campaign, the Habs recalled him for a three-game stretch, the maximum an amateur could play, before the holidays the following year.

Playing in his third NHL match on December 18, 1952, Béliveau scored a hat trick in a 6–2 victory over the Rangers. A few days later, in his final appearance before being sent back, he collected two more goals. Looking to ensure that Béliveau was back in a Habs sweater sooner than later, in 1953 the Canadiens bought the entire QSHL and turned it into a professional circuit so they could call up "le Gros Bill" and keep him in Montreal.

DECEMBER 19

HABS PLAY FIRST NHL GAME, 1917

B y the time Jack Darragh and Hamby Shore joined their Ottawa teammates, it was almost too late. The pair of Senators had refused to lace up their skates for one of the first NHL games on December 19, 1917, until their contracts were renegotiated, and the Canadiens' Joe Malone took advantage of their absences. When the first period came to a close, the elusive Phantom Joe had already scored two goals and the Habs were leading 3–0.

Darragh and Shore were able to join their teammates for the second frame and help cut the deficit, but Malone added two more. It would have been the first hat trick in league history had it not been for the Wanderers' Harry Hyland, who had a three-goal performance in the first period of a game against the Toronto Arenas that started 15 minutes earlier that day. Malone would find the back of the net for a fifth time in the final session, guiding the Canadiens to a 7–4 victory, their first in the new circuit.

DECEMBER 20

GUY LAFLEUR SCORES 500TH GOAL, 1983

G uy Lafleur was just happy it was over. Now he could finally go back to playing hockey. On December 20, 1983, Lafleur recorded his 500th career goal in a 6–0 victory against the Devils, becoming just the third player in franchise history to accomplish the feat, joining Maurice Richard and Jean Béliveau. Prior to that game, Lafleur had just two tallies in his previous 18 games and was feeling the pressure not only for himself but also for his teammates, who were constantly trying to put him in position to notch the milestone goal.

But it wasn't just Lafleur who was relieved that night. Steve Shutt also had a breakthrough of his own, scoring his 400th career goal early in the third period. Following the game, Lafleur said, "We're just two guys with no pressure now." When asked if he had another mountain he wanted to climb, Lafleur said it was important for him to reach Richard's record of 544 goals before he retired. Lafleur would indeed get there, but it wouldn't be in a Habs jersey.

DECEMBER 21

YVAN COURNOYER RECORDS
FIRST HAT TRICK, 1966

Yvan Cournoyer was a power-play specialist. Early in his career with the Canadiens, he was used sparingly and saw most of his ice time on the man advantage. In his second full campaign in Montreal, the speedy right winger recorded 18 goals, 16 of which were on the power play. By the time he was in his third season with the Habs, not much had changed. "I have to make the most of my chances," Cournoyer told reporters. "Unless there are a lot of penalties, I don't get much ice time."

The Roadrunner certainly made the most of his opportunities in a game against the Maple Leafs on December 21, 1966. He scored three goals, his first career hat trick, all with the extra man. Cournoyer would finish the year with 20 power-play goals, the most in the NHL that season. While he remained lethal on the man advantage, Cournoyer was soon utilized more broadly by the Canadiens and became a key part of the club's dynasty in the 1970s.

DECEMBER 22

RED LIGHT RACICOT GETS
FIRST NHL WIN, 1990

André Racicot had a rough start to his NHL career. In his debut, he allowed three goals on just six shots in just over a period of play against the Leafs and was yanked by head coach Pat Burns. Following this dismal performance, the goaltender was saddled with the nickname "Red Light." There's debate as to who bestowed the unfortunate, but fantastic, moniker on the netminder. Some say it was legendary Canadiens beat writer Red Fisher; others say it might have been Don Cherry.

After his brief appearance against the Leafs, Racicot returned to the minors but was called back up to the Habs the following year. In his third big-league start, on December 22, 1990, Racicot made 28 saves against the Rangers to earn his first NHL victory. While Michael Farber from the *Montreal Gazette* said maybe it was time to retire "Red Light," since Racicot had allowed only three goals in three games so far that season, the nickname hung around, even when he became a serviceable backup for the Habs a couple of years later.

DECEMBER 23

MARK RECCHI PLAYS IN 500TH CONSECUTIVE GAME, 1997

Mark Recchi's iron-man streak looked to be in jeopardy. After he was slashed in the elbow by Greg de Vries during a game against the Oilers, it appeared that Recchi might miss Montreal's match the very next night with the Ottawa Senators. But when X-rays revealed there were no broken bones in the joint, Recchi breathed a sigh of relief. He hadn't missed a day of work since the start of the 1991–92 season, when he was still with the Penguins.

Despite not sleeping much overnight at the hospital and complaining he had trouble closing his left hand just a few hours before puck drop, Recchi was in the lineup in Canada's capital. Skating out onto the ice on December 23, 1997, he made his 500th consecutive game appearance. Although he was still a long way from catching former Canadien Doug Jarvis's record of 964 straight games, Recchi was holding on to the longest active streak in the NHL. He eventually pushed it to 570 games, the eighth longest streak in league history at the time.

DECEMBER 24

CHRISTMAS EVE GOALTENDING DUEL, 1949

The fans at the Montreal Forum may not have been gifted a goal on Christmas Eve 1949, but they were treated to an incredible goaltending duel when the Habs' Bill Durnan and the New York Rangers' Chuck Rayner, two of the league's best tenders of the twine, squared off. While Durnan turned in his fifth shutout of the season, it was Rayner who really stood on his head, stopping all 30 shots he faced in a scoreless draw.

The Rangers' netminder fended off a barrage in the first period, and the closest the Habs got to solving him was as the frame came to a close. After Maurice Richard collided with Rayner, Billy Reay tapped the loose puck into the net while the Broadway goaler was still sprawled on the ice. But referee Hugh McLean reportedly blew the play dead and called the goal back. The Canadiens argued McLean was too eager with his whistle, but that was as close as they'd get to lighting the lamp. Durnan added three more shutouts down the stretch and finished the season with his sixth Vezina.

DECEMBER 25

LAST CHRISTMAS GAME
AT THE FORUM, 1966

f this is the first story you're reading because you received this book as a Christmas gift, well, Merry Christmas! It actually wasn't that long ago that you could have watched the Canadiens play on Christmas Day. The practice, however, stopped after 1971 when the NHL decided it was important to provide a more generous holiday break, a move that was heralded by the players and their families.

The Habs were part of that final round of festive games, losing 4–2 to the Penguins that year, but the last Christmas game played in Montreal was on December 25, 1966. The fans brought the holiday cheer to the Forum and watched their beloved Habs take on the Red Wings. Although Detroit got on the board first, the teams exchanged goals until it was deadlocked at three markers apiece late in the third period. With just over two minutes remaining, Henri Richard, who assisted on all three of Montreal's tallies, buried the game-winner, giving the Canadiens a 4–3 victory in what would be the last Christmas game at the Forum.

DECEMBER 26

MARCEL BONIN PICKS UP FIVE POINTS IN ROUT, 1959

Marcel Bonin could shoot just as accurately off the ice. When he started his NHL career with the Red Wings, he became friends with a Detroit police officer and got into target practice. After joining the Canadiens in 1957, Bonin continued to hone his shooting skills. During the off-season, when he was away from the rink, he even served as a pistol instructor for the Joliette police force, just north of Montreal.

Bonin would not have been considered a sniper by hockey standards, but he regularly approached the 20-goal mark and could light the lamp when he needed to. In a Boxing Day rout of the Black Hawks on December 26, 1959, he chipped in three goals, his second big-league hat trick, and added two assists, matching his career benchmark for the most points in a game. It proved to be one of Bonin's last great offensive performances. A couple of years later, Bonin, who had a nagging back for nearly a decade, suffered a slipped disc in a collision that became a career-ending injury.

DECEMBER 27

GUY CARBONNEAU RECORDS HAT TRICK, 1993

G uy Carbonneau was not exactly known for scoring in bunches. Regarded as one of the best two-way players in the game, he had won three Selke trophies for his defensive play. During his first full season with the Canadiens in 1982–83, Carbonneau notched three goals in an 11–3 shellacking of the Kings, but it would be more than a decade before the defensive forward matched the feat again. On December 27, 1993, in a match against the Blues, he recorded his second career hat trick.

And while it was uncharacteristic of Carbonneau, the team desperately needed it. The Canadiens got off to a sluggish start that season, going 14-14-6 as they appeared to battle through a championship malaise after winning the Stanley Cup. Carbonneau, who had just 13 points so far, hoped it might be the shot in the arm that both he and the club needed. The Habs did improve down the stretch, finishing with 41 victories, but they were unable to defend their title, bowing out in the first round to Boston in seven games.

RICHARD NOTCHES EIGHT POINTS, 1944

Maurice Richard's feats were legendary. There is even a Heritage Minute that immortalizes one of his most extraordinary performances. Before the Canadiens hosted the Red Wings on December 28, 1944, Richard spent the day moving his family into a new home in Montreal. The campy vignette features him dragging a sofa up a staircase before going out that evening and racking up eight points, an NHL record that stood for more than three decades. It's a great yarn, but it didn't unfold quite that way.

Many years later, Dave Stubbs, a columnist for NHL. com, stumbled upon comments Richard made to the French-language newspaper *La Presse*, in which he divulged that he actually made the move across town the day before the game and not the day of. It doesn't diminish Richard's achievement in any way, since five goals and eight points in a game is still an incredible feat no matter what. But if anybody could've pulled off lugging furniture all day and collecting eight points a few hours later, it would've been the Rocket.

DECEMBER 29

STÉPHANE RICHER SCORES
100TH GOAL, 1988

S téphane Richer was on the cusp of another milestone. Heading into a game against the Flames on December 29, 1988, he was sitting at 99 career goals. Drafted 29th overall by the Canadiens in 1984, the right winger quickly rewrote the club's record books. In his third season, Richer, just 21 years old, reached the 50-goal mark, becoming the youngest Hab and the first since Guy Lafleur to accomplish the feat.

Coming off that record-setting season, Richer got off to a slower start in 1988 but was soon set to make history again. Late in the second period of that match against the Flames, Richer potted his 100th career goal on the power play, becoming the youngest Canadiens player to reach the benchmark. He finished the year with just 25 goals but returned to the 50-goal mark the following year, joining Lafleur as the only other Hab to record multiple 50-goal campaigns. Richer spent another year with the Canadiens before he was traded to New Jersey for Kirk Muller, but he returned to Montreal in 1996 for a second and final stint.

RICK WAMSLEY RECORDS
FIRST NHL SHUTOUT, 1980

Rick Wamsley was making the most of his time in the big leagues. Drafted 58th overall by the Canadiens in 1979, he was recalled from Montreal's affiliate in Nova Scotia early the next season when goaltenders Bunny Larocque and Richard Sévigny went down with injuries. Wamsley made his first start on December 23, 1980, stopping 21 shots in a 2–2 tie with the Nordiques. The 21-year-old rookie then picked up victories in his next two outings. Exactly a week after making his NHL debut, Wamsley turned aside all 23 shots he faced to record his first shutout.

Despite his string of impressive performances, once the Canadiens' crease was healthy again, Wamsley was sent back to the minors in January. He returned to Montreal the next year and, along with Denis Herron, was the inaugural winner of the William M. Jennings Trophy for the fewest goals against. Wamsley split the starting duties for a couple more seasons before he was traded to St. Louis as part of a package of draft picks that would net Shayne Corson and Stéphane Richer.

DECEMBER 31

NEW YEAR'S EVE BATTLE AGAINST THE SOVIETS, 1975

S omewhere out there, in an alternate hockey history timeline, Ken Dryden and Vladislav Tretiak were teammates. They would have made quite the goaltending tandem. Both were erudite, and both were incredible netminders. When they first squared off during the 1972 Summit Series, which pitted the Soviet Union against Canada for hockey supremacy, they immediately developed a mutual respect for each other. When some of Russia's top teams came to North America a few years later for an exhibition tournament against NHL clubs, billed as the Super Series '76, Dryden and Tretiak went head-to-head again at the Forum on December 31, 1975.

Dryden didn't face much action, but Tretiak dazzled the fans, stopping 35 shots and earning their adoration in a 3–3 tie. Exactly seven years later, Tretiak and CSKA Moscow returned to Montreal for another New Year's exhibition, but it wasn't Dryden at the other end of the ice. The bespectacled goaltender had retired a few years earlier.

Even if Dryden had been there, Tretiak once again stole the show. He stopped all 40 shots he faced in a 5–0 victory.

Following the game, Tretiak, along with Russian coach Viktor Tikhonov and an interpreter, reportedly visited Canadiens GM Irving Grundman. It was not clear what was discussed, but Tretiak supposedly left with a Dryden jersey.

Later that year, the Habs shocked the hockey world when they selected Tretiak 143rd overall at the NHL Entry Draft. While Tretiak was only 31 years old at the time, he would have had to defect from the Soviet Union to fulfill his aspirations of tending the twine for the bleu, blanc, et rouge. He played another season for Moscow before he also hung up his pads.

Although Dryden's other passions drew him away from the sport, it's not inconceivable that had he stuck around for a few more years and had Tretiak been given permission to join the Canadiens, the two could have shared the same crease.

ASSISTS (ACKNOWLEDGEMENTS)

Writing a book is a lot like winning the Stanley Cup. Sure, it's not as glamorous or as lucrative, but you can't do it without a good team.

Thanks to the fine folks at Dundurn Press, chiefly Chris Houston, Meghan Macdonald, Kathryn Lane, and Elena Radic, for allowing me to once again expand the Hockey 365 universe.

If you picked up the book because you judged it by its cover, then I have Ron Beltrame to thank for that. You may not recognize my name on bookstands, but Ron always ensures that the cover catches your eye.

Stick tap to Patricia MacDonald for bagging a hat trick with me on *Habs 365*. This is my third edit with her, and the books are always stronger after she moves my words around like a good power-play quarterback cycling the puck.

Thanks to Michael Carroll for doing the final proofread and fact check. Michael edited my second *Hockey 365*, so it's great to have him back on the team. Any errors you may find, however, belong to me and me alone.

Early in this process, I reached out to some Habs fans I know for guidance. One of those trusted allies was Blain Potvin. Thanks to Blain for suggesting some of the stories you found in these pages. Blain's had me on his podcast over the years, often to end up talking about the Leafs, but now he can finally have me on to talk about the Canadiens.

There are too many people to name, but I received a lot of feedback on social media about what stories to include. Many of them are in here because of your recommendations, so thank you. You know who you are.

I owe my cousin Matt a beer or two for getting his friend Andrew to connect me with Canadiens owner Geoff Molson. I had the chance to chat with Geoff, and his support for the idea of the project inspired me to keep going down the path. Geoff also connected me with a number of former alumni, including Larry Robinson, Yvan Cournoyer, Réjean Houle, and Chris Nilan. Thanks to those Habs legends for sharing their stories with me and informing some of these pages.

Special thanks to Terry Ryan for taking a stroll down memory lane with me for his entry in the book. I really wanted to include the story he's told elsewhere about his pet tarantula, but I'll have to find a way to sneak that into another book.

My mom, Patti, always prides herself on being the first one to pre-order a copy of my book, but this time it was a struggle. I have no doubt that she was still the first, but I know that, as a dyed-in-the-wool Leafs fan, it pained her to make the purchase. She and my dad, Tony, may not cherish all the stories in this one, but I can always count on them to support my work.

This book has scored me some serious points with my father-in-law, Moe. Sure, I've given him two beautiful granddaughters, but this is a book about the Montreal Canadiens. Moe's talked to me about the Habs over the years, and that definitely came in handy for this project. See, Sue, I knew those stories would pay off.

People often ask me, "How do you find the time to write another book?" After claiming it's thanks to a woeful dereliction of duty at my day job, I tell them the real answer: I have a very patient and loving wife. These books don't happen without her, and I appreciate everything she does so I can chase my hockey dreams. *Je t'aime.*

To my *filles*, Zoe and Sophia. You both make me want to be the best version of myself in everything I pursue. I can only hope that one day you'll look back on these words and be proud of your *papa*.

Finally, thanks to all the Habs fans who will read these pages and the Leafs fans who will use this book as a doorstop.